JOURNAL FOR THE STUDY OF THE OLD TESTAMENT
SUPPLEMENT SERIES

350

Sheffield Academic Press
A Continuum imprint

Witch-hunts, Purity and Social Boundaries

The Expulsion of the Foreign Women in Ezra 9–10

David Janzen

Journal for the Study of the Old Testament
Supplement Series 350

Published by
Sheffield Academic Press Ltd
The Tower Building, 11 York Road, London SE1 7NX
370 Lexington Avenue, New York, NY 10017-6550

www.SheffieldAcademicPress.com
www.continuumbooks.com

British Library Cataloguing-in-Publication Data

A catalogue record for this book is available from the British Library

Typeset by Sheffield Academic Press
Printed on acid-free paper in Great Britain

ISBN 1-84127-292-2

For Kim and for all of those who know who they are.

Contents

ABBREVIATIONS

AASOR	Annual of the American Schools of Oriental Research
AB	Anchor Bible
AfO	*Archiv für Orientforschung*
ANET	James B. Pritchard (ed.), *Ancient Near Eastern Texts Relating to the Old Testament* (Princeton, NJ: Princeton University Press, 1950)
AOAT	Alter Orient und Altes Testament
AOS	American Oriental Series
ASOR	American Schools of Oriental Research
ASORER	American Schools of Oriental Research Excavation Reports
AUSS	*Andrews University Seminary Studies*
BA	*Biblical Archaeologist*
BAR	British Archaeological Report
BARev	*Biblical Archaeology Review*
BASOR	*Bulletin of the American Schools of Oriental Research*
BE	Babylonian Expedition of the University of Pennsylvania, Series A: Cuneiform Texts
Bib	*Biblica*
BHS	*Biblia hebraica stuttgartensia*
BIS	Biblical Interpretation Series
BWANT	Beiträge zur Wissenschaft vom Alten und Neuen Testament
CAT	Commentaire de l'Ancien Testament
CBQ	*Catholic Biblical Quarterly*
CIS	*Corpus inscriptionum semiticarum*
CRAIBL	*Comptes rendus de l'Académie des inscriptions et belles-lettres*
CT	Cuneiform Texts from Babylonian Tablets
DJD	Discoveries in the Judaean Desert
DMOA	Documenta et Monumenta Orientis Antiqui
EI	*Eretz Israel*
ESI	*Excavations and Surveys in Israel*
HAT	Handbuch zum Alten Testament
HSS	Harvard Semitic Studies
ICC	International Critical Commentary
IEJ	*Israel Exploration Journal*
JBL	*Journal of Biblical Literature*

JNES	*Journal of Near Eastern Studies*
JSNT	*Journal for the Study of the New Testament*
JSOT	*Journal for the Study of the Old Testament*
JSOTSup	*Journal for the Study of the Old Testament*, Supplement Series
JTS	*Journal of Theological Studies*
KAI	H. Donner and W. Röllig, *Kanaanäische und aramäische Inschriften* (3 vols.; Wiesbaden: Harrassowitz, 1962–64)
NCBC	New Century Bible Commentary
NEAEHL	Ephraim Stern (ed.), *The New Encyclopedia of Archaeological Excavations in the Holy Land* (4 vols.; Jerusalem: Carta, 1993)
OTL	Old Testament Library
PEQ	*Palestine Exploration Quarterly*
PF	Richard T. Hallock (ed.), *Persepolis Fortification Tablets* (UCOIP, 92; Chicago: University of Chicago Press, 1970)
PR	R.A. Brown, *Aramaic Ritual Texts from Persepolis* (UCOIP, 91; Chicago: University of Chicago Press, 1970)
PT	George Cameron (ed.), *Persepolis Treasury Tablets* (UCOIP, 65; Chicago: University of Chicago Press, 1948)
RB	*Revue biblique*
RES	*Repertoire d'epigraphie semitique*
SBLDS	SBL Dissertation Series
SBLMS	SBL Monograph Series
Sem	*Semitica*
TA	*Tel Aviv*
TAD	Bezalel Porten and Ara Yardeni (eds.), *Textbook of Aramaic Documents from Ancient Egypt* (4 vols.; Jerusalem: Carta, 1986–99)
TBC	Torch Bible Commentaries
Trans	*Transeuphratène*
TransSup	*Transeuphratène* Supplement Series
TynBul	*Tyndale Bulletin*
UCOIP	University of Chicago Oriental Institute Publications
VT	*Vetus Testamentum*
WBC	Word Biblical Commentary
WMANT	Wissenschaftliche Monographien zum Alten und Neuen Testament
ZAW	*Zeitschrift für die alttestamentliche Wissenschaft*

Introduction

1. *The Problem and its Background*

a. *The Problem under Consideration*

Ezra 9–10 is the story of a mass divorce, and this work is an attempt to come to grips with why the Persian period temple community centered at Jerusalem believed that it had to force its members to divorce and expel from the community all women designated as foreign. The chapters under consideration are part of the larger narrative of the book of Ezra–Nehemiah which tells of the return of the exiles from Babylon to Yehud (the Aramaic name of the Persian province of Judah) and their reconstruction of the temple and the walls of Jerusalem. The particular part of this story under consideration here states that the postexilic community, under the leadership of Ezra, decided, for reasons that the text does not make immediately clear, that all exogamous marriages contracted by men within the community must be ended. This results, the text says, in the divorce of all foreign women who had married into the community and their expulsion from this social body. Scholars have, in light of the fact that the text itself does not appear to give a good rationale for these divorces, suggested a number of causes for the divorces chronicled in Ezra 9–10, ranging from matters of economics, ethnic identity, *Realpolitik* and theology. Why should the reader be burdened with yet one more work that attempts to get at the cause behind these divorces and expulsions? Because, I will argue, in order to understand an action undertaken by a social group we must be aware of the social composition, structure and worldview of that group, and this is a matter that no scholar has yet seriously considered in reference to the divorces of Ezra 9–10.

Let me be more specific. What I will argue below in this introduction is not that we should discount all previous scholarly explanations, but that none of them should be understood as the root cause of the expulsion of these women, and so some explanation must be advanced for the precise actions that the community took. The Jerusalem temple community of postexilic Yehud obviously believed that the divorce of these women solved one (if not more) of the community's problems, and these problems may well have included such issues as apostasy or syncretism, one of the explanations offered by other scholars to explain the divorces. These suggestions in themselves, however, do not explain why the community took the *particular* action of divorcing foreign women. Suppose, for a moment, that the Jerusalem community was concerned that foreigners were inducing apostasy. Why not simply mandate monolatry? Surely this seems a less drastic solution than forcing all members married to foreign women to divorce their wives. What I will argue here, in short, is that solutions proposed by other scholars do not explain why the community took the specific action of mandating the divorce and expulsion of the foreign women. Furthermore, a number of the proferred explanations have not taken the social and economic context of ancient Near Eastern marriage and divorce customs into account, and have not fully grasped the relation of marriage and land-ownership in ancient Israel. However, I believe that with a full consideration of the social structure of the community, with a specific emphasis on its external boundaries, internal social integration, and worldview, we should be able to explain why this particular social group took this action and not any other. Within the social consciousness of the community, something formed and maintained by the group's social structure, these women that it designated as 'foreign' were considered dangerous; so dangerous, in fact, that their expulsion from the community was viewed as the most logical way to relieve the danger they posed. What this investigation of the community's structure can show is that the action that the group took was the most likely one it could have taken, of all the infinite number of actions theoretically open to it.

A fuller statement of this work's thesis will follow below, after I have summarized the viewpoints of other scholars on this matter. I should make this point here, though, and I will reiterate it later: my argument that the structure and worldview of the community made it likely that it would expel these women does not compel me to argue that the community, or at least a significant number of its members, was not concerned about issues such as whether or not people in its midst were worshiping gods besides YHWH or neglecting the Jerusalem temple cultus. What I do argue is that concerns such as this one are epiphenomena of the social structure of the community, and so if we cannot explain the latter then we cannot explain why its members would have been worried about such issues to begin with. That the community insisted on the expulsion of the foreign women means that it believed this was the most logical and best way to solve the problems besetting it, and that merely passing laws regarding monolatry simply would not do. What I am compelled to demonstrate is that the social consciousness or worldview of the community portrayed the women as dangerous, and that particular strains on social boundaries triggered the expulsion of these women as narrated in Ezra 9–10. In the presentation of my thesis I shall refer to this expulsion as a ritualized act of purification or, more specifically, a witch-hunt, which is a kind of purification ritual.

b. *Excursus: The Social Basis of Epistemology*

I have already mentioned such issues as external boundaries and internal social integration and social consciousness and worldview, and it will be difficult to continue until readers are familiar with what I mean by these terms. The first two I will address below, and at this point I will address only the issue of social consciousness or worldview. A point generally taken for granted in the fields of sociology and anthropology is the existence of a social consciousness, an idea that may not be entirely familiar to biblical scholars. By 'social consciousness' I mean a worldview taken for granted by the members of a particular society, a way of looking at things that needs no justification because it is considered to be common sense. Aspects of one society's worldview may overlap with those of others—quite a number of societies may believe, for example, that personal and social misfortune is the direct result of a person or society having engaged in actions displeasing to the divine—but many of these aspects will be unique to the society in question, and so each one has a distinct worldview. Individuals within the society are formed by this worldview in the sense that it determines, to a large extent, how they think and how they understand natural and social phenomena. The anthropologist Clifford Geertz has pointed out that during the period of the Enlightenment scholars assumed that a human nature existed independent of time and place and circumstance, and that culture—both material and mental—was simply one more layer that the individual puts on.[1] Anthropologists no longer work with such assumptions, however. We should approach culture, writes Geertz, as a set of 'control mechanisms' for governing social behavior. Although as infants we have the equipment to live a thousand possible lives, it is culture that narrows it down to one in particular. The idea of culture as a control mechanism, then, implies that thought is fundamentally a public, not a private mechanism, and that without culture

1. C. Geertz, *The Interpretation of Cultures: Selected Essays* (New York: Harper-Collins, 1973), pp. 34-40.

patterns—the way the worldview is socially manifested in language, morality, social institutions, and so on—experience would be 'virtually shapeless'.[2] It is these culture patterns that make up what I have called social consciousness or worldview. The thought of individuals is formed by this worldview, and this is why Geertz writes that '[h]uman thought is consummately social: social in its origins, social in its functions, social in its forms, social in its applications. At base, thinking is a public activity…'[3] What one can think and how one interprets experience is determined, to a large extent, by social consciousness or worldview.

Why should Geertz and many other scholars have come to such a conclusion? In part because of the overwhelming evidence of sociological and anthropological fieldwork, but also because of conclusions reached through a study of culture within the framework of human evolution. Culture was one of the ingredients that produced the relatively large-brained *Homo sapiens*, writes Geertz, part of the evolutionary process that led to the genesis and extinction of numerous species from *Australopithecus* through *Homo*, our evolutionary ancestors. Those most able to take advantage of the benefits of culture were more likely to survive. The human neocortex thus evolved in interaction with culture and cannot direct behavior without the guidance of the worldview and language produced by culture. There is no such thing as human nature apart from culture.[4] 'Like the cabbage it so much resembles', writes Geertz, 'the *Homo sapiens* brain, having arisen within the framework of human culture, would not be viable outside of it'.[5]

2. Geertz, *Interpretation*, pp. 44-46. See also pp. 213-14 where Geertz also makes the argument about the fundamentally public character of thought.

3. Geertz, *Interpretation*, p. 360.

4. Geertz, *Interpretation*, pp. 47-49.

5. Geertz, *Interpretation*, p. 68. The human brain is about seven times the expected size for an animal of its weight, and the brain size within the genus *Homo* has doubled over the last million years (R. Foley, *Humans before Humanity: An Evolutionary Perspective* [Oxford: Basil Blackwell, 1995], pp. 162-65). The development of brain size is, evolutionarily speaking, an extremely expensive bit of development, as the human brain amounts to only three percent of body mass but uses twenty percent of the body's energy (Foley, *Humans*, p. 170). What purpose could such development serve? The answer to this question accepted by most biological anthropologists is that it permits a greater degree of social complexity which itself promotes the perpetuation of particular species with such large brain masses. The larger the brain size in a species, the larger will be the size of the group in which individuals of that species may cluster. With a larger intellect, one is better equipped to predict the behavior of another

Culture is a universal phenomenon of human social complexity, and it is culture that creates the symbol systems that synthesize a people's ethos and worldview. It is by means of ethos—meaning, broadly speaking, the cultural morality or way of living—and worldview that individuals within a society are able to predict each others' behavior and coordinate their activities. Ethos, as Geertz says, is shown to be reasonable because it is demonstrated to be ideally adapted to the world as the worldview describes it, and the worldview is made convincing by being shown to be an image of the world that accommodates the way of life implied by the ethos. Style of life and metaphysic thus sustain each other in this circle.[6] That is, a society will advocate a particular moral structure to which its members are expected to adhere, and it will reward those who do so. This morality is advanced because, according to the social worldview, it describes the best possible way to act given the way the world is. The worldview prescribes a social morality that is rewarded; because adherence to this morality brings reward, it seems to vindicate the worldview's ability to describe the cosmos. People in a particular group will thus act in stereotyped ways because these are seen to be the best ways to act given the way the world is. In this way is common sense created. People who do not follow the way of life urged by cultural symbol systems, writes Geertz, are generally seen to be stupid rather than evil. The symbol systems of a society urge that people live in conformity with the way the world is—to live by the rules of common sense as the society perceives it—and since lives ruled by common sense tend to succeed, the worldview's metaphysic is vindicated.[7]

So culture, as Peter Berger puts it, is a human product that acts upon its producers.[8] Unlike other animals for which the world is a given, humans must construct their own world, and nothing is understandable for humans outside of the worldview through which they comprehend things.[9] Society

individual (Foley, *Humans*, pp. 165-70). The function of intellect, then, is to solve social problems. As Geertz has argued, there can be no such thing as a human that exists outside of culture, for as a species our brains developed in order to permit the existence of culture, the means by which humans live in society.

6. Geertz, *Interpretation*, pp. 89-90.

7. Geertz, *Interpretation*, pp. 129-30.

8. P. Berger, *The Sacred Canopy: Elements of a Sociological Theory of Religion* (New York: Anchor, 1969), p. 3.

9. Berger, *Canopy*, pp. 3-28.

thus orders and norms human activity[10] since, as we have seen, the activity prescribed by cultural symbols is, within its cultural context, common sense. Notably, both Geertz and Berger refer to a social group's entire set of symbols as religion. Religion, as Geertz defines it, is 'a system of symbols which acts to establish powerful, pervasive, and long-lasting moods and motivations in men [*sic*] by formulating conceptions of a general order of existence and clothing these conceptions with such an aura of factuality that the moods and motivations seem uniquely realistic'.[11] This is simply a systematic statement of his views on lifestyle and worldview that I have already summarized; but what these two scholars are arguing by referring to the system of cultural symbols as religion is that the actions urged by these symbols is grounded by the social worldview in the depths of reality. Symbol systems make things understandable by placing them within a cosmic framework that transcends reason because it is the source of social reasoning. As Paul Tillich rather nicely puts it, '[f]aith is not an act of any of [humanity's] rational functions, as it is not an act of the unconscious, but it is an act in which both the rational and the nonrational elements of [humanity's] being are transcended'.[12] Quite simply, it is religious faith that grounds worldview and dispositions, and as such cultural symbols tend to be rather difficult things to challenge if one's worldview has been formed by them. Religious faith (as Geertz, Berger and Tillich understand the term) transcends and grounds reason, which means that reasonable thought will have to challenge its very basis if it is to challenge the social worldview.

Pierre Bourdieu has focused on the dispositional or practical side of this argument, noting that practice, the actions that people in a society undertake, embody the values of the society without explicitly communicating them.[13] Nothing, he writes, seems more ineffable and incommunicable

10. Berger, *Canopy*, p. 19.

11. Geertz, *Interpretation*, p. 90.

12. P. Tillich, *The Dynamics of Faith* (New York: Harper & Row, 1957), p. 6.

13. P. Bourdieu, *Outline of a Theory of Practice* (trans. Richard Nice; Cambridge Studies in Social Anthropology, 16; Cambridge: Cambridge University Press, 1977). Bourdieu refers to the *habitus*, as he calls it, which consists of systems of durable dispositions, structures predisposed to creating and forming practices and representations that are regular and regulated without being the result of obedience to rules, an adaptation to goals without a conscious verbalization of goals (p. 72). The *habitus* is the 'socially constituted system of cognitive and motivating structures' (p. 76), 'the durably installed generative principle of regulated improvisations' (p. 78). It is through practice, he argues, that a society promotes goals of life without explicitly stating them.

than such values, for they are beyond consciousness. In this way there can be a whole cosmology and metaphysics instilled in a statement such as 'stand up straight'. 'The whole trick of pedagogic reason', he claims, 'lies precisely in the way it extorts the essential while seeming to demand the insignificant'.[14] Social morality, the way people act, is so deeply ingrained that the most quotidian activities mirror and reinforce it. The smallest of actions, because it is in conformity with a social worldview that provides the basis for an understanding of morality, reflects the social worldview; and in such actions the actors demonstrate their absorption of and conformity to these goals and worldview. Actions performed by individuals within society are the product of a method of acting that they did not devise and of which they have no conscious mastery. Through repetition of actions that they have been taught, a common sense world is produced for the actors, and in this way the experiences of individuals within a society are continually harmonized and continually reinforced. As if impelled by an invisible hand, people in a society perform actions by the same laws. This is not through any conscious homogenization of purpose, but simply because each individual's law seems to agree with everybody else's.[15] This is not to say that practice creates worldview, simply that it regenerates and maintains it. I will argue in the section on the function of ritual at the end of this introduction that worldview and social order can also be regenerated and maintained through more formal and liturgical means.

Not every anthropologist agrees with Bourdieu's conception of how practice facilitates unconscious absorption of social worldview. Here I mention only one challenge to Bourdieu's conclusions, that of Maurice Bloch. I choose Bloch's challenge to Bourdieu because it addresses the important notion of ideology and its social function, a matter that must be understood when the text of Ezra 9–10 is approached. Bloch develops the Marxist distinction between cognition and ideology, arguing that 'non-ideological cognition', the pre-linguistic cognition advanced by some developmental psychologists, is a universal phenomenon in infants, and only later is the product of this process standardized by the social worldview, what Bloch calls ideology.[16] Unlike Geertz or Bourdieu, Bloch is

14. Bourdieu, *Outline*, pp. 94-95.

15. Bourdieu, *Outline*, pp. 79-81. 'The *habitus* is precisely this immanent law', writes Bourdieu (p. 81).

16. M. Bloch, *Ritual, History and Power: Selected Papers in Anthropology* (London School of Economics Monographs on Social Anthropology, 58; London: Athlone Press, 1989), p. 134. For his development of this argument, see pp. 106-36.

arguing that at a very early stage of life, the human thought process begins prior to the imposition of the socially constructed worldview. Ideology, for Bloch, is the imposition of this worldview on the thought patterns of individuals after a period of non-ideological cognition. The point that Bloch is trying to get at is that ideology is directly linked to a society's acceptance of instituted hierarchy. The greater and more defined the social order, the more interest in ideology we are likely to find. For Bloch, as for Marx, ideology legitimates power.[17] Ideology for Bloch fights to impose the social worldview and its concomitant view of social structure on individuals, countering the view of the world developed in pre-ideological cognition.

There is no space here for a full discussion of Bloch's views, so I will note only that his argument is not entirely incompatible with the views of Geertz and Bourdieu, especially in regard to the interest of this present work, which simply regards the imposition of a social worldview at *some* early point in the individual's life. Ideology is meant, like ritual, to dramatize the social worldview, and so ritual and ideology have much in common.[18] Since I have referred to the divorces of Ezra 9–10 as a ritualized act of purification, I will discuss the function of ritual at the end of this introduction. Here I will only make the obvious point that ideology must be persuasive if it is to be successful, and it can be persuasive only if it points people's attention to a worldview and social order that they already take for granted. Too often ideology is viewed along Marxist lines as a sort of 'ethereal medium which veils the hard reality of material production',[19] a conscious falsification of reality perpetrated by those who control the means of production to maintain this control. (Bloch's view of ideology, I should point out, does not imply this.) But ideology can only function if it appeals to ideas found within the social worldview that everyone takes for granted as common sense.[20] And while the social order and the ideology that dramatizes it may well benefit some groups in society more than others, this does not mean that it is a consciously promoted lie. Instead of seeing ideology as a mask that the dominant class consciously wears in order to hide its power, argues J.B. Merquior, we should view it

17. Bloch, *Ritual, History and Power*, p. 123.

18. So R. Wuthnow, *Meaning and Moral Order: Explorations in Cultural Analysis* (Berkeley: University of California Press, 1987), p. 145.

19. J.B. Thompson, *Studies in the Theory of Ideology* (Berkeley: University of California Press, 1984), p. 16.

20. See Geertz, *Interpretation*, pp. 193-229.

as a veil, something that unintentionally veils the sources of power, as 'a set of unchallenged, normally tacit, value-orientations which, once translated into the language of purpose, amounts to that "manipulation of bias" in favor of privileged groups'.[21]

What this view of ideology excludes is what Geertz has dubbed the 'interest theory', the notion that people's actions can be explained solely by 'rational calculation of their consciously recognized personal advantage', what Geertz refers to as 'superficial utilitarianism'.[22] We should not assume that the causes of human action may be traced to the sole desire to gain control over the means of production. The reasons why the interest theory will often fail to explain why people act the way they do should be clear from the preceding. People act the way they do because they have been socialized into acting that way, and, writes Geertz, to assume that social action is fundamentally a struggle for power is to ignore the complexity of social interaction and social order.[23] Actions and motives are shaped not simply by an actor trying to solve a problem, but by the things and values the actor believes to be good, and these are matters implied by social worldviews. This is not to say that people do not try to advance their own positions, simply that they will do so on the patterns that are traditionally available, and this will vary from group to group.[24] Two different individuals in two different societies attempting to solve the same problem may well do it in different ways because their thinking is grounded in two different worldviews. To understand why particular people in particular societies do what they do, one must understand more about the society than simply its economic and political settings, even if these are important elements in any investigation of the social.

To understand why the Jerusalem temple community undertook to expel the foreign women in its midst, then, we must look beyond explanations that focus solely on one group's desire to maintain power, land or wealth. We should not ignore such explanations entirely, as an understanding of the economic and political setting of the action can only contribute to our knowledge of that community's social structure. In order to understand fully the actions a social group undertakes and the arguments and ideology

21. J.B. Merquior, *The Veil and the Mask: Essays on Culture and Ideology* (London: Routledge & Kegan Paul, 1979), pp. 27-29.

22. Geertz, *Interpretation*, p. 202.

23. Geertz, *Interpretation*, pp. 202-203.

24. S.B. Ortner, 'Theory in Anthropology since the Sixties', *Comparative Studies in Society and History* 26 (1984), pp. 126-65 (151-55).

that it finds compelling we must understand, to the highest degree possible, the structure of the society and its worldview. What types of practice did that society value, and why? Why were foreign women considered so dangerous that at one point the ideology advanced to expel them was convincing to the society at large? What social factors shaped that society's worldview such that this ideology became convincing? These are questions that must be addressed as thoroughly as the economic and political make-up of the temple community.

c. *Previous Scholarship on Ezra 9–10*

Generally speaking, scholarly study believes that the issue at stake in this passage is boundary maintenance. This is hardly surprising, since Ezra 9–10 is the story of the divorce and expulsion of a particular group of women, a case of the community redefining its boundaries to keep out a particular group of people. The question, then, is what motivated the boundary maintenance, and scholarly opinion on the matter may be divided into three basic categories: (1) Ezra was simply enforcing the law in order to prevent apostasy; (2) there were issues of ethnic identity at stake that the divorces and bans were designed to address; or (3) the motivating factor behind the social boundary maintenance was really an economic or political issue.

That scholars have proposed such various interpretations of the text—and some scholars believe that issues in two of the categories are responsible—is a testament to the difficulties that the text presents. The main difficulty, I will show in Chapter 1, is that scholars have implicitly concluded that the text seemingly provides little good evidence for why the community takes the actions that it does, where 'good evidence' is what an outside observer from a different social context might consider good. After I briefly examine the various scholarly interpretations of the texts in this introduction, I will ask what support each explanation can garner from the texts themselves, and point out the lacuna of evidence that each category of explanation encounters. This does not imply that at least some of the issues that scholars believe were the reasons for the community's actions were not live issues within the community at the time, but that these issues did not lie at the root of the divorces and expulsions. At best, they can be considered epiphenomena of the basic cause of these divorces and expulsions. In Chapters 2 and 4 I do argue that we should expect the community to be anxious about such issues as apostasy and cultural assimilation within the temple assembly (categories 1 and 2, respectively); yet the examination of the text in Chapter 1 points out that the community does not offer such explanations for the expulsion of the women. The text does in fact offer an explanation, but it can only be understood when the social boundaries and worldview of the community are understood.

F.W. Schultz's explanation of Ezra 9–10 is anomalous within the scholarship regarding this passage, but reflects the difficulty interpretation of it has faced, because it falls into none of the categories listed above. The presence of the foreign women threatens Israel's existence, he writes.[25] He does not explain why this is so, but the text does not seem very forthcoming on the matter, either. This is what lies at the root of the various proposals for the basic cause of the expulsion of these women: if the text does not give an explanation, one must be constructed. In fact, the text does give a reason—foreign peoples are impure, and mixture with them on the part of Israel is illegitimate—but the significance of this seems to have escaped scholarship.

Those who propose apostasy as an explanation often believe that the presence of the foreign women threatened widespread apostasy or syncretism, and that the future existence of YHWHism was at stake. Mark Throntveit argues that the list of peoples from whom the foreign women allegedly come (Ezra 9.1) suggests a parallel to the laws of Exod. 34.11-16 and Deut. 7.1-6[26] that proscribe intermarriage with foreigners because apostasy will result and that contain a similar list of nations.[27] D.J.A. Clines takes the same tack as Throntveit, arguing that while it is true that Exodus and Deuteronomy prohibit marriage only to non-Israelites from Palestine (the list of Ezra 9.1 mentions nations from outside of Palestine), the actions of the Persian period community adhered more closely to the spirit of the Pentateuchal provisions.[28] Jacob Myers agrees, arguing that

25. F.W. Schultz, *The Book of Ezra* (J.P. Lange Commentaries, 7; trans. C.A. Briggs; New York: Scribner, Armstrong and Co., 1877), p. 99.

26. Essentially, scholars believe that if Ezra did follow some law or combination of laws known in the Torah as we have it, they may have been the following: (1) Deut. 7.1-6 (H.G.M. Williamson, *Ezra, Nehemiah* [WBC, 16; Waco, TX: Word Books, 1985], p. 131; L.W. Batten, *The Books of Ezra and Nehemiah* [ICC; New York: Charles Scribner's Sons, 1913], pp. 334-35; and others); or (2) Deut. 7.1-6 and Exod. 34.11-16 (D.J.A. Clines, *Ezra, Nehemiah, Esther* [NCBC, 15; Grand Rapids: Eerdmans, 1984], pp. 116-17; J.M. Myers, *Ezra–Nehemiah* [AB, 14; Garden City, NY: Doubleday, 1965], p. 76; and others).

27. M.A. Throntveit, *Ezra–Nehemiah* (Interpretation; Louisville, KY: Westminster/John Knox Press, 1992), pp. 50-51.

28. Clines, *Ezra, Nehemiah, Esther*, pp. 116-17.

the danger to the Persian period community in such marriages was 'compromise and idolatry'.[29]

Closely related to the first category of explanation is the second, in which we find many scholars who believe that there is more going on than a straightforward application of the law where there had been no such application before. For them the matter is not purity of religious beliefs and practices but ethnicity. The issue turns around the necessity of boundary maintenance to maintain the ethnic or cultural distinctiveness of the community. The explanation offered by Peter Ackroyd could be said to fall in both the first and second categories, for he argues that the purpose of expelling the foreign women from the community was 'the preservation of the life and faith of the community'; specifically, it represented an attempt to keep the priests free of marriages to foreigners.[30] H.G.M. Williamson finds the root of the divorces in the community's need for a 'distinctive self-identity', where 'the clinching factor' for this identity was conceived to lie along racial lines.[31] Wilhelm Rudolph makes a similar argument,[32] as do C.F. Keil and Franz Delitzsch, who believe that the expulsions represented an attempt to cut social and civil ties with the surrounding population.[33] In a similar vein, Daniel Smith-Christopher argues that the marriages to foreign women may have resulted from attempts on the part of males in the Jerusalem temple community to marry into a higher economic bracket. The divorces, then, were an attempt to re-create the ethnic purity of the society.[34]

29. Myers, *Ezra–Nehemiah*, p. 77.

30. P.R. Ackroyd, *I and II Chronicles, Ezra, Nehemiah* (TBC; London: SCM Press, 1973), pp. 261-63.

31. Williamson, *Ezra, Nehemiah*, pp. 160-61. Williamson believes that the community followed the Pentateuchal law regarding miscegenation, but misconstrued it to refer to race, not religion, as was (in his opinion) its original intent.

32. W. Rudolph, *Esra und Nehemia* (HAT, 20; Tübingen: J.C.B. Mohr, 1949), p. 89.

33. C.F. Keil and F. Delitzsch, *The Books of Ezra, Nehemiah, and Esther* (trans. S. Taylor; Edinburgh: T. & T. Clark, 1888), pp. 135-36. Their point really deals more with culture than ethnicity or race, but I include it here by broadly interpreting ethnicity to include cultural specificity.

34. D.L. Smith-Christopher, 'The Mixed Marriage Crisis in Ezra 9–10 and Nehemiah 13: A Study of the Sociology of the Post-Exilic Judaean Community', in T.C. Eskenazi and K.H. Richards (eds.), *Second Temple Studies: 2. Temple and Community in the Persian Period* (JSOTSup, 175; Sheffield: JSOT Press, 1994), pp. 243-65.

Perhaps the most striking problem faced by all of these categories of interpretation—including the third one, the varieties of which I will examine below—is that the text does not mention these issues as explanations proposed as a motivating factor for the divorces. What all such interpretations must assume, then, is that the author of Ezra 9–10 either felt no reason to justify the action the community took or that he or she consciously obscured the reason. Yet if the community believed that it had good reason to force its members to divorce all foreign wives then why would the author of these chapters try to hide the reason? And why, in the telling of the story, would the community's own justification for expelling the women be omitted? I will argue below—specifically in Chapter 1—that through an investigation of the problem by means of the social boundaries and worldview we can come to an understanding of this action on the basis of the explanation the author has left for us in Ezra 9–10. That is, my approach assumes that an explanation for the divorces has been provided in the text. It is simply a matter of how to understand what the text says.

Another problem that the text poses to the first two categories of explanation is the list of Ezra 10.18-44, a record of all of those men in the community who had married foreign women and divorced them. It is quite short and contains only about 110 names.[35] It is difficult to see how YHWHism could be threatened by about 100 women within a sizable community like that of Persian period Yehud, where the population was likely around 20,000.[36] This also poses a difficulty for those readings that fall in the second category: it is hard to believe that a handful of women could seriously threaten the community's cultural or ethnic integrity. The small number of foreign women is a notorious problem for scholarship dealing with Ezra 9–10 because it seems incongruous with the importance with which the community treats the issue. Both Ezra and the whole community go into a state of mourning over the matter, and Ezra claims that the very existence of the community is at stake. This is why some scholars have suggested that the list refers only to marriages within the upper

35. The MT of Ezra 10 contains the names of 111 men who divorced their wives, while the LXX of 2 Esdras has 109 (or 111 or 112, depending on whether some individuals are listed with two names), and the LXX of 1 Esdras has 109 or 110.

36. This is the figure for the population of Yehud in the latter part of the Persian period (450–332) proposed by C. Carter (*The Emergence of Yehud in the Persian Period: A Social and Demographic Study* [JSOTSup, 294; Sheffield: Sheffield Academic Press, 1999], pp. 195-213), who relies on the most recent archaeological evidence and methods of estimating population.

classes,[37] or that the list is incomplete.[38] Such suggestions, however, should only be considered testaments to one of the vexing problems that the passage poses, for the text gives no indication that this is anything but a complete list—it states that the list refers to '*all* the men who married foreign women' (10.17)—and there is no text-critical evidence to support them.

Many of the explanations that fall within the first category assume that Ezra compelled the community, which had long ignored Pentateuchal law, to expel the women. Such explanations run afoul of the text's narrative, however, for Ezra 9–10 makes it clear that the initiative to compel the men to divorce comes from the community, not from Ezra. Moreover, I will argue in Chapter 1, Ezra does not seem to have occupied a position within the community where he could have forced it to take such an action against the will of its members. While the text makes it clear that Ezra was there to teach the law (and there is no reason to doubt this assertion, as I shall show), he could not enforce his private will on the people. The divorces did not occur because a charismatic man with the power of the Persian administration suddenly arrived in the province and mandated the action. What this kind of explanation cannot explain, furthermore, is why the community would have undertaken divorces as opposed to a less disruptive form of action. Why would it not have simply passed a law mandating monolatry? What it cannot show, in short, is why this action on the part of the temple community was likely. I am arguing that when one understands the social composition and worldview of this particular social group one can see why it would undertake precisely such an action.

To move to explanations that fall in the third category, the category that looks to economic or political explanations, Jon Berquist argues that the list of men who divorced women 'leans heavily toward the priests and leaders'.[39] This being the case, he continues, the divorces would have served the interests of the economic elite who would have been concerned that land and political control not leave their circle. The first difficulty with this explanation, beyond the fact that it has no textual support, is that the list of men divorcing hardly seems weighted to priests and leaders. Of the 110 names mentioned, only 26 are temple employees, a figure that

37. So, e.g., J. Blenkinsopp *Ezra-Nehemiah: A Commentary* (OTL; Philadelphia: Westminster Press, 1988), p. 197.

38. So, e.g., Rudolph, *Esra und Nehemia*, p. 97.

39. J.L. Berquist, *Judaism in Persia's Shadow: A Social and Historical Approach* (Minneapolis: Fortress Press, 1995), p. 118.

includes gatekeepers and singers as well as priests and Levites. Second, Berquist does not explain how land and political power would escape the elite should a rich man of the temple community marry a poor woman. His sons would inherit any land that he owned when he died, and it is difficult to see how this would diminish the economic and political power of the temple community elite. The transfer of land in marriage and divorce in the ancient Near East is a question that touches upon almost all the explanations of this category, and so I shall comment further upon it below.

Tamara Eskenazi and the sociologist E.P. Judd have drawn a parallel to the divorces of Ezra 9–10 with the situation in the modern state of Israel.[40] In the latter case, when the Orthodox Rabbis took religious power in Israel, they deemed some marriages as illegitimate when one of the marriage partners was not, according to their definition, Jewish. Eskenazi and Judd suggest that a similar situation may have occurred in Persian period Yehud, when marriages could have been declared invalid as more conservative religious elements gained power in society. The suggestion is intriguing, yet it has almost no support from the text. Ezra 9.4 does refer to the support Ezra received from *kl ḥrd bdbry 'lhy yśr'l*, 'all who tremble at the words of the God of Israel', but the text says nothing about their religious views or the role they played in effecting the divorces.

Harold Washington, in an attempt to locate a social and economic background to the evil 'foreign woman' of Proverbs 1–9, finds it in the attempts to free the community of all foreign things in Ezra–Nehemiah.[41] Noting that the law of Num. 27.1-11 and 36.1-9 gives women in Israel the right to inherit should their deceased father have no living sons, he concludes that the community saw marriage to foreign women as a problem because inheritance could lead to alienation of property from the community. Joseph Blenkinsopp[42] and Tamara Eskenazi[43] (in a different article

40. T. Eskenazi and E.P. Judd, 'Marriage to a Stranger in Ezra 9–10', in T.C. Eskenazi and K.H. Richards (eds.), *Second Temple Studies: 2. Temple and Community in the Persian Period* (JSOTSup, 175; Sheffield: JSOT Press, 1994), pp. 266-85.

41. H. Washington, 'The Strange Woman of Proverbs 1–9 and Post-Exilic Judean Society', in T.C. Eskenazi and K.H. Richards (eds.), *Second Temple Studies: 2. Temple and Community in the Persian Period* (JSOTSup, 175; Sheffield: JSOT Press, 1994), pp. 217-42 (230).

42. J. Blenkinsopp, 'The Social Context of the "Outsider Woman" in Proverbs 1–9', *Bib* 72 (1991), pp. 457-73, esp. p. 470.

43. T. Eskenazi, 'Out from the Shadows: Biblical Women in the Post-Exilic Era', *JSOT* 54 (1992), pp. 25-43 (27-31).

than that mentioned above) have pointed to the same issue. The point that none of these scholars addresses, however—and we can include Berquist in this discussion—is how marriages to foreign women would lead to an alienation of land. Should the husbands of foreign women die the children, not the foreign wives, would inherit from him. This was the case throughout Israel and the ancient Near East, as I have shown elsewhere.[44] The foreign women would inherit nothing. Should a husband predecease his wife, his sons inherit his property immediately, and the wife is dependent upon them.[45] If the community had been worried that a man's daughters might inherit and marry outside of the community it would have proscribed marriages of its women to foreigners (something that happens elsewhere in Ezra–Nehemiah); but causing the men to divorce their present wives would not affect the movement of land except, as we shall see below, in a matter deleterious to the community.

Finally, Kenneth Hoglund has argued that the Persian government structured groups of displaced ethnic nationalities into collective units, and strove to keep these units ethnically separate.[46] Hoglund does not suggest why the Persian administration might find such an arrangement beneficial, nor does he offer much in the way of parallels from the Persian period. He notes a number of texts from the Persepolis Fortification tablets that refer to disbursement of goods to particular groups referred to by ethnicity, and to one group mentioned in Herodotus that was conquered by the Persians and deported.[47] The divorces of Ezra 9–10, he concludes, served to prevent any 'diminution of collective privileges or property' enjoyed by the temple community.[48] Since he offers no convincing rationale as to why the

44. D. Janzen, 'The Meaning of *porneia* in Matthew 5.32 and 19.9: An Approach from the Study of Ancient Near Eastern Culture', *JSNT* 80 (2000), pp. 69-83.

45. One example of this tradition is an Aramaic wedding contract from Murrabbat that dates sometime before the First Roman-Jewish War and which reads, in part, 'if I [the husband] go to that house [i.e. if I die] before you, you may be a resident and be nourished from my possessions all the days (in) their house, the ho[use of our son]s'. Text and translation in J.T. Milik, 'Textes hebreux et araméenes', in P. Benoit *et al.* (eds.), *Les grottes de Murabba'at* (DJD, 2; Oxford: Clarendon Press, 1961), pp. 67-205, no. 21.14-15 (114-15). This was standard practice in the ancient Near East, as we shall see below.

46. K. Hoglund, 'The Achaemenid Context', in P.R. Davies (ed.) *Second Temple Studies:* 1. *The Persian Period* (JSOTSup, 117; Sheffield: JSOT Press, 1991), pp. 54-72.

47. Hoglund, 'The Achaemenid Context', pp. 65-66.

48. Hoglund, 'The Achaemenid Context', p. 67.

Persians might benefit from such ethnic purity, and since he offers minor and unconvincing parallels, it is rather difficult to accept his conclusions. But even if one should accept his argument, it does not explain why a man from the Jerusalem temple community who married a foreign woman would have been considered less a part of the ethnic group settled there. Nor does it explain how, as Hoglund puts it, a marriage to a foreign woman 'raises the potential for the transfer of one ethnic group's property to the control of another'.[49] The only manner in which such a transfer could occur would be in the case of a temple community man who divorced his wife without just cause.

The question of the movement of property in an ancient Near Eastern divorce is an important one that touches all of the scholarly suggestions that fall within the third category. In the marriage contracts and legislation concerned with divorce in the ancient Near East it is clear that a man must have just cause to divorce his wife, where just cause amounts to matters such as adultery or theft from his estate upon his wife's part. Armed with cause, he can divorce her with no monetary penalty, and even retains possession of her dowry. Such, at any rate, was the case in Old Babylonian law,[50] and the same situation applied to first-century Judaism and, it would seem, to ancient Israel.[51] A man could also divorce without just cause, although in that case he was obliged to repay the dowry (*Code of Hammurapi* 138). If his wife had borne him children, he was also obliged to forfeit his own property (*Code of Eshnunna* 59), since his property is, in some sense, for the purpose of providing his sons with inheritance and his daughters with dowry. When a woman is divorced without just cause she takes her dowry and her husband's property (or a part of it, if he is married to more than one partner) and raises the children. When her sons became of age to inherit, they are then bound to support her with the inheritance (*Hammurapi* 137).

While the Pentateuchal laws and literature of ancient Israel tell us almost nothing about divorce, it is clear that first-century Judaism and ancient Israel differentiated between divorce with just cause and without, and handled the financial issues in the same manner as their cultural neighbors.[52] The significance of this observation is that if the temple

49. Hoglund, 'The Achaemenid Context', p. 67.

50. R. Westbrook, *Old Babylonian Marriage Law* (*AfO* Beiheft, 23; Horn: Ferdinand Berger & Sohne, 1988), pp. 71-78.

51. Janzen, 'The Meaning of *porneia*'.

52. Janzen, 'The Meaning of *porneia*'.

community of the Persian period was concerned about the loss of land, the last thing it would do would be to force its members married to foreign women to divorce them without just cause and so send these women away holding the ownership to the land as a divorce settlement in order to support the children.[53] Instead, they would have forbidden families from marrying out their daughters to foreigners, for land was often a component in dowries, as is clear from the marriage contracts of the neo-Babylonian period.[54] This in fact occurs in Nehemiah 10 and 13, but this is not the issue in Ezra 9–10. Had possession of land been an issue, the community would have encouraged its male members to marry foreign women, for that would have increased the land holdings of the community.[55] The divorces and expulsions would have led to a communal loss of land.

Besides the difficulties I have mentioned with the various individual interpretations of the third category, I should reiterate those that apply to

53. The MT of Ezra 10.44 does seem to say that the women and the children from the mixed marriages were forced from the community in accordance with the group's statement that it would do so in 10.3, but the Hebrew here is difficult. Blenkinsopp (*Ezra–Nehemiah*, p. 197) believes the latter part of this verse in the MT—*wyš mhm nšym wyśymw bnym*—is 'corrupt beyond repair', and simply reads with LXX^{AB}: *kai egennēsan ex autōn huious*, 'and some of them had borne sons'. Williamson (*Ezra, Nehemiah*, pp. 144-45), on the other hand, argues that the MT is not impossible, and translates 10.44 as 'and some of the women had even borne children'. A number of emendations have been suggested (for which see the *BHS* footnote). It would appear that LXX^{AB} reads with MT, if it takes the verb *śym* to mean 'to bear (children)'. This would also seem to be the case with LXX^{L}, Old Latin, Ethiopic and Vulgate, which all follow the MT (again, assuming the same translation of *śym*). *śym* has this meaning nowhere else in the Hebrew Bible, but there appears to be no other way for the ancient translators to make sense of it without emending the text. The Vorlage of 1 Esd. 9.36 did in fact emend the text, and its *kai apelusan autas sun teknois*, 'and they sent them away with the children', assumes a reading of *wyšlḥwm nšym wbnym*. This is clearly the lectio facilior; but what is noticeable about it is that it appears to assume a reading consonant with the cultural practices of the time: women divorced without just cause are sent away with the children.

54. M. Roth (*Babylonian Marriage Agreements 7th–3rd Centuries B.C.* [AOAT, 222; Neukirchen–Vluyn: Neukirchener Verlag, 1989) notes that of the extant marriage agreements from the neo-Babylonian period (they date from 635 to 203), the transfer of property in the dowry is one of the main purposes for the composition of the texts (pp. 25-26). A number of them actually refer to themselves as a 'dowry agreement' (pp. 26-27).

55. For the inclusion of land in dowries in the neo-Babylonian period see, e.g., Roth, *Babylonian Marriage Agreements*, nos. 1.3-18 (pp. 34-35); 9.3-9 (pp. 42-43); 15.5-7 (pp. 47-48) and 22.3-9, 11-13 (pp. 56-58), among others.

all three categories: they do not follow the rationale for the divorces and expulsions offered by Ezra 9–10 itself, and they do not explain why they ignore this rationale. Further, in positing alternative explanations, they give no indication as to why such grounds for the expulsions are not mentioned in the text. In the remainder of this work I will argue that the text does indeed include a clear explanation of why the community effected the expulsion of these women: they were impure. The real difficulty that confronts us is to understand what this explanation means.

2. *Statement of Thesis and its Methodological Corollaries*

a. *The Thesis*

The thesis of this work is that the Jerusalem temple community's decision to force its members to divorce their foreign wives and expel them from the community was a ritualized act of purification, and a specific kind of this action, commonly called a witch-hunt. For the purposes of this work I define a witch-hunt in the following way: the act of a social group to blame a sub-group for social dissension for which this sub-group is not responsible, occurring when there is no obvious candidate to blame for social dissension. It purifies the society of a perceived social evil. Because the witches—the sub-group in question—have not committed any crime, charges against them have to be manufactured, if any are offered at all. Witches can be blamed for a particular social crisis when there is no obvious candidate to blame. They are blamed because of who they are, not because of what they have done. When problems arise within society and responsibility for them cannot be attached to any obvious party, common sense stipulates that the witch is the most obvious responsible party. No probative evidence—where 'probative evidence' refers to evidence that people outside of that social worldview would find compelling—need be presented to condemn the witch since there is none, because it seems obvious to the social group that the witch is guilty. So the community carrying out the witch-hunt will truly believe that the witches are guilty, although the action will hardly seem rational to someone with a different worldview. We may think of a witch-hunt as a type of social purification, since it attempts to heal the social body by means of removing or purifying from it one or a number of persons whose presence is thought to endanger its integrity. For the witch-hunt to take place, then, one individual or sub-group that was formally considered to be part of the community must be regarded as foreign and dangerous. The ideology employed in a witch-hunt must convince the participants that the witches are people who had only been masquerading as community members, and unless they are removed the community lies in danger.

The purpose of a ritualized act of purification is to enforce the moral order of a society and thereby strengthen the social order. It will be triggered by anxiety within the society that the social order is collapsing. In such an act, one particular group is defined by the community as outside of the social body. In such an identification the rest of the people are implicitly defined as authentic community members, members who have an obligation to adhere to social morality. In the act of expelling the group identified as foreign, the community also acts concretely to enforce the social order, and so provides evidence of its subjugation to it. The community members thereby commit themselves to adhering to social institutions and morality with their concomitant norms, roles and obligations. This is a matter that I will take up in the excursus on ritual at the end of this introduction.

The self-diagnosis that leads to the solution of a ritualized act of purification such as a witch-hunt may not be accurate. That is, what the social body as a whole perceives to be the imminent destruction of the community may simply be a minor crisis. What matters is how the group sees the matter. If anxiety is high a witch-hunt will, under certain circumstances, be the result. What matters is perception, not reality, since perception becomes the reality for the social group. As I will argue, anxiety about social disintegration may not be fully justified, but will reflect a widespread feeling that people are failing to observe the norms and expectations of the society, what I call internal boundaries or internal integration. A society that perceives itself to have weak internal boundaries—that believes that people are failing to observe social morality at an alarming rate—and that has strong external boundaries is likely to engage in a ritualized act of purification. The practical benefit of a witch-hunt, as I just mentioned, is that it dramatizes and actualizes subjugation to the moral order of society. If I can show that the Persian period temple community was a society with strong external boundaries and weak internal ones, then I can conclude that its action of expelling the women as narrated in Ezra 9–10 was precisely the type of action we would expect that social group to take. The anxiety within the community may have manifested itself in concrete ways that included concerns about who was worshiping foreign gods, but such concerns cannot rightly be called the causes of the divorces and expulsions. They are merely epiphenomena of the group's internal and external boundaries and the worldview that existed with them once internal integration was sufficiently weak. I will attempt to explicate these points in the next section, but one final point should be made clear here. I will argue that this act functions, as I have mentioned, as an act of social purification, and the language of the text of Ezra 9–10 contains the language of purity. One of the main advantages that this approach holds over other scholarly approaches is its ability to find evidence for its argument in the explanation that the text itself offers.

b. *The Methodological Corollaries of the Thesis*

I have argued that the text of Ezra 9–10 does not lend unequivocal support to the theses of other scholars who have addressed this issue. The text appears to remain stubbornly ambivalent as to the reasons that might explain why the women are such a danger that they must leave the community. This in itself can be taken as evidence of a witch-hunt, since such an act is unconscious. Social groups do not consciously mark out subgroups as dangerous and foreign for no reason. Yet in a witch-hunt no reason is needed, because the social worldview makes the action seem self-evident and eminently necessary. To ask those involved in such an action what justification they have for expelling the witches would be rather like asking them what justification they have for assuming two plus two equals four. The reasons are grounded in the way the world is. Yet, lest readers believe that I am embarking upon an argument from silence, I devote Chapter 1 to an analysis of the text in question. While Ezra 9–10 does not say that the Jerusalem temple community expelled the foreign women without evidence and because this was the only group to blame for social anxiety because no obvious candidate could be found—a witch-hunt, as I have defined it, precludes such recognition—these chapters leave us clues beyond a failure to mention any crime on the part of the women that a witch-hunt is precisely what happened. The text continually uses terms associated with purity, suggesting that it is advancing an ideology that its readers are to find convincing: the women are an impure and thus a dangerous foreign body that threatens the health of its social host. The ideology employed here, then, hints that a ritualized act of purification is underway, and a witch-hunt, as I will argue, is a kind of purity ritual. In short, Chapter 1 will make the argument that there is enough evidence in the text itself that we are faced with a witch-hunt that the matter deserves further investigation. In the second part of Chapter 1 I will show that there is no reason to doubt the historical validity of Ezra 9–10.

Chapter 2 will focus on two major points: first, communities likely to engage in ritualized acts of purification such as witch-hunts are those with weak internal integration and strong external boundaries; and second, women are the most likely victims of witch-hunts. By strong external social boundaries, I am referring to societies that take great pains to distinguish themselves from surrounding communities. Social groups with strong external boundaries will be obsessed with keeping foreigners and foreign influences out of their midst. They may rely on genealogies to clearly distinguish who belongs within the community. They may discourage the importation of foreign goods. They will look upon foreign cultures and religions and mores with suspicion. They may obsessively use the language of purity in order to talk about the necessity of keeping such foreign substances out. The foreign is equated with the impure and the dangerous. When I write of internal boundaries or internal integration, I refer, as I have already mentioned, to the degree of adherence to social expectations and norms and obligations and institutions and the social moral order. Every society has some range of behavior expected from its members, although naturally this will vary greatly from group to group. My focus here is particularly on social groups anxious that the expectations and norms and morality held up as good by the social worldview are not being met by members. People may have begun abandoning the traditional religion, challenging the accepted structures of authority, turning to outside sources of wisdom and healing, refusing to respect their elders. In such societies we find a great deal of internal ambiguity, as people become uncertain whether traditional structures of power and culture and religion are valid, or whether they can stand at all. They may be uncertain as to which voices to listen to, whose instructions to obey, which set of values to honor. As I will show in the section below on the function of ritual, ritual is meant to resolve such situations of ambiguity, to communicate in a persuasive manner to community members the validity and goodness of traditional social power structures and religion and culture. It is, as Wuthnow has pointed out, meant to regulate and define social relations.[56]

There is a certain logic to this. Ritual demands the participation of community members, so simply the fact that people are present and speaking, singing or acting in such a situation indicates assent to—if not necessarily belief in[57]—the traditional social structures with which they are associated.

56. Wuthnow, *Meaning and Moral Order*, p. 107.

57. This is a matter that will be addressed below, but on the difference between assent and belief in ritual contexts see R.A. Rappaport, *Ritual and Religion in the*

Not only does the community act here as a group, it does so on the basis of a liturgy that portrays reality and social worldview in a unified way. When the group acts as a whole it implies, at the very least, that it thinks as a whole and shares the same values. In ritual, social worldview is dramatized, communicated and assented to, and this is why Wuthnow has pointed out that rituals are more meaningful at times of uncertainty[58] and why Geertz has stated that ideology will have more impact when the general cultural orientations of a society appear to be lost.[59] By dramatizing the social order and worldview and by having community members participate in its dramatization, ritual acts, if it works, to clear up ambiguity in social relations, to make it clear how people should act and think. It acts, as Wuthnow writes, as a 'social thermostat' that informs members how to behave.[60] I will have more to say on the function of ritual at the end of this chapter.

Why would a community with strong external boundaries and weak internal integration be likely to engage in a ritualized act of purification? I delay a fuller explanation until Chapter 2, but, basically speaking, societies with strong external boundaries remain constantly vigilant in defining themselves in opposition to outside groups. However, within such societies that also have weak internal integration, there will be ambiguity regarding social roles and relations, adherence to traditional values and social worldview, and so on. Should such ambiguity reach unacceptable levels—should a significant number of people within the community become anxious that lack of adherence to traditional norms and behavior will lead to social disintegration, in other words—this society that is obsessed with defining itself against other social groups will quite naturally find the root of its problems as stemming from an illegitimate mixing with other peoples. Whatever factors caused our society in question to maintain such strong external boundaries, we may logically infer that it does so because it views any mixture with other societies as dangerous and bad. The worldview of that society makes it clear to community members that contact with outsiders is to be avoided. When situations of social ambiguity arise, then, it will be read by society's members through the social worldview that demands strong external boundaries because of the

Making of Humanity (Cambridge Studies in Social and Cultural Anthropology, 110; Cambridge: Cambridge University Press, 1999), pp. 119-24.

58. Wuthnow, *Meaning and Moral Order*, pp. 111-14.

59. Geertz, *Interpretation*, p. 219.

60. Wuthnow, *Meaning and Moral Order*, p. 107.

dangers that foreigners pose to the group. We should thus expect the belief to arise that these external boundaries have not been strong enough, that foreign influences have slipped through the cracks in the external guards, and the hunt for foreign infiltrators will be on. The hunt will end with the group that, in the worldview of the community, is most easily associated with the dangerous and, thus, the foreign. There is a logic to such actions even if, as Bourdieu has put it, it is 'fuzzy' logic.[61] The actions that the community takes are completely in keeping with its worldview and the unspoken connections that it can draw that seem to defy scientific logic. The result of the hunt, however, is that a group of people once considered part of the community will be regarded as foreign and dangerous. The worldview of the community insists that a foreign group is responsible for social ambiguity, and a foreign group will be found, even if it has to be manufactured.

The second point that I will make in Chapter 2 is that women are the most likely victims of scapegoating. I will present a number of studies that suggest reasons why particular societies regard women as especially dangerous and linked to the foreign pollutants that are thought to threaten the integrity of the social body. When societies exercise control over their members, when they promote particular modes of behavior and morality as right, they link such control to the way the world is as seen through the social worldview. When Geertz writes that moral disposition and worldview reinforce each other, he means that in the circular logic created by social groups mores can be vindicated by comparing them to the way the cosmos functions. When, in the social worldview, the social claims the power to control even birth and death, one obvious challenge to this worldview is that women give birth to children, and as such they represent a challenge to the social worldview. Quite often, as Nancy Jay has pointed out, many societies emphasize an opposition between childbirth, associated with impurity, and sacrificial rituals of the social, associated with

61. Bourdieu, *Outline*, pp. 112-25. What Bourdieu means by fuzzy logic is that in many cases people simply do not have the luxury of logical speculation, and so perform actions informed by an internal logic of social symbolism. A relationship is established between practice and the worldview of a society by means of a symbolism that can metaphorically connect such diverse things as pregnancy and the germination of wheat in the ground. This metaphorical power of social symbols is an especially important matter when the social body needs to find a witch, as particular groups are more closely associated with the dangerous and the impure by social symbolism.

purity.[62] Ritual, dramatizing and communicating the social order, will at times align the social order against women. They are suspect because of the challenge they pose to the worldview, and so will be obvious candidates when the worldview is seen to be under challenge.

This is why we are so unlikely to find particular criminal charges drawn up against witches, for they are simply the candidates to whom common sense dictates that society turn when no one more obviously guilty can be found. They are being blamed, we could say, for social disintegration, but the social body need bring no actual charges against them, since the implication of their guilt stems from who they are, not what they have done. If there is one particular cause of the collapse of social integration, the anxiety this triggers may easily locate those responsible for causing the social evasion of morality, and so will purify the society of those people. But if the causes are many and diffuse, if there is no one group truly responsible for introducing foreign elements into society, then there is really no one guilty party. At this point we expect a witch-hunt, a particular kind of purification act, one that simply aims to purge the group most easily associated with anti-social tendencies from the social body in order to increase social integration.

If these are the societies that are likely to engage in acts of purification, then I am obliged to show that the Persian period temple community was a group that meets the criteria of weak internal integration and strong external boundaries. This is the purpose of Chapter 3, where I set out to show that the biblical texts produced during this period betray such boundaries. They indicate anxiety about social integration. Again, we expect this anxiety to be expressed through fears in the community regarding the collapse of adherence to social norms. Do the young people disregard the religion of their ancestors? Does the loyalty of the citizens to the nation waver? Have people begun to ignore the usual codes of politeness? Do they go outside of the community to find wisdom and marriage partners?

We should also expect to find evidence that this is a community obsessed with maintaining strong external boundaries between itself and other social groups. Such boundaries may be drawn by means of genealogies (one must trace a pedigree in order to be considered a community member), or by physical distance (we need as much separation from other peoples as possible), or by ideology (no other group is as good as we are;

62. N. Jay, *Throughout your Generations Forever: Sacrifice, Religion, and Paternity* (Chicago: University of Chicago Press, 1992), p. xxiii.

all other peoples worship false gods and association with them must be avoided at all costs lest they turn us from true worship), or by all three. In Chapter 3 I will argue, through a consideration of some of the biblical texts produced in the exile and in the Persian period, as well as through an examination of the distribution of settlements in Persian period Yehud, that the Jerusalem temple community employed all three of these strategies. I do not really attempt to explain why this group was obsessed with strong external boundaries, with keeping itself pure of outsiders, I merely point to the fact that there is strong evidence for it.

By this juncture in the work, I hope to have made the following points: the text of Ezra 9–10 gives us hints that we are faced with a witch-hunt, a kind of ritualized act of purification; that societies with weak internal integration and strong external boundaries tend to pursue such acts if internal ambiguity becomes too high; and that the Persian period temple community centered at Jerusalem appears to be just such a community. The point that I wish to address in Chapter 4 regards the causes that contributed to the anxiety within the community that internal ambiguity had reached the point that something must be done; that, as we outside observers could say, a witch-hunt should take place. I can offer no single event to serve as the cause of the anxiety, but can suggest a range of factors that would contribute to weak internal integration, and that would thus raise social anxiety and consequent demands for greater adherence to social norms, the anxiety and the demands that resulted in a witch-hunt.

Some scholars, as we have seen, have explained the divorces by pointing to a fear within the community that apostasy or syncretism was becoming widespread. The abandonment of the national religion is an obvious example of weak internal integration. While this particular issue is not explicitly raised in Ezra 9–10 (although the text does allude to it), the situation within Persian-ruled Palestine was amenable to the spread of foreigners and their religions. Trade blossomed in the region at this time, and the Persian army established small forts that protected trade routes and, in some cases, resupplied travelers. Foreigners, of course, will bring not just goods when they come to trade, but all sorts of cultural products that include such things as religions, worldviews, religions and morality. Given what we know of the temple community's strong external boundaries and weak internal ones, given that the text of Ezra 9–10 offers us clues that the divorces and expulsions were effected as a ritualized act of purification, it seems at the very least likely that the presence of foreigners in Yehud due to the free flow of trade in Palestine and the cultural products that they brought with them was one cause of the anxiety in the community about adherence to cultural norms.

We may trace another cause to the geographical spread of the community. While I argue in Chapter 3 that settlements in Persian period Yehud are closely clustered around Jerusalem, a distribution of sites that creates a physical distance between the community and other peoples, we know from the text of Ezra–Nehemiah and from epigraphical evidence that members of the Jerusalem temple community lived outside of the province. They lived among foreigners, and were daily subject to their religions, worldviews and mores. At such points the external boundary between the community and other peoples was actually weak, and the community members in such areas would have been constantly exposed to ideas that gave them different perspectives on reality than that provided by their own social group. When we remember that moral dispositions are vindicated when they can be shown to be in conformity with reality as seen through the social worldview, exposure to different worldviews can weaken adherence to expected modes of action. Even the presence of the Persian administration itself within the province, made up of foreign bureaucrats and soldiers, represents a foreign presence and a source of worldviews and culture that differed from that of the temple community.

An overview of the method I employ—one could call it a social anthropological approach—shows that it is comparativist. I ask, specifically in Chapter 2, what the Persian period temple community had in common with societies that scapegoat and engage in witch-hunts, and come up with the answer of weak internal integration and strong external boundaries where no easily identifiable cause of weakening social integration could be located. So I do not wish to dismiss the insights of other scholars on this matter, but I do wish to point out that by themselves they are insufficient to explain the divorces. If the community had only been concerned about apostasy, or had only fought to control ethnic purity, there were a thousand possible courses of action open to it. My investigation of the social boundaries of the community, its worldview, and its economic and political setting shows that a witch-hunt was the action that it was extremely likely to take.

c. *Excursus: The Function of Ritual and Ritualized Acts*

The Function of Ritual. If social worldview is the means by which people make sense of experience, ritual reinforces this worldview. Ritual functions as a means of communication that makes the worldview plain, that informs participants about the way the world is put together and how they should act as a consequence. I mentioned above that the community's decision to mandate the divorces and that the divorces themselves are a ritualized act, and I shall presently distinguish between ritual and ritualized act. I will first draw upon the work of anthropologists, however, to show how, as Edmund Leach put it, humans use rituals to transmit messages to themselves.[63]

Mary Douglas makes the same point: 'Ritual is pre-eminently a form of communication', she writes.[64] As children learn to speak, she points out, they learn specific codes that create order and relevance, permitting communication with others. And since language is a social phenomenon and a creation of social groups, the social worldview is encoded in this language and becomes the substratum of experience within each particular group. Every time people speak and listen to speech, in other words, their social identity is shaped because their social worldview is shaped.[65] Ritual is a particular kind of speech and a particularly limited kind of speech, as we shall see. By communicating information about worldview, by appealing to ultimate principles of humanity and the cosmos (as the society understands them) it makes social structures seem reasonable and so creates social solidarity.[66] As Valerio Valeri puts it, ritual dramatizes a state of affairs that reinforces experience as filtered through the social worldview, and rituals 'are reflective experiences in which the constitutive concepts of action are apperceived'.[67] Without awareness of the fundamental social concepts communicated through ritual, in other words, experience and action are directionless and meaningless. Rituals attempt to show why the social structure and its authority are necessary and desirable, what moral dispositions are consequently necessary, what types of actions individuals owe to each other, and so on.

The very limited grammar and structure of ritual, its extremely formal style, focuses participants' assent to the authority and social structure that they communicate. Many scholars concur with Roy Rappaport's

63. E. Leach, *Culture and Communication: The Logic by which Symbols are Connected* (Cambridge: Cambridge University Press, 1976), p. 45.

64. M. Douglas, *Natural Symbols: Explorations in Cosmology* (New York: Vintage Books, 1973), p. 41.

65. Douglas, *Natural Symbols*, pp. 43-44.

66. Douglas, *Natural Symbols*, pp. 79-80.

67. V. Valeri, *Kingship and Sacrifice: Ritual and Society in Ancient Hawaii* (trans. Paula Wissing; Chicago: University of Chicago Press, 1985), p. 347.

characterization of ritual as 'the performance of more or less invariant sequences of formal acts and utterances'.[68] Ritual actions are repetitive and consist of stereotyped elements, rituals are often performed with specific regularity, and they transmit information by means of redundancy.[69] In Valeri's point of view, ritual's redundancy and regularity functions as a drill for its participants as they act in dramas to reinforce and reproduce socially sanctioned and desirable dispositions.[70] Bloch has pointed out that human language is powerful because of the vast creativity of its syntax that can articulate almost any notion.[71] The formality and stylization of ritual language, on the other hand, drastically reduces linguistic freedom and the number of responses available to participants.[72] Ritual drastically restricts loudness patterns, choice of intonation, syntax, vocabulary, sequencing of speech acts, sources from which illustrations may be drawn, and maintains strict stylistic rules. There are very few proper responses to the sentence 'The Lord be with you' when it is uttered in the context of a religious service. This impoverishment of language through the formalization of ritual makes the course of rituals fairly predictable, and it makes the utterances and actions of its leaders and participants equally predictable. In this way, argues Bloch, ritual functions as a form of social control. One speaker can coerce the response of other speakers, and '[i]t is really the type of communication where rebellion is impossible and only revolution could be feasible'.[73] Of course, the speech of those leading the ritual is also radically restricted, and so all participants acknowledge the traditional authority communicated by the ritual.

Because the formalization of ritualized speech rules out the potential of nearly infinite responses to one statement and the potential of contradiction, both prerequisites of logic, it is impossible to represent such language as logical. Rather, writes Bloch, following J.L. Austin, ritual language is illocutionary or performative. It is language that does not report facts but that influences people. The grammar of ritual does not lend itself to explanation the way that ordinary, logical language does,[74] but through its structure it can communicate certain social desiderata and

68. Rappaport, *Religion and Ritual*, p. 24.
69. Rappaport, *Religion and Ritual*, pp. 33, 46, 77.
70. Valeri, *Kingship and Sacrifice*, p. 344.
71. Bloch, *Ritual, History and Power*, pp. 22-33.
72. Bloch, *Ritual, History and Power*, p. 20.
73. Bloch, *Ritual, History and Power*, p. 29.
74. Bloch, *Ritual, History and Power*, p. 37.

aspects of the worldview. In describing social dramas, Victor Turner argues that they contain four main phases: a breach of social norms, a mounting crisis, a period of redressive action that attempts to repair the social system, and final reintegration.[75] Rituals are a kind of social drama, albeit an extremely stylized and predictable kind. A ritual has a perfectly predictable outcome unless it fails entirely. It dramatizes particular aspects of the social order to its participants and commands their assent. Bloch, writing of the circumcision ritual among the Merina of Madagascar, refers to it as a drama with two 'acts'.[76] The ritual begins by bringing the boys out of the house, the realm in Merina society that is associated with women. It is where the boys have spent their time before their initiation into manhood, and it is the area associated with their mothers. The feminine in the Merina worldview is associated with the biological, the material part of life that passes away, and that is set in opposition to the masculine, associated with social unity and the ancestors who live eternally and who truly control the sources of life. As the boy leaves the realm of his mother and, by association, that which is impermanent, he enters the realm of men and the ancestors; and as he is taken away the women crawl about on the floor and throw dirt on their heads, an extremely polluting action in Merina society. This is the first act.

What the ritual emphasizes in this moment of chaos is that biological birth, obviously linked with the feminine, is of no worth when compared to the true birth of the boy into the realm of the ancestors. The power and life and beneficence of the Merina ancestors is implicitly contrasted with the biological power of women to give birth, and the ritual is unsubtle in pointing out that it is the ancestors who truly control the sources of life. When the boy is finally circumcised, the second act of the ritual, the message conveyed is that this is his true and more important birth. It is the birth into society by way of the ancestors that takes precedence over his biological birth by way of his mother. In this small drama, a particular aspect of the Merina worldview is emphasized. The ability of the ancestors to control the source of life stands in apparent contradiction to the simple biological fact that it is women, not the dead, who give birth, and so the acts of the ritual dramatize the social place of women in relation to the boy and the rest of society, as well as the social place of the boy in relation to

75. V. Turner, *Dramas, Fields, and Metaphors: Symbolic Action in Human Society* (Symbol, Myth, and Ritual Series; Ithaca, NY: Cornell University Press, 1974), pp. 37-42.

76. Bloch, *Ritual, History and Power*, pp. 158-61.

the rest of society. Social hierarchy has been demonstrated, as has the metaphysic that underlies it.

The very grammar and structure of ritual, then, forces participants' assent to the social order and depicts parts of it. Both Bloch and Rappaport have noticed that rituals do vary to some extent, and both have noticed that the part that varies will represent the current state of the participants.[77] Rappaport refers to this as the self-referential aspect of ritual, and it acts, he claims, to boil down the various feelings of the participants into one in order to signal a 'general condition of the group'. In this way any ambiguity within the group about assent to the social worldview is eliminated. Rituals take various and unstable dispositions and force assent to the social aspects being communicated.[78] While not all participants may be in agreement with the unambiguous sign of the ritual nor believe the metaphysic of the worldview it dramatizes, the ritual 'filters out' such feelings, making them private phenomena with no place in the social system.[79] 'By participating in a ritual the performer reaches out of his [*sic*] *private* self, so to speak, into a *public* canonical order to grasp the category that he then imposes upon his private processes'.[80]

The invariant aspects of ritual Rappaport calls its canonical aspects. By performing in a ritual, participating in 'a more or less *invariant* sequence of formal acts and utterances *encoded by someone other than the performer*', members of a society acknowledge the social authority by which that ritual is established and the worldview that it portrays.[81] The result is assent to this social worldview and order, and this becomes the social basis of morality. Participation in ritual cannot determine if people believe in the social order on display, but it does assume consent. Even if the acceptance is insincere, obligations and conventions and roles have been established and participants are bound by participation to observe them.[82] Should someone be found to be in violation of social norms and obligations they may be judged because of the public assent demonstrated by participation in ritual. Actions are judged by the degree to which they conform to the social order as expressed and accepted in ritual, and so

77. Rappaport, *Religion and Ritual*, pp. 52-54, and Bloch, *Ritual, History and Power*, p. 32.

78. Rappaport, *Religion and Ritual*, p. 95.

79. Rappaport, *Religion and Ritual*, p. 103.

80. Rappaport, *Religion and Ritual*, pp. 105-106. His emphasis.

81. Rappaport, *Religion and Ritual*, p. 118. His emphasis.

82. Rappaport, *Religion and Ritual*, pp. 117-26.

ritual drama constructs an 'ought' by which the 'is' of behavior may be judged.[83]

Such assertions as to the function of ritual are, in their own ways, expansions upon Emile Durkheim's assertion that ritual creates a sense of dependence upon and need for moral harmony with the social.[84] In ritual a worldview is presented along with its associated social morality, norms and obligations, and if there is dependence here it is simply on the part of individuals who need to make sense of the way the world is. Ritual provides them with this sense, and participation in it forces assent to the social order and its consequent morality. As Geertz has pointed out, when a ritual or any other type of explanatory cultural pattern fails, deep disquiet will result.[85] In a case study of a ritual that failed, Geertz comes to the conclusion that it could not be performed successfully—that is, people refused to participate—because the worldview on which it was based was at odds with the organization of society. The worldview did not correspond to the way things actually were and the way people acted, and the polity it attempted to dramatize no longer existed.[86] People will only participate in ritual—and so give their assent to the social worldview and system of morality—when they believe that it tells them something true about the way the world is, and so is useful for informing them as to how to interpret experience and to act.

As Rappaport pointed out, rituals eliminate ambiguity. An initiation rite signals that a girl has become a woman or that a boy has become a man. While the biological process of such developments takes place over the course of years, a ritual signals that, socially speaking, the individual in question is, at this one point, no longer a child but an adult. The new man or woman now knows how he or she is viewed by other members of society, what their new roles are, and so what is expected of them as a result. In some rituals, writes Wuthnow, ambiguity is exaggerated simply in order to more fully dramatize the lack of it when the ritual is over, thereby reinforcing the moral order.[87]

83. Rappaport, *Religion and Ritual*, pp. 132-33.

84. E. Durkheim, *The Elementary Forms of the Religious Life* (trans. J.W. Swain; New York: George Allen and Unwin, 1915), pp. 235-72.

85. Geertz, *Interpretation*, p. 100.

86. Geertz, *Interpretation*, pp. 142-69.

87. Wuthnow, *Meaning and Moral Order*, pp. 122-23.

Ritualized Acts and Ezra 9–10. I should now distinguish between ritual and ritualized act. Ritual, as I have been using the term, refers to either a regularized liturgy (such as Sunday Mass) or to a fairly set liturgy that may be repeated whenever necessary (such as a Bar Mitzvah). Catherine Bell, however, has suggested that there are many activities which, while the people who practice them would not recognize them as ritual, still function 'to distinguish and privilege what is being done in comparison to other, usually more quotidian, activities'.[88] Unlike Wuthnow, she would not call left-hand turn signals examples of ritual simply because the people who make them would not recognize them as such.[89] There are many actions that are not rituals as I have been using the term, however, that do construct certain types of power relations within social organizations. A ritualized action 'produces and objectifies constructions of power (via the schemes that organize its environment), which the social agent reembodies'.[90] In this way, Bell writes, participants in such actions construct a view of the world that lays out the hierarchy of the universe as produced by the social and that is employed in practical actions.[91] What Bell points toward, in short, is a whole scale of actions that run the gamut from activities just more than quotidian to rituals that alert members of a society to an authoritative ordering of the world and the power relations of the society that go along with such an ordering. If rituals can accomplish this, so can less formal activities.

I raise the difference because the scene narrated in Ezra 9–10 is obviously not a ritual in the strict sense but may be considered a ritualized act. Yet the performative functions of ritual that I have noted, its ability to force assent to the social order and its creation of morality thereby, are dependent, as scholars have shown, upon ritual's redundancy. Can we attribute the same functions to a ritualized act which lacks such repetition? Bell states that the purpose of ritualized act 'is to ritualize persons, who

88. C. Bell, *Ritual Theory, Ritual Practice* (Oxford: Oxford University Press, 1992), p. 74.

89. Bell, *Ritual Theory*, p. 205. Wuthnow includes a much broader range of activities under the rubric of ritual than Bell. He considers left-hand turn signals to be rituals (or at least a prototype of ritual) because they take place under particular circumstances within a network of social obligations in order to eliminate ambiguity. Cf. Wuthnow, *Meaning and Moral Order*, pp. 111-12. See also p. 109 for his definition of ritual.

90. Bell, *Ritual Theory*, p. 206.

91. Bell, *Ritual Theory*, p. 208.

deploy schemes of ritualization in order to dominate (shift or nuance) other, nonritualized situations to render them more coherent with the values of the ritualizing schemes and capable of molding perceptions'.[92] We can see how the divorces in the Jerusalem temple community functioned to 'ritualize' community members in order to mold their perceptions and make their actions coherent with social values. First, the action focuses on a particular group in society and brands them as foreign. In this way it emphasizes who does and does not belong to the community, and so reduces ambiguity in regard to the external boundaries of the community. Like a ritual, then, it functions to reduce ambiguity. Second, those within the community are obliged to conform to social obligations and norms—to work to sustain internal social integration—and in this way the action, like some rituals, does not just symbolize the social order, it does something about it.[93] In agreeing to divorce these women the men who do so (and all community members who agree that this is the proper course of action to take) produce a concrete example of their willingness to conform to social norms. In the action, the word of morality is made flesh.

Finally, in the subordination to the social order there is assent to the social order. True, the matter at hand concerns only the divorce and expulsion of a small number of women, but, as Bell writes, ritualized actions mold people and help them direct future actions by means of social values. In this way her point is not terribly different than Bourdieu's, since both believe that the actions of daily praxis that mold individuals without conscious intent direct them toward social goals. How does this happen? In the particular case of Ezra 9–10 the community members assent to the social worldview that marks out a particular group of women as outsiders and that marks the rest of the members as insiders, true community members. As community members they have social roles to play which entail certain obligations that are grounded in the same social worldview that marks the women as outsiders. So if in Ezra 9–10 the social hierarchy is not explicitly mentioned, if a wide variety of social norms and obligations are not expressed, the community decision to demand the divorce and expulsion of these women works because the community members subscribe to a common worldview. In participating in the action, whether as husbands who divorce or as the members of the temple assembly that demands that the husbands do so, the community reminds itself of its external boundaries and it forces itself to make a concrete example of

92. Bell, *Ritual Theory*, p. 108.

93. On this point see Rappaport, *Religion and Ritual*, pp. 141-49.

subjugation to the social order. In this way are people made aware of their society's worldview, their need to subjugate themselves to it, and the necessity to admit that their actions must be formed by the roles and obligations it requires. It is clear, then, that the act of purification in Ezra 9–10 is a moral issue: it alerts community members to the boundaries of their community and gives them an opportunity to express their subjugation to the moral order. Such actions, as I shall argue in Chapter 2, increase social integration.

This is why I argue that the causes that other scholars have offered for the divorces are, if they were actually live issues at the time, epiphenomena of the worldview that accompanied the temple community's social boundaries. Although there is no evidence that links the community's divorce and expulsion of the women to a fear that they would cause apostasy, such a fear may have existed. Why would the community worry about apostasy? While the question may sound inane, remember that religion is a social creation even when its rituals are performed in private.[94] Since religion and its rituals instruct social members in worldview and social obligations, the abandonment of the religion of your culture is a sign of a weakening allegiance to society and its norms and roles. It is as much a social and moral decision as it is a religious one. As Rappaport argues, it is ritual participation that creates morality and obligation and the standard by which actions may be judged. As people refuse to engage in such rituals they do not bind themselves to the moral standards of judgment of their society and so reject its worldview and its ethical structure. From the point of view of others within the society, this rejection of the religion of the ancestors will be taken as an obvious rebellion against social heritage and so as a sign of social disintegration.

Why would a society worry about ethnicity? As I mentioned above this is another cause suggested by scholars for the divorces and expulsions, even though the evidence for it is quite limited. If the temple community was concerned about ethnic purity then all this demonstrates is the fact that it was a community with strong external boundaries and was worried that these boundaries had been breached. It is only a community

94. Rituals in this sense function just the way language does. Language is a social invention that functions by means of a socially constructed grammar which individuals obey even if they are talking to themselves. So, argues Wuthnow, when rituals are performed in private they represent individuals' internalization of collectivity. See Wuthnow, *Meaning and Moral Order*, pp. 103-104, as well as Geertz, *Interpretation*, pp. 360-64.

concerned with keeping foreigners out that will worry about ethnic purity, and such a society will only actively search for foreigners when it believes that it has been alerted to their presence within the community. Anxiety about weakening social integration functions as an alert; and so a society concerned about ethnic purity is a society with strong external and weak internal boundaries. The boundaries and the worldview that accompanies it are the cause of any concerns about ethnic purity.

The approach I bring to this material has the benefit of being able to take the explanation offered for the divorces in the text at face value: it is a matter of social purity. This work is dedicated to explaining the significance of social purity within the context of the Jerusalem temple community's social boundaries, and it can answer questions that other scholarly approaches beg. Why would the community be concerned about social purity? Why are foreigners, especially foreign women, understood as a danger? Why does Ezra 9–10 not charge the women with any offenses? Why did the community expel the women and not take another action? The approach I suggest to explain the action can answer these questions.

Chapter 1

The Narrative of Ezra 9–10: Some Interpretive Difficulties

1. *Introduction*

In the first part of this chapter I will examine the narrative of Ezra 9–10 in order to point out that the text levels no charge against the foreign women, and that it contains a number of references to purity and impurity. The point of this chapter is to show that the narrative of Ezra 9–10 gives us enough evidence that we are faced with a witch-hunt that we should pursue the matter farther. We shall see that these chapters make it clear that the very existence of the community is seen to hang in the balance, that at least a significant number of its members believe that continued survival depends on how the society deals with the presence of the foreign women. While the women are charged with no crime, their husbands appear to be: they have caused foreigners to dwell (the text uses the hiphil of *yšb*) within the community, and that has endangered the community's existence. Throughout these chapters, the impurity of foreigners is contrasted with the community's need to be pure, to be separated (the text uses the niphal of *bdl*) from all peoples.

It would appear, if the community is not charging the women with any wrongdoing, such as causing others to worship foreign gods—or even doing so themselves—then it does not expel the women because of what they have done. The danger they pose is their impurity, and Ezra 9–10 contains language that deals with purity. This is our first bit of evidence that these chapters deal with a ritualized act of purification, and, with the help of the work of Mary Douglas, I shall discuss the bearing such language of purity has on the social boundaries of the group. Yet if the women are charged with no crime, their husbands are: they have caused the impure to dwell in the midst of the holy and must act, with the rest of the community, to separate this illegitimate and dangerous intermingling.

The issue, as we shall see, is both ontological and moral. The impure and pure, according to Israelite theology, must be kept separate because of their opposed essences. On the other hand, these expulsions are also a test of the community's loyalty to its social morality: will it subjugate itself to social morality or not? The community expresses its anxiety theologically, making an argument for separation based on ontology. But what the anthropologist sees is a concern to shore up internal integration in the society by involving the community in a ritualized act of purification, clearly indicated by the language the text employs. So the text makes the community's rationale for the expulsions clear; our only difficulty lies in interpreting the significance of the purity language it uses.

In the second part of this chapter I shall show that there is no reason to doubt the historical validity of Ezra 9–10. No evidence exists to argue that the actions portrayed in these chapters on the part of the community as a whole and on the part of Ezra would not be in keeping with the actions of the Jerusalem temple community and its administrative head (the role, as I shall show, of Ezra). This is not to claim that Ezra 9–10 is a verbatim report of what happened, but the narrative does alert us to the possibility of a witch-hunt, as the initial investigation of the passage will show. If in the following chapters I can show that we are faced with a society that is likely to engage in an act of purification, then it would seem that the story accurately reflects the community's worldview.

2. *An Analysis of the Narrative of Ezra 9–10*

a. *Analysis*

The crisis involving the foreign women first appears in Ezra–Nehemiah when officials of Yehud report to Ezra that the people of Israel and the priests and the Levites had not *nbdlw*, 'separated themselves', from the peoples of the lands (Ezra 9.1), and that *zr' hqdš*, 'the holy seed', had 'mixed itself' with them (9.2). Ezra's response to the message is to tear his clothes and pull out some of the hair of his head and beard, the symbols of mourning. Then he begins his prayer of 9.6-15, which contains a number of interesting notions. He begins by noting his shame due to 'our iniquities' and 'our guilt', both apparently due to the community members who had married women from the peoples of the lands. In 9.7 Ezra goes on to say that this situation is hardly unique: 'From the days of our ancestors we have been in great guilt until this day, and in our iniquities we have been given, we, our kings, [and] our priests, into the hand of the kings of the lands'. The situation of guilt and iniquity is, in his opinion,

Israel's normal state. However, as he continues his prayer, he states that Israel's situation is somewhat different now, even if it is still a nation of guilt and iniquity. 'But now', says Ezra, the community has been shown grace from its God, which has left over a surviving group *bmqm qdšw*, 'in his holy place' (9.8). Still, in the same verse Ezra calls the community's situation one of slavery, and one gets the idea that he perceives its current status as a kind of probationary period: instead of the punishment that it deserves due to the sins of the nation, past and present, the people has been shown grace, but has not been restored to its former station. And in case the reader has missed the point, Ezra uses the terms 'slaves' and 'slavery' to open the next verse: 'For we are slaves, yet in our slavery our God did not abandon us', and instead showed loving kindness to the community (9.9).

The notion of Israel's past guilt met with God's present grace may roughly be said to be the theme of 9.7-9. But in 9.10 Ezra returns the reader to the present, for in the present, of course, lies more guilt and iniquity, as he has already informed us in 9.6. 'And now, what shall we say, O our God, after this? For we have abandoned your commandments' (9.10). Even though in the present God has shown the community grace with probation instead of destruction (9.8; and remember that that verse also began with the word 'now'), in the present the community has met this grace with disobedience. Although God did not 'abandon' the community (9.8), the community has 'abandoned' God (9.10). While Ezra speaks of commandments in the plural in 9.10, in 9.11-12 he cites only one commandment that the community has abandoned: intermarrying with the people of the lands. The motivation clause (9.12) is directly related to the idea of probation that he has already introduced. Israel must not intermarry if it wishes to keep the land. And the consequences of violating probation are laid out in 9.14, after Ezra once more underlines the fact of Israel's guilt by stating yet again that even though Israel has committed 'evil deeds' in its 'great guilt', God has still left a remnant despite its 'iniquities' (9.13). Should Israel continue in this way, he says, God will destroy the community and leave 'no remnant nor surviving group', an apparent reference to a final exile that will put a complete end to Israel. The notion of the current community being a remnant or a surviving group has already been mentioned in 9.8, and appears to suggest that while God did not destroy all of Israel through exile to Babylon, one more occurrence of guilt might cause the divine anger to destroy even the remnant that is left. 9.15 concludes the prayer by restating its two salient features: God's righteousness has left over a surviving group, but this group is guilty. In a sense, this verse lays out the problem as Ezra sees it, the cause and effect process that has brought the community to its dangerous situation. By intermarrying with these people, the community has incurred guilt that will activate God's destructive wrath and cause another exile.

Another point of interest in this prayer is the specific vocabulary that Ezra uses to describe the peoples of the lands. He refers to them by using the language of impurity, and speaks about *niddat 'ammê hā'ᵃrāṣôt*, 'the impurity of the peoples of the lands', and about *ṭum'ātām*, 'their impurity' (9.11). Impurity (*ṭum'â* or *niddâ*) and things and people that are impure (*ṭāmē'*) are contagious. Numbers 19.13 notes that those who touch a corpse defile (*ṭimmē'*) the tabernacle because they are *ṭāmē'*, 'impure'. Haggai 2.10-14 makes the same point: one who is impure because of coming into contact with a dead body (*ṭᵉmē' nepeš*; cf. Num. 5.2; 9.6, 7, 10) can defile anything that he or she comes into contact with. Once impurity enters into pure social structures, it is very dangerous. The noun *ṭum'â* is, in the main, a priestly term, with most of its occurrences scattered throughout Leviticus, Numbers and Ezekiel. While an investigation of the word's precise significance is outside of the scope of this chapter, it is perhaps enough to note here P's warning that those who approach the sacred precincts in a state of *ṭum'â* will die (Lev. 15.31). H adds the grim admonition that those who, while *ṭum'â*, approach the sacred things that Israel has sanctified for YHWH, will be put to death (Lev. 22.3). The impure is irreconcilably opposed to the holy and dangerous to life.

The term *niddâ*, 'impurity', that Ezra also uses to describe the foreign peoples, has similar connotations. Its primary use appears to be in reference to the time of a woman's menstruation, when she is said to be *bᵉniddātāh*, 'in her impurity' (cf. Lev. 15.19-24). Like the root *ṭm'*, this word appears mostly in priestly works, generally in P or Ezekiel. And like people or objects that are *ṭāmē'*, the impurity of *niddâ* is very contagious. Whatever a woman touches while menstruating becomes impure (*yitmā'*), and whoever touches her or any object that she has touched also becomes impure. Once impurity enters into the social system, in other words, it is infectious and a danger that must be stemmed. At the end of a law regarding a woman's discharge of blood that does not appear in the normal menstrual cycle (Lev. 15.25-31), the text of Leviticus states that by following the stipulations for cleansing included therein, 'you will separate[1]

1. Reading *whzrtm* with MT, *Targum Pseudo-Jonathan* and *Targum Onqelos*, and not *whzhrtm* with the Samaritan Pentateuch, the Syriac and LXX. The latter reading

the Israelites from their impurity [*miṭṭum'āṭām*] and they will not die in their impurity in their making impure (*bᵉṭammᵉ'ām*; the piel of *ṭm'*] my tabernacle which is among you' (15.31). Impurity leads to death because it is unalterably opposed to the holy presence of God.

As Ezra ends his prayer, he continues weeping and prostrating himself before the temple, and is joined in these activities by the people (10.1). This symbolic acceptance of their guilt is verbalized when a spokesperson admits the community's sin. 'We have acted treacherously against our God, and we have caused to dwell [*wnšb*] foreign women' (10.2). While the use of *yšb* in the hiphil here is often translated as 'we have married' rather than 'we have caused to dwell', the latter translation seems more appropriate. The author uses the common Hebrew terms for marriage in Ezra's prayer (the verbs *nś'*, *ntn* and *ḥtn* in 9.12, 14), and the sense of this causative verb is obviously somewhat different. The problem that the community sees and acknowledges is one of people—specifically, the foreign women—being in a place where they should not be. It was their action in causing these foreign women to dwell in the community that they interpret as treachery against God. The people also pick up on the temporal language that Ezra used. Just as Ezra claimed that the grace shown by God to the community 'now' was 'now' being threatened by the community's own guilt, the spokesperson states that even now all is not lost. 'Now there is hope for Israel concerning this', he says, 'for now let us make a covenant with our God to send away all the women and their children' (10.2-3). The community recognizes with Ezra the serious nature of the offense. Even as Ezra reacted to the news of the intermarriages by warning of another and final exile that would completely destroy even the remnant of Israel left over from the last exile, the people admit their culpability. The solution that they themselves propose is severe and urgent. Like Ezra, they realize that time is of the essence and that the matter must be solved immediately. There is a pervading sense of anxiety that the community's guilt, both present and past, which brought them to their current dismal state of probation, might destroy the community together. The solution, 'to send away all the women and their children', was really hinted at when the story began. 'The people of Israel and the priests and the Levites have not

('you will warn the Israelites from their impurity') does not really seem to fit the context. As J. Milgrom points out, there hardly seems to be any reason to warn the people from impurities that are unavoidable (*Leviticus 1–16* [AB, 3; New York: Doubleday, 1991], p. 945).

separated themselves [*nbdlw*] from the peoples of the land' (9.1), the leaders of the community had warned Ezra.

The problem here is apparently one of separation from impurity, and so it is no wonder that the solution is to force the women out. The very nature of the community, of course, is that it is the polar opposite of what is impure, that it should be separate from such people. The community is 'the holy seed' that dwells in God's 'holy place'. This is the point of the use of *bdl* in the niphal ('to be separate, to separate oneself'). Like the roots dealing with purity and impurity, *bdl* is found mainly in priestly sources, such as P, H and Ezekiel. P employs it to indicate cosmic order in its story of creation. God separates (*wybdl*) the light and the darkness (Gen. 1.4), the waters above and below the firmament (1.6), and the day and the night (1.14, 18). The verb is also used in the sense of setting apart or distinguishing the clean from the unclean, as it is when God tells Aaron *lhbdyl byn hqdš wbyn hḥl wbyn hṭm' wbyn hṭhwr*, 'to separate between the holy and the profane and between the impure and the pure' (Lev. 10.10). *bdl* occurs a number of times with words from roots designating the pure and the impure. We might think of the difference as an ontological one: what is pure must be separated from what is impure, for their essential characters or essences are completely incompatible, just as light and darkness must be separated because they are polar opposites. And, as we saw in the discussion of the purity language used by Ezra, the impure that makes contact with the pure is dangerously contagious. So it is that when Ezra formally charges the community with wrongdoing—'you have acted treacherously and caused to dwell [*wtšybw*] foreign women, to increase the guilt of Israel'—he exhorts them to 'separate yourselves [*hbdlw*]' from the women and their people (10.10-11). The people agree to this measure, and a list of all those who had married foreign women, about 110 in all, concludes the account (10.18-44).

In this narrative, both Ezra and the community use the languages of purity and morality to describe Israel's very current state of very real danger. Purity vocabulary expresses the community's past and present disobedience that has led it to its dreadful state before God. What is holy—the community and the place in which it dwells—may have no contact with the impure, or death will result. This is as clear in Ezra 9–10 as it is in a priestly law such as the one that contains Lev. 15.31 which states that impurity within the Israelite camp leads to death if it makes the tabernacle impure. Every single purity law must be fully obeyed; Israel is to be holy because YHWH is holy and, God says in Lev. 20.26, 'I separated [*w'bdl*] you from the peoples to be mine'. Holiness is the absence of impurity and so demands separation. In the case of the community in Ezra 9–10, then, its present disobedience stems from its causing of foreign women to dwell where they should not. The language of purity and impurity vividly illustrates the community's danger: foreign and impure contaminants threaten the community's destruction.

And yet, if it is the impurity that threatens the community's existence, the moral question regarding the culpability of those who caused them to dwell in the midst of the holy seed is also in question. The ideology the text advances appears to work this way: we are already in danger because our ancestors angered God with their loose morality, and by disobeying this law of God we threaten to wear out God's extraordinary patience completely. So the community and Ezra demand and receive a radical example of communal subjugation to social morality. It is not just the offending husbands who are involved, but the entire community that assembles to hear, judge and conform.

What I mean to point out in the concluding section of this part of the chapter and in Chapter 2 is that ritualized acts of purity and manifestations of submission to the moral order are closely related, since the former aims to produce the latter. The anxiety we see is caused by a lack of social cohesion (a declining commitment to the moral order) and a society with strong external boundaries (one obsessed with keeping itself pure of foreign influences) will, because of its worldview, look for foreign influences—the impure—that have contaminated the social body. A purification rite thus urges the community to reject the foreign for the native social order, and so questions of purity and morality are inevitably intertwined. This is why Ezra 9–10 makes no good distinction between them.

Once again, the benefit of the approach of this work is that it finds the basis of its evidence in the texts themselves. It takes the purity language and high communal anxiety in Ezra 9–10 seriously since we expect to hear such language from a community with strong external boundaries which is anxious that its social coherence is collapsing. The Persian period temple community was just a society, I will show in Chapter 3, and so we should not be surprised to find the language of purity and impurity in its writings as it attempts to alleviate the anxiety surrounding weak social integration.

b. *Conclusions: The Significance of Purity Language*

This analysis of Ezra 9–10 has raised four basic issues. First, the community levels no charges against the women. It clearly feels that the danger that it faces stems from the mere presence of foreigners, a matter that the text conveys with the language of impurity and with the solution of expulsion that it chooses. The women appear to pose a threat because they are impure, and any mixture of the impure with the holy—the language that the text uses to describe the community—can potentially lead to death and destruction. This would appear to explain the use of *yšb* in the hiphil and *bdl* in the niphal.

Second, the text places ultimate guilt for this infraction upon the community itself. Its guilt, iniquity and treachery are constantly emphasized. What is not clear, however, is why causing foreign women to dwell within the community is thought to be such a terrible action. Is it an ethical question—which is to say a matter of community members disobeying a law given to them by God—or is it an ontological matter—which is to say the presence of impurity in the place of the holy? The text draws no clear distinction between the two issues.

Third, despite the fact that this text stresses the community's guilt in causing the foreign women to dwell within it, it is the women who are sent away. No sanctions for the community are mentioned, unless one counts the emotional and financial losses to the men who are forced to send away their wives and children.[2] It is clear that the expulsion of the women is a satisfactory conclusion to the episode.

Fourth, this story portrays a community filled with anxiety, in whom the language of the danger of impurity resonates with success. In the narrative the ideology of Ezra's prayer works because it appears to tap into communal feelings of guilt and anxiety and into a social belief that the presence of foreigners, especially foreign women, is dangerous.

To begin with the first issue, I mentioned in the introduction that many scholars believe that the community's concern was one of apostasy or syncretism, that these foreign women were causing their husbands and families to worship other gods. However, I noted, it is rather difficult to find evidence for this in the text of Ezra–Nehemiah itself. There are hints and allusions to this as a problem, but no outright claim of this as a danger. For example, the anachronistic identification of the peoples of the lands with 'the Canaanites, the Hittites, the Perizzites, the Jebusites, the Ammonites,

2. As I mentioned in the introduction, in Israel and the ancient Near East men who divorced their wives without providing just cause for the action (just cause consisting of some legally recognized unacceptable action on the part of the woman, such as adultery) were obliged to repay the dowry, and often an added financial penalty. See Janzen, 'The Meaning of *porneia*'.

the Moabites, the Egyptians, and the Amorites' in Ezra 9.1 recalls the law banning all covenants and marriages with 'the Amorites, the Canaanites, the Hittites, the Perizzites, the Hivites, and the Jebusites' in Exod. 34.11-16, which specifies that such marriages will lead to apostasy. The parallel law in Deut. 7.1-6 also gives a list of nations with whom Israel should make no covenants or marriages, since apostasy would be the result. But if apostasy is the concern then why not state that fact directly? If, in Ezra 9.11-12, Ezra is citing Exod. 34.11-16 or Deut. 7.1-6 (he is clearly not quoting either one of them), why does he not say that such marriages to foreign women 'will make your sons also prostitute themselves to their gods' (Exod. 34.16), or that the women 'will turn your children from following me to serve other gods' (Deut. 7.4), or that they will 'teach you to do according to all their abominations that they do for their gods' (Deut. 20.18), or some such thing?

The text makes no claim that the women must be expelled because of things they have done, it states that the community must be separate from them because of their impure nature. Although Ezra appears to rely on Pentateuchal law, the rationale for enforcing the law in Ezra 9–10 is not the same as in Exodus and Deuteronomy. I do not mean to state here that we can, with absolute certainty, rule out the notion that the community feared that the presence of such women would lead to apostasy, but I do mean to point out that there is little evidence in the texts themselves that can be used to say that such women had been involved in turning people away from YHWHism. The text does support the case that such women were linked in the social mind of the community to apostasy—the reference to the laws from Exodus and Deuteronomy is a case in point—and that even without formally charging these women with any crime, the community can paint them as a dangerous influence. There may have been cases of apostasy in the community, and I argue in Chapters 2 and 4 that this would not be unexpected in a society like that of the Persian period temple community, and in Chapter 3 I point to evidence of neglect of the Jerusalem temple cult by its members. In Chapter 4, however, I show that there were many sources by which foreign ideas and religion could enter Yehud, and if apostasy was a widespread phenomenon, or at least perceived to be, it might make more sense to blame the other sources than the foreign women, against whom no such charges are actually laid and who made up a tiny percentage of the population. The connections that are drawn between foreign women and foreign worship seem to function more as justifications for the community's actions of mandating the divorces and expulsions than as charges on which the women are brought up. That is, if community members were abandoning YHWHism, or at least neglecting their duties toward the temple cult, then the community blames the women for this without offering evidence of it.

I have already mentioned that societies with strong external boundaries and weak internal ones are likely to engage in witch-hunts, actions that I have described as ritualized acts associated with purity, since they are purifying the social body of what is considered to be a dangerous foreign group (this is the focus of the next chapter). I have also shown how the foreign women are associated with impurity in Ezra 9–10 and how the language of this text reflects the Israelite belief that the impure will cause destruction when it comes into illegitimate contact with the holy. The significance of such language is that it is precisely the kind of vocabulary we would expect to hear from a society engaged in or close to engaging in an act of purification, and so suggests that we should look for further evidence which can demonstrate that this is a ritualized act of purification. As Mary Douglas has pointed out, concern with purity arises in societies that are exerting pressure on their members to conform to social norms.[3] Strong purity boundaries, she writes, are indicative of societies with strong external integration.[4] This is why it stands to reason that societies anxious that social coherence is collapsing will become concerned with notions of purity. This, I will argue, was precisely the situation of the Persian period temple community.

Yet why is there no clear distinction between concerns about social morality and obligations and purity, the second main observation that we have gleaned from the reading of Ezra 9–10? And why is it, to pick up on the third observation, that the text lays guilt upon the society yet responds to the apparent crisis by sending away the impure women? Douglas has laid out a connection between purity and the social use of it in order to enforce communal morality. The human body, she writes, is a frequent locus of purity regulations, and so a good microcosm of the social body. The body is something that individuals can, for the most part, control, and so Douglas's 'purity rule' is that in situations where the social body wishes to exert a great deal of control it will demand that individuals control their bodies according to specific social dictates, as well.[5] For the

3. Douglas, *Natural Symbols*, p. 12.
4. Douglas, *Natural Symbols*, p. 91.
5. Douglas, *Natural Symbols*, p. 12.

most part, people can control what foods they eat and when they will excrete waste products. The more a society wishes to control and enforce social integration, Douglas has observed, the more it will demand that individuals control what and when they eat and when and where they will excrete.[6] The individual and social bodies become mirrors of each other, so that bodily control becomes an expression of social control. Interest in what goes in and comes out of the biological body results from a concern with social entrances and exits.[7] The first point to be made, then, is that issues of purity arise when a society is attempting to enforce adherence on the part of its members to the social moral order.

The understanding of purity and impurity, of cleanliness and dirt are, Douglas has shown, social constructions. What a society designates as clean or pure is what it understands to be orderly. What a society designates to be dirty or impure is what it understands to be chaotic and opposed to order.[8] In any society dirt and pollution is what a society excludes from the socially acceptable (whether this involves morality or food or social relationships) because it does not fit into the categories established by the social worldview.[9] In her examination of the purity laws of the Pentateuch, Douglas concludes that holiness is an attribute of the divine and that is irrevocably opposed to impurity. Blessing, she finds, results from adherence to holiness,[10] a conclusion consonant with my comments above. Purity and holiness imply conformity to one's place as defined by the social worldview. The matter is an epistemological one as much as a moral one. The animals that the Israelite laws designate as impure, Douglas states, are those that did not fall within the basic Israelite manners of classification.[11] What falls outside of the social epistemological order—the worldview—is as unclean and dangerous as what falls outside of the social moral order.

6. Douglas, *Natural Symbols*, p. 101.

7. Douglas, *Natural Symbols*, pp. 95-100.

8. M. Douglas, *Purity and Danger: An Analysis of the Concepts of Pollution and Taboo* (London: Routledge & Kegan Paul, 1966), pp. 2-3.

9. Douglas, *Purity and Danger*, pp. 36-41.

10. Douglas, *Purity and Danger*, pp. 51-52.

11. Douglas, *Purity and Danger*, pp. 55-58. The categories established by the Israelite worldview fit the animals most commonly encountered by the people. Since animals of their herds chewed their cud and had cloven hooves, animals that chewed their cud and did not have cloven hooves, or animals that had cloven hooves but did not chew their cud, were considered to be impure. Other basic categories are involved in adjudging whether animals were pure or impure, but what this shows is that it is

It is difficult for the social order to function if social roles and obligations are ambiguous, and purity laws act to draw sharp lines between order or purity and disorder or impurity. What is impure, what lies outside of the social order, is recognized to have power that threatens social stability. What provides purity categories with their suasive power is the belief that what is impure is posed against the social and will destroy it.[12] This is why, writes Douglas, purity laws and distinctions will be emphasized in the areas of society where social authority and order are ambiguous and threatened. Pollution is seen to exist where the social order has been attacked, and so purity laws are employed by that order to protect itself.[13] Purity laws and distinctions guard against ambiguity in the social order, and they will be emphasized and enforced where the social order has been challenged and threatened. For this reason witches are associated with impurity. They are believed to wield a power that is un- and anti-social, power that does not come from accepted sources and that is used against the society.[14] By means of witch-hunts a society charges a certain group or individual with wielding power that causes social disintegration. By purifying the society of such people the social order protects itself, and this is why issues of purity are raised when the social moral order is under attack.

The significance of the purity language in Ezra 9–10 and the worldview that it reflects should be clear. A society will believe that its social purity is at stake when its internal integration is threatened, when, one could say, the belief arises that the social order can no longer control all aspects of society. Where adherence to the social morality is ambiguous purity laws will be emphasized and enforced, for they point out where the impure—points of power posed against the social order—has infected society, and so call on the social body to purify itself of such contaminants. Social order may thus be restored, and ambiguity in regard to following social norms and obligations eliminated. When a society believes that its social order is threatened *and* it is a society with strong external boundaries (and so one that fears the presence of foreigners), its purity laws will focus on foreign influences as the source of impurity, that which endangers the social. Since I will argue in Chapter 3 that the Jerusalem temple

confirmation to epistemological categories established by the worldview that defines order and purity.

12. Douglas, *Purity and Danger*, pp. 95-100.
13. Douglas, *Purity and Danger*, pp. 100-14.
14. Douglas, *Purity and Danger*, pp. 100, 110.

community was just such a society, we should not be surprised to find a piece of its literature refer to foreign women and foreigners in general as impurities. The fact that Ezra 9–10 uses the vocabulary of impurity to refer to the foreign women and to contrast them with the holiness of the temple community provides evidence that the temple community had strong external boundaries and weak internal ones.

This explains the four apparent oddities of the text of Ezra 9–10—its use of purity language, its inability to draw a sharp distinction between the moral and ontological, the blame it casts upon the community itself while insisting the only solution is to send away the women, and the high communal anxiety about the issue it relates—and their significance. The purity language points to a group concerned about its internal integration and the unwillingness of its members to adhere to the moral order. Purity is ultimately concerned with separation based on categories established by the social worldview and so issues of morality are not really distinct from issues of ontology. What is impure is ontologically excluded from the pure and belongs to the anti-social. Behavior that ignores social morality is by definition anti-social and therefore impure. The society expels the women and not the offending husbands, the ones primarily responsible for increasing the guilt of Israel, because a society with strong external boundaries immediately looks to foreigners as the source of its problems. Finally, the high level of anxiety suggests a community concerned that it is near destruction because of a failure to adhere to social morality. As Ezra puts it, the community's abandonment of God's law could lead to God's abandonment of the community.

I should be clear that these observations, given what we know of the significance of purity language, is evidence for my thesis, although not proof of it. I still need to show more clearly why societies with strong external boundaries and weak internal ones tend to rites of purification, and that the Jerusalem temple community was such a society. What I have shown is that the use of purity language should alert us to the issue of witch-hunts, and what I will argue in the next chapters is that there is enough evidence to prove that this was one.

3. *The Historicity of Ezra 9–10*

Having said that the textual account of Ezra 9–10 provides us with evidence of a society with strong external boundaries and weak internal ones and that is engaged in a witch-hunt, how may we be certain that it is historically accurate and that the divorces ever occurred? The best historical evidence that we can draw upon shows that there is no good reason to doubt the historical veracity of the Ezra narrative, and Ezra 9–10 is no exception. In general, most scholars accept the historicity of the Ezra narrative (broadly defined as Ezra 7–10 and Neh. 8). H.G.M. Williamson, for example, sees the basis of this narrative as an account of his activities that Ezra wrote to the Persian court after his first full year in Yehud.[15] D.J.A. Clines, while viewing these chapters as redactional efforts by the Chronicler, believes that the first-person sections have reproduced Ezra's wording almost exactly, and that the third-person sections were drawn at least partially from Ezra's own work.[16] There is no reason to doubt the veracity of this narrative, writes Clines, for '[o]nly historical implausibilities or impossibilities could tell strongly against the supposition of an Ezran substratum to the narrative and it, in my opinion, tells a coherent and plausible story'.[17] Joseph Blenkinsopp believes that the narrative has been more heavily edited than Clines does, but also sees no reason to discount its contents.[18] Franck Michaeli, like Clines, believes that these chapters were produced by the Chronicler who sometimes quotes an original document from Ezra and sometimes draws from it.[19] C.F. Keil and Franz Delitzsch even suggested that Ezra may have been the author of Chronicles; but whatever the case they saw no reason to doubt the historical nature of the material in Ezra–Nehemiah.[20]

Not all scholars have been so sanguine about the historical character of the Ezra narrative. One of the most forceful proponents of the work as fiction in the early twentieth century was C.C. Torrey, who claimed that the story of Ezra was a pure work of fiction by the Chronicler.[21] The Ezra narrative, he believed, was composed in imitation of the Nehemiah Memoir, and he referred to the story of Ezra as 'the Chronicler's masterpiece'.[22] Torrey's evaluation of the Ezra narrative received followers in

15. Williamson, *Ezra, Nehemiah*, pp. xxxi-xxxiii.

16. Clines, *Ezra, Nehemiah, Esther*, p. 6.

17. Clines, *Ezra, Nehemiah, Esther*, p. 7.

18. Blenkinsopp, *Ezra–Nehemiah*, p. 46.

19. F. Michaeli, *Les livres des Chroniques, d'Esdras et de Nehemie* (CAT, 16; Neuchâtel: Delachaux & Niestlé, 1967), p. 19.

20. Keil and Delitzsch, *The Books*, pp. 14-18.

21. C.C. Torrey, *Ezra Studies* (New York: Ktav, 1970), pp. xxi-xxii.

22. Torrey, *Ezra Studies*, pp. 238-40. In Torrey's view, the Chronicler was so inventive that he or she would have preferred to have been a novelist rather than an editor (p. 250).

the later part of the century, as well. Jacob Myers accepted his evaluation uncritically.[23] Ulrich Kellermann argued that only Ezra 7.12-26—a letter purportedly written by Artaxerxes, the Persian monarch, in order to commission Ezra for royal service in Yehud—is authentic, and the rest of the Ezra narrative is simply the Chronicler's midrash on the letter.[24] Martin Noth came to the same conclusion.[25]

Most scholars have recognized the letter as authentic even if, as Wilhelm Rudolph noted, it has a distinct 'Jewish coloring'.[26] Williamson argues that its use of Imperial Aramaic, Persian loanwords, and agreement with known Persian administrative policy implies its authenticity.[27] E. Meyer suggested that the letter-writer's obvious familiarity with the details of the Jerusalem cult may simply mean that Ezra wrote it and had the Persian monarch sign it.[28] What Lester Grabbe, among others, has pointed out, however, is that Artaxerxes's alleged commission for Ezra in the letter appears to be at odds with Ezra's activities in the rest of the narrative. He is sent to enforce the law in Yehud and yet in the narrative it is the community that exercises legal authority. He is sent to restore the cult, and yet it had long been functioning. He is told to appoint judges and yet is never recorded as doing so. All of this, writes Grabbe, makes Ezra's mission a bit of a puzzle.[29] He has, like Torrey and others, suggested that Ezra may never have existed.[30]

The real difficulty in resolving the question of the historical plausibility of the Ezra narrative would appear to lie in untangling the knot of the discrepancies between the Artaxerxes letter and the rest of the narrative. The scholarly consensus that the Chronicler is responsible for Ezra–Nehemiah has collapsed thanks to linguistic studies over the last few

23. Myers, *Ezra–Nehemiah*, pp. l-li.

24. U. Kellermann, *Nehemia: Quellen, Überlieferung und Geschichte* (Berlin: Alfred Töpelmann, 1967), pp. 68-69.

25. M. Noth, *The Chronicler's History* (trans. H.G.M. Williamson; JSOTSup, 50; Sheffield: JSOT Press, 1987), pp. 63-64.

26. Rudolph, *Esra und Nehemia*, p. 75.

27. Williamson, *Ezra, Nehemiah*, p. 98.

28. E. Meyer, *Die Entstehung des Judenthums* (Halle: Max Niemeyer, 1896), p. 65.

29. L.L. Grabbe, 'What was Ezra's Mission?', in T.C. Eskenazi and K.H. Richards (eds.), *Second Temple Studies: 2. Temple and Community in the Persian Period* (JSOTSup, 175; Sheffield: JSOT Press, 1994), pp. 286-99 (297-98).

30. L.L. Grabbe, *Judaism from Cyrus to Hadrian*, I (2 vols.; Minneapolis: Fortress Press, 1992), pp. 92-93.

decades,[31] and without this assumption of responsibility one cannot argue that the Chronicler composed the Ezra narrative as a non-historical piece of fiction. The matter of fiction, however, appears to lie with the letter of 7.12-26 allegedly composed by Artaxerxes, not the rest of the Ezra narrative. I have argued elsewhere that the Artaxerxes letter lacks the typical stylistic components of official Persian correspondence in Aramaic, and that there are no significant parallels to the supposed 'mission' upon which Ezra is sent by the Persian crown elsewhere in the Persian empire. Lacking parallels in style and content, in short, the letter appears to be a complete fabrication.[32]

On the other hand there are no such objections to the historical validity of the rest of the Ezra narrative. What Ezra is portrayed as doing therein—teaching the law and leading the community in divorces—is perfectly in keeping with what we know of the office of priest and scribe—the two titles applied to Ezra—in the temple communities of the Persian period. He appears to act the way the *šatammu*, the administrative head of Babylonian temple communities acted. The *šatammu* could guide the temple assembly in making decisions but could not mandate particular actions.[33] This is precisely the way Ezra functions in the narrative of the divorces. In Ezra 8 he is portrayed as teaching the law, a matter in perfect conformity with his role as priest in ancient Israel.[34] It is worth noting as well that some scribes in Babylonian temples were also priests, while others were administrators. Such appears to be the case in the Persian period Jerusalem temple community also, where Levites are mentioned as acting in scribal

31. See S. Japhet, 'Supposed Common Authorship of Chronicles and Ezra–Nehemiah Investigated Anew', *VT* 18 (1968), pp. 330-71; H.G.M. Williamson, *Israel in the Book of Chronicles* (Cambridge: Cambridge University Press, 1977); and M. Throntveit, 'Linguistic Analysis and the Question of Authorship in Chronicles, Ezra and Nehemiah', *VT* 32 (1982), pp. 201-16.

32. D. Janzen, 'The "Mission" of Ezra and the Persian-Period Temple Community', *JBL* 119 (2000), pp. 619-43. Sara Japhet has noted that Ezra 1–6 seems to have been composed with an eye to equating the will of the Persian king with the will of God ('Sheshbazzar and Zerubbabel: Against the Background of the Historical and Religious Tendencies of Ezra–Nehemiah', *ZAW* 94 [1982], pp. 66-98; 95 [1983], pp. 218-29), and the letter of Artaxerxes may have been composed with the same intent.

33. G.J.P. McEwan, *Priest and Temple in Hellenistic Babylonia* (Freiburger Altorientalische Studien, 4; Wiesbaden: Franz Steiner, 1981), p. 25.

34. It is clear that in ancient Israel the priest was associated with the teaching of the law. See Deut. 17.18; 31.9-13; Jer. 18.18; and 2 Chron. 15.3.

capacities (1 Chron. 24.6; 2 Chron. 34.13). To paraphrase Clines's comment, there is no reason to doubt the historicity of the Ezra narrative (with the exception of the Artaxerxes letter) since there is no evidence that argues against the historicity of his activities. Indeed, he seems to act in perfect conformity with the role of temple administrator known from other parts of the ancient Near East.[35] The discrepancies between the letter and the activities of Ezra in the narrative can be explained by positing the letter as a fabrication. It is extremely unlikely that Ezra was ever sent on a mission by Artaxerxes. On the other hand, the activities and power ascribed to him in the narration fit the role of Israelite priest and ancient Near Eastern temple administrator quite well.

In the narrative of Ezra 9–10, Ezra acts like an administrative head. He does not force the community to do anything; indeed, he does not even initiate the discussion about the foreign women. While he orders the assembly to be gathered, it is ultimately its decision, not his, as to what to do about the crisis. Nehemiah, who was a governor appointed by the Persians, acts much differently when faced with complaints about the dire financial situation in the province in Nehemiah 5. When people complain to him that loans incurred from meeting tax payments have forced them into poverty, he forces those within the temple assembly who have loaned out money to forgive the interest and to restore confiscated collateral (5.6-13). Ezra, however, is portrayed as having no such power, but this is in keeping with his role as the equivalent of the Babylonian *šatammu*.

There is no reason, then, to doubt the historicity of Ezra 9–10. I have made no claims, however, to the effect that Ezra is responsible for this first-person narrative. It is certainly possible, but even if true it would not prove that these chapters are a verbatim account of the event. Are there reasons to doubt its details? This is a matter that remains to be seen, but the investigation of the text certainly suggests that we are faced with a ritualized act of purification and, specifically, with a witch-hunt. If the investigation of the social boundaries of the community in the following chapters does indeed inform us that the Jerusalem temple community was prone to witch-hunts, then we will have our answer.

35. Janzen, 'The "Mission" of Ezra', pp. 638-43.

Chapter 2

SOCIAL STRUCTURE, WITCH-HUNTS AND WOMEN

1. *Introduction*

My contention in this chapter is that societies with strong external boundaries and weakening internal integration will engage in acts of purification when social anxiety about the failure of community members to observe social morality, norms, obligations and roles reaches a critical level. They will engage in the particular kind of act of purification commonly called a witch-hunt when there is no obvious group to blame for the perceived lack of adherence to social morality. Precisely what level will count as critical will depend on the particular society under observation. Nonetheless, this is the social structure we can point to as the cause of ritualized acts of purification. In such a society most people will be wary of foreign influences and will be cautioned against any sort of affiliation with them. This will include, but will not be limited to, foreign individuals, ideas, religions, systems of morality, sources of wisdom, and material culture. It stands to reason that any society with strong external boundaries—a society that takes pains to separate and distinguish itself from foreigners, in other words—has such boundaries because it does not wish to associate with foreigners. Foreign societies and all things associated with them are regarded as dangerous, as people and things that will harm the society should it come in contact with them. As I mentioned in the introduction, external boundaries may be realized: (1) geographically, by keeping a certain amount of space between the community and the foreign; (2) by means of genealogies, where it is necessary to trace one's pedigree in order to be considered an authentic member of the community; and (3) ideologically, by strongly contrasting the good beliefs and religion and morality of the society in question with the dangerous ones of other peoples.

A society with weak internal boundaries, or weak internal integration, is one in which the worldview of the society commands little loyalty. Social morality, roles, norms and obligations will be only loosely and vaguely defined, and people will often be free to pursue a wide range of lifestyles and occupations. They will not be trammeled by a strongly ingrained morality that places severe limits on actions. Their choice of possible occupations will be great since social roles are constantly open to redefinition, or lack much definition. Since there will be few well-defined obligations to others in their community, they can act toward others with some impunity. Codes of politeness may be lax, and actions of respect and honor toward parents and elders may not be highly valued. To invoke a rather well-known example, one could argue that the internal integration of American society is much weaker than that of Japanese society.

My interest here is in communities that believe that their social integration has grown so weak that society itself is about fly apart. Should a large section of Japanese begin to act like Americans, anxiety in Japan about social disintegration might rise. The notion of the strength of social boundaries, naturally, is a relative one. Dispositions and codes of conduct that may be taken for granted in one society will be considered odd and dangerous in another. The focus of this chapter will be on societies that have come to the conclusion that the behavior of many of its members has become so odd and dangerous that the society seems to be on the verge of collapse. The traditional norms and obligations are not being observed, according to the anxious social body, and unless the situation is reversed the community may cease to exist.

Why would this be considered a problem? Why would the society not welcome new and innovative ways of thinking and acting as a breath of fresh air, as a way to shake up the traditional social status quo? In part, the answer to such questions can simply point to the power of tradition, but this merely begs the question. What is at issue here is why tradition and not innovation that disregards tradition is revered. I propose a twofold answer that depends both on worldview, the way of understanding and explaining the world that supports tradition, and power. The social worldview, as I mentioned in the introduction, really needs no justification. When members of a social body have been conditioned to think and act in particular stereotyped ways, people who violate the acceptable range of variations permitted within each stereotype will likely be considered to be stupid.[1] When they suggest that the world is not really flat (or not really spherical), when they claim that God does not exist (or that only one God

1. On this point see Geertz, *Interpretation*, p. 129.

exists), when they argue that all people should be considered as equals (or that some are naturally inferior to others), their beliefs will stand in such stark opposition to the social worldview—to common sense—that they will seem immature and perhaps humorous. When, instead of following the social roles laid out for them they insist that worship of their ancestors' gods is irrelevant, or that they will not pursue the career their teachers have chosen for them, or that they will not marry the spouse picked out by their parents, people may simply regard them with some astonishment. Their actions and beliefs are so at odds with the social worldview that everyone takes for granted that they appear to be thwarting their own best interests in such fecklessness.

Difficulties will arise, however, when a large number of people exhibit such oddities. At this point the matter will no longer appear primarily to be one of stupidity but one of outright rebellion. It is no longer one or two individuals throwing their lives away on vain pursuits but a large group seemingly intent on drastically changing the social order. For the rest—the orthodox, we might call them—it will appear that their own well-being is threatened. Since, as social anthropologists such as Geertz have shown, the social worldview is made convincing because it appears to be an image of the world that best explains why traditional ways of life are the best ways of life and so succeed, a strong challenge to tradition—interpreted here both as worldview and as praxis—threatens to change all of society. The orthodox may no longer be allowed to pursue the way of life that they know through common sense to be the best way to live. Unless the threat is quelled, the society as a whole will change, and to the orthodox such change appears disastrous. All of society may end up believing wrong and harmful things and acting in wrong and harmful ways. Social destruction will be the result.

Intertwined with this part of the explanation is the question of power. In the roles and obligations prescribed by the social worldview certain people have more power than others. Their positions legitimate certain actions that they may take, certain obligations that they may reasonably expect others to perform that will benefit them. Should people within society begin to ignore the obligations they owe to their superiors, people in positions of social power will suffer materially. They will begin to lose the benefits of their power, and they may lose their power altogether. This is not to suggest, as I noted in the introduction, that the actions which people take may be explained solely by a desire to increase or maintain control over the means of production. How they decide to do so, which will be governed by the worldview that has shaped them, will depend upon the society from which they come. Should people in positions of power argue that those who ignore their social obligations are out of line, we should not believe that such arguments are motivated solely by material interests, even though they may take such issues into account. Their arguments will be convincing to no one, as I pointed out, unless they can make them convincing, unless they can appeal to ideas that most people in society take for granted and believe to be good and true. When certain people in a social group are charged with witchcraft, this is in part a charge (as we shall see in the case studies in this chapter) that they are challenging the accepted sources of social power and that such challenges are illegitimate, but such charges cannot be laid and the social group as a whole will not collude in their punishment or execution unless they are convinced by such charges. Ideology is convincing, as Geertz and other pointed out, only when it draws on social common sense. Power does not underlie worldview, as Marxists believe, it is intertwined with it.

In the rest of this chapter I shall present the theories of Richard Fenn and Mary Douglas who independently arrived at the conclusion that societies with strong external boundaries and weak internal ones are likely to engage in acts of purification. In order to illustrate their ideas I shall then move to three case studies of witch-hunts from three different societies on three different continents. In each instance the social group involved in the activity is one with strong external boundaries and weak internal ones. Witch-hunts, I will point out, are really a kind of social purification, insofar as they function to increase social integration by targeting for expulsion or execution a particular group of people who are charged with no probative evidence. Finally, I will draw on anthropological studies that can shed light on the question of why women are almost always the group singled out in witch-hunts.

2. *Social Purification and Social Structure*

a. *Social Boundaries and Ritualized Acts of Purification*

Richard Fenn has pointed out that a society that wants to engage in acts of purification must have boundaries that are clear and strong enough to distinguish it from other societies. There must be a fairly clear idea of who belongs if a society is going to purify itself of a group it singles out as foreign. These external boundaries, however, must be permeable enough if they are to allow foreign influences through in the first place, assuming that the integrity of a society weakens because foreign influences have entered in the first place.[2] The first characteristic of a society that involves itself in ritualized acts of purification such as witch-hunts, then, is one with strong, although not absolutely strong, external boundaries. A society that fears the influence of outsiders, a fact made manifest in the simple existence of its strong external boundaries, will blame them when the social body seems on the verge of disintegration. The result of such a fear, writes Fenn, will be the attempt to purify the body of foreign ideas, experts and religion, and this will result in 'intensified demands for the discipline of the emotions and for constraints on behavior so that individuals will interact in ways that support social institutions and the larger society itself'.[3]

This is precisely what I have referred to as the strengthening of internal social integration. A society can fly apart if there is no conformity to social morality and institutions, and if enough of its members believe this to be a real possibility, the whole community will be urged to act for society. What is foreign and dangerous will be contrasted with what is native and good, and the point will be made that the foreign is about to destroy the native. It is easiest to blame any anti-social desires within the social body on foreigners, especially when the society views the foreign with deep suspicion to begin with, notes Fenn. From such a worldview the foreign is the simplest suspect, and its indictment prevents placing ultimate blame for social collapse on the society itself, even if social members may be picked out as contaminated by the foreign.[4] If no foreign influences are readily available to be singled out, foreigners must be created, and individuals once considered insiders, even if only marginally so, will be redesignated as outsiders. One way to do this is to brand a certain group of people as witches.[5] Witches, as we shall see, are people who are charged with drawing on illegitimate sources of power, and what is illegitimate in a society with strong external boundaries is foreign. What witches want, as a consequence, is opposed to the needs and goals of the social. Witches are social creations, people who are believed to draw on foreign sources of power, sources of power that do not spring from legitimate social centers and so are opposed to the social.

2. R.K. Fenn, *The End of Time: Religion, Ritual, and the Forging of the Soul* (Cleveland: Pilgrim, 1997), p. 128.
3. Fenn, *The End of Time*, pp. 131-32.
4. Fenn, *The End of Time*, p. 142.
5. Fenn, *The End of Time*, p. 144.

For this reason, writes Douglas, a witch is often considered to be the opposite of human.[6] A human, socially defined, is someone who fulfills his or her social obligations and gives due obeisance to social morality and institutions. A society will need to find witches—identify figures within its boundaries who do not do such things—during periods of anxiety about social ambiguity in such matters. Problems will arise, Douglas points out, when individuals within a society are exposed to a number of different classification systems,[7] what I have been calling worldviews. When worldviews besides that of the society become available to members of the social body, when they have exposure to various systems of metaphysics and morality, internal social ambiguity will be the result.[8] They can question the received wisdom and common sense of their own society, they can question the legitimacy of social institutions and norms and obligations. Dispositions and social ambiguity such as these are precisely what lead to charges of witchcraft.

So far I have focused on what Fenn and Douglas have to say about the role of social worldview in ritualized acts of purification. A society with strong external boundaries and anxiety about weakening social integration has a worldview that tends to look for foreigners who threaten its internal integration. They will demand strict adherence to the moral order. Witch-hunts, a search for the illegitimate presence of foreigners, are what we should expect. Issues of power, however, are also involved. Again, I hasten to point out that charges of witchcraft cannot be credibly laid unless those who bring them can convincingly appeal to the social worldview. Not only does the social body have to believe in the existence of witches, it must be convinced that there is some evidence for their existence at that particular time. This evidence, I am arguing, is anxiety about social disintegration in a society with strong external boundaries. If these conditions do not exist then a charge of witchcraft is unlikely to succeed. So while there will be some within the social body who will benefit materially from expelling certain groups of people, they will not be able to do so unless there is social support for the move. Witch-hunts can occur only when there is a certain amount of public sentiment for them.

This is not to claim that issues of power or control of the means of production do not figure into such actions, merely that they are intertwined with and not exclusive of worldview. A ruler who believed that his or her

6. Douglas, *Natural Symbols*, p. 139.
7. Douglas, *Natural Symbols*, p. 82.
8. Douglas, *Natural Symbols*, pp. 82-83.

power could be increased by killing or expelling a particular group of people, and who could carry out such actions without public support, would not need to bother with charges of witchcraft. Any charges would do, and the action could be carried out regardless of public sentiment. Witch-hunts, by contrast, are social actions. Ritualized acts of purification affect social integration, and when such charges are laid we may assume that there is real social anxiety that lies behind them, even if issues of material and political power are involved. Such issues may well be at stake in a society with strong external boundaries and weak internal ones, as Douglas points out. In a social group that has strong internal integration, social norms and roles and obligations will be well defined. What one owes to one's parents, gods, teachers, political leaders, army commanders, and so on will not be in doubt. In cases where that is not the case and ambiguity exists in such matters, one encounters, as Douglas notes, a competitive society.[9] A person in a position of authority will not be guaranteed the loyalty, honor and material rewards that would be due to him or her in a society with stronger internal integration. Different social leaders and social institutions may compete for people's loyalty, and the social world-view and system of morality of the society as a whole may have to compete with those of other cultures. In a society with strong integration who owes what to whom is highly regulated, but where integration is weak such matters are constantly negotiable.

The result is not simply competition, says Douglas, but a sense that the world is full of sinister powers. When people in such a society do not receive what they believe they are owed—whether this be money, respect, prestige or loyalty—it becomes easy to believe that their due has been stolen from them by illicit means, means that have not been sanctioned by social powers. Such illegitimate power is what Douglas defines as witchcraft, and all societies with strong external boundaries and weak internal ones have some sort of belief in it.[10] Having the public convict one of witchcraft is to be finished politically, for in a competitive society nothing is worse than someone who does not play by the rules and who draws on illegitimate sources of power. So when a society experiences a period of deviancy—a social recognition that internal integration is weakening further—it will embark upon a witch-hunt, for witches are understood to be those who go so far in competition that they are willing to go outside

9. Douglas, *Natural Symbols*, p. 137.
10. Douglas, *Natural Symbols*, p. 138.

socially sanctioned centers of power. As Douglas notes, it will be the obvious dissidents who will be expelled as a result of the hunt, those who have most obviously flaunted social norms and roles.[11] Yet Douglas also agrees with Fenn when she argues that in societies with strong external and weak internal boundaries evil is seen as something that is introduced from the outside by disguised foreign agents; and while group members—insiders—may be accused of allowing these foreigners to infiltrate, it will be those 'foreigners' themselves who are branded as witches (since they are believed to draw on power and espouse a worldview that runs counter to that of the society in question).[12] In some incidents, as we shall see in the case studies below, foreigners are not always easy to identify, and then foreignness must be created in order for the witch-hunt to succeed. And, I will argue in the last section of this chapter, women universally seem to be those most easily associated with the anti-social, and so it should not be surprising that the overwhelming majority of victims of witch-hunts are women.

To sum up, then, societies with strong external boundaries and weak internal ones are likely to blame foreigners for fears of social disintegration. The worldview of such societies, as both Fenn and Douglas point out, sees the foreign as suspicious and poised against the social. When things go wrong on a large scale within the society it is simply easier to believe what has always been believed: foreigners are evil and their presence endangers society. Witches are foreigners, if only because they are associated with foreign, and so dangerous, sources of power. Before being regarded as foreigners, they are considered to be members of the society. Now they have been chosen by the social group in order to function as the main players in a ritualized act, the object of which is to increase social integration. Intertwined with this explanation is that of power. In such societies where competition will be strong, those who prosper at others' expense may be seen as benefiting from illegitimate—which is to say, foreign—sources of power. They have won by cheating, and the power to cheat does not come from socially sanctioned sources of power. They are impure since, as Douglas has shown, the impure is associated with the anti-social or chaos. Society must purify itself of them. A call for purity often goes hand in hand with charges of witchcraft since both are, in the end, calls for conformity, calls for people to behave in an acceptable

11. Douglas, *Natural Symbols*, p. 139.
12. Douglas, *Natural Symbols*, p. 169.

manner, adhere to social morality and obligations, and abandon all illegitimate sources of power.[13]

A witch-hunt is, on one level, just a witch-hunt, an illogical activity engaged in by particular societies attempting to confront powers of the occult that do not really exist. From the point of view of the social anthropologist, though, a witch-hunt is an effective way to increase social integration. It indicates that sources of power and morality that are not socially approved are wrong; it extracts social assent to the veracity of this claim from the social body by having it participate in the witch-hunt, a concrete act that indicates assent; and in this action the community subjugates itself to the social order. In the action, the community signals its agreement to the notion that only the power, worldview, and morality approved by the social order, and all the things that accompany them—norms, roles, obligations, institutions—are acceptable. Social integration has been increased, although the social body engaged in the action would not put the matter this way. From its standpoint it has purified itself from a dangerous foreign influence that threatened to destroy it; from the standpoint of the anthropologist it has engaged in a ritualized act that has garnered assent from its members to observe social morality, norms and obligations, and to grant legitimacy to social institutions.

b. *Case Studies*

The Massachusetts Bay Colony of the Seventeenth Century. I have included here three separate case studies from three societies on three separate continents in order to show readers how the theory laid out above plays out in actual social groups. The first comes from Kai Erikson's study of the three 'crime-waves' (as he puts it) of the Massachusetts Bay Colony from 1636 to 1692. Each of these incidents is helpful in shedding light on the relationship between witch-hunts and social integration, and, more importantly, in shedding light on the particular incident of Ezra 9–10. The first two crime-waves have one main dissimilarity to the case of Persian period Yehud, but the third, the witch-hunt of 1692, is remarkably similar in some respects to the events narrated in Ezra.

While Erikson does not distinguish between external and internal boundaries, there is enough documentation gathered on the Massachusetts Bay Colony that we can state with some certainty that the society had strong external boundaries. Its isolation was both geographical and

13. Douglas, *Purity and Danger*, p. 103.

ideological, being both a great distance from England and a great theological distance from the established church there. When Erikson writes that his study of the colony focuses on how it controlled its boundaries by means of controlling the behavior of its members and the networks of interaction that link its members together in social relations,[14] it is clear that he writes about what I have been calling internal boundaries. How much deviancy or variation from the social norms a society allows—when it acts to control such deviancy, in other words—indicates how much diversity it is willing to tolerate before it believes that its unique identity will be lost.[15] When feelings of anxiety in a society rise because it believes that this uniqueness is being lost—when there is fear of social disintegration due to weak internal boundaries, in other words—the community will move to censure activities that have been going on for some time but had not previously attracted attention.[16] Anxiety rises when these activities are taken up by a significant number of people.

The first crime wave that Erikson documents is the matter that became known as the Antinomian controversy of 1636. At the time the new colony was in the midst of establishing an apparatus to keep order within its congregations. This was a necessary operation, since the Puritans were no longer a minority in Anglican England but the dominant group in their part of the New World. The particular area of contention in this matter was the directive that the ministers of the church were to decide who was truly converted, and thus who deserved the privileges of franchise in the colony. The group that became known as the Antinomians averred that no person could judge whether another had been converted.[17]

Obviously, this was, on one level, a dispute over where power was to lie in the new community. The position of the Antinomians was a theological argument, and yet even the principals of the dispute, including John Winthrop, the colony's first governor and one of the prosecutors, admitted that the theological distinctions being drawn were so fine that almost no one could understand them.[18] The issue came to a head with the prosecution of Anne Hutchinson, the woman singled out as the leader of the Antinomians. Curiously, no charges were laid against her when she was brought

14. K. Erikson, *Wayward Puritans: A Study in the Sociology of Deviance* (New York: John Wiley & Sons, 1966), pp. 10-11.

15. Erikson, *Wayward Puritans*, p. 11.

16. Erikson, *Wayward Puritans*, p. 69.

17. Erikson, *Wayward Puritans*, pp. 72-74.

18. On this point see especially Erikson, *Wayward Puritans*, pp. 74, 82 and 91.

to trial, and yet her opinions, which the court was unable to summarize, were thought to be so dangerous that she was banished from the colony.[19]

From the point of view of the colony, the matter was a theological one. Hutchinson and her supporters (all of whom renounced their support as the trial wore on) held a theological position that was said to be heretical. From the standpoint of the participants—and this includes the judges and the clergy who brought her to court, those who abandoned Hutchinson, the colony members who attended the trial and those who said nothing; the entire community, in other words—such deviancy was a danger to the social body. From the standpoint of the anthropologist the matter was not, at its core, theological, but social. Hutchinson and her fellow Antinomians challenged the social boundaries that the society was attempting to establish. The power of the clergy to decide upon enfranchisement and the power of those who had received it was at stake. The theological issues were real insofar as that was the way the colony decided to see the problem, but no actual charges were drawn up against Hutchinson, nor could the court state with any certainty at the end of the trial what her theological position was or why it was dangerous. Since it was the firm belief of the colonists that it was necessary to expel her, however, it seems clear that this was a ritualized act of purification. As Erikson puts it, the outcome of this ritual was never in doubt, 'the problem was to find a meaningful way to register it'.[20] That is, to maintain the tenuous social order that had been established the society needed agreement from its members that they would adhere to it, and this was accomplished by means of making an example of Hutchinson. In their collusion in her expulsion, the members of the society did not have to grasp the minute theological nuances of the trial. They merely had to assent to the veracity of the court's verdict, which they did, since no one spoke against it. In their silent participation, then, they have acknowledged the legitimate sources of power and morality. Their assent to them comes in their participation in the act of expelling Hutchinson, and this signals their subjugation and allegiance to the order. Since she is deemed anti-social, she must be expelled by the community. The punishment of expulsion—as opposed to corporal punishment or imprisonment—suggests that the social body saw her as an alien, and so returned her to the foreign where, given her anti-social views, she really belonged. In this manner are ontology and morality related in rituals of purification.

19. Erikson, *Wayward Puritans*, pp. 93, 101.
20. Erikson, *Wayward Puritans*, p. 104.

The colony's Quaker crisis of 1656 to 1661 may be analyzed along much the same lines. Within this period, many Quakers made their way to the Massachusetts Bay Colony and were imprisoned and subjected to corporal and capital punishment. Those who insisted on returning after initial beatings and expulsions were put to death. Quakers were usually expelled as soon as they arrived, even before the colony passed laws against their presence in the community. When two Quaker women arrived at the colony in 1656 they were immediately imprisoned and the windows of the jailhouse were boarded up so that there could be no contact between them and passers-by.[21] As in the Antinomian controversy, there were few theological differences between the Quakers and the Puritans, although in this case the magistrates showed no real interest in defining the few that existed. Instead, they identified Quakers primarily by their refusal to remove their hats when in the presence of superiors, an act that signaled their lack of respect for the authority of the community.[22]

In some respects the Quakers were the focus of punishment simply because they were foreign and represented the influx of strange and dangerous ideas into the community. Again, from the standpoint of the Puritans the matter was theological: like Hutchinson and the Antinomians the Quakers were said to possess heretical ideas that could endanger the community. And again, from the standpoint of the anthropologist, the real danger posed by the Quakers was, like the Antinomians, their refusal to acknowledge the legitimacy of the society's structures of power. It was not really their theology that was the focus of Puritan fear and punishment but their unwillingness to recognize their betters by removing their hats, a sign of their disregard for the colony's social norms and obligations. The fear, of course, is that the presence of enough Quakers in the colony would contaminate the entire populace and so the society would collapse altogether; thus even the prison windows were boarded up when Quakers were there.

The final crime-wave that Erikson documents is the witch-hunt of 1692. In the decades before this time, ambiguity surrounding internal integration ran high. The clergy and magistrates quarreled about their respective areas of power, dissension among the colonists themselves took the form of land disputes and personal litigation, and sermons of the time focused on the decline of morality within the community.[23] In the midst of this, a number of young girls in Salem began behaving strangely. The town doctor,

21. Erikson, *Wayward Puritans*, pp. 114-16.
22. Erikson, *Wayward Puritans*, pp. 126-31.
23. Erikson, *Wayward Puritans*, pp. 137-41.

lacking any physiological explanation for their disorders, pronounced them bewitched. As the search began for the witches who controlled them, the girls initially accused three local women of witchcraft: a slave originally from Barbados, a beggar, and one woman of somewhat higher social standing who had lived with a man for several months before marrying him.[24] The first two were marginal members of the community and the third was a woman who had violated an obvious social norm in her choice of cohabitation before marriage. The hysteria lasted for a year and spread outside of Salem as the girls began accusing more and more people higher and higher up the social ladder. Even some men were accused. The process was only called into question when the girls accused eminent people within the community: the wife of Governor Phipps, and Samuel Willard, the pastor of the First Church in Boston and the president of Harvard College. The court refused to indict them, and the hysteria quickly dissipated. Only three of the 350 still in prison on charges of witchcraft or accused of such at that time were subsequently put to death.[25]

What allowed such a state of affairs to continue until almost 30 persons, almost all women, were put to death on the sole evidence of a number of young girls? Why would the colony put up with, believe and execute the charges and punishments of such a large number of people when their primary accusers were girls who had not yet reached the age of majority? Clearly this was a society with weak internal integration—its leaders struggled for power against each other, its citizens quarreled and sued, community values were widely believed to be on the decline. In such a society where external boundaries are still strong, Fenn points out, the community will find it far easier to believe that the foreigners everyone fears are responsible for the propinquity of the society's disintegration. The hundreds of people charged with witchcraft in the colony were not foreigners in the strict sense of the term, but what is native and what is foreign are social designations. One's neighbor may appear perfectly normal until it is discovered that she is an enemy spy. So it is with witches: they are accused of wielding an illegitimate power that has as its goal the destruction of society. In the argot of the colony, witches were consorts of the devil, and drew on his power. Only once their disguises are penetrated can they be seen for the anti-social creatures they are, drawing upon a power that does not come from socially approved centers and that

24. Erikson, *Wayward Puritans*, pp. 141-43.
25. Erikson, *Wayward Puritans*, pp. 143-53.

aims at destroying the society. This is why in the case of the witchcraft hysteria as well as the other two crime-waves the culprits were either killed or expelled from the social body. They represented a threat to society that came from the outside (in the worldview of the colonists, at any rate), and so they could not simply be imprisoned. They were put to death or returned to their true place of origin.

What differentiates the latter crime-wave from the two that preceded it in the Massachusetts Bay Colony was its choice of accused. In the cases of the Antinomians and Quakers there were obvious candidates the social body could blame for its anxiety. Anne Hutchinson and her followers truly did challenge the social structure of the colony, as did the Quakers in their refusal to acknowledge the presence of social superiors. Such was not the case during the witchcraft hysteria. At that time ambiguities within the social order were vague and diffuse. Clergy and magistrates struggled for power, personal animosities within the colony ran high, and all of this was reflected in a belief that the social morality as a whole was declining. There was no one easily identifiable source of the ambiguity as was the case during the Antinomian controversy and Quaker persecution. There were a whole number of causes of social dissent, and yet not one was easily identifiable; certainly the conglomeration of them could not be blamed on a single party as it could in the case of the Quakers and Antinomians. At such times the sources of social disintegration may be manufactured, and this was the case with the witches of 1692.

It is true that in the first two crime-waves there was no probative evidence presented against the accused—Hutchinson's theology was thought to be heretical, and yet the court could not define it; the Quakers were also heretics from the colony's standpoint, and yet they were expelled before any laws were passed against them and theology was rarely invoked when they were subject to expulsion and capital punishment—but charges are not needed when the social body is convinced that the guilty party is obvious. To the anthropologist the issues at stake were social ones that the community articulated theologically. In resolving those two crises social ambiguity in the colony was reduced. The matter concerning the witches was different, because the witches had to be made into the obvious guilty party. They became manufactured foreigners, but the anxiety within the community was obviously high enough such that they could be manufactured with the flimsiest of charges. The original three accused of witchcraft—a black slave, a beggar woman, and a woman who had recently and publicly flaunted social norms surrounding sexuality—existed near the boundaries of the social group, and so were (again, from the point of view of the social body) obvious candidates for the channeling of the power of the occult that comes from outside the boundaries of the social. Only once the accusations touch those close to the centers of power does the social body realize that they cannot be true. The power associated with witches does not come from the centers of power, it comes from the outside and is opposed to the social and its center.[26] Why witches are almost uniformly women is a matter that will be addressed in the last part of this chapter.

Only so much diversity will be tolerated within a society until the social body moves to limit it, Erikson points out. Charges of witchcraft will appear when internal ambiguity is seen to be enough of a problem that the society may collapse, and witches will be suspected and seen where the cause of this ambiguity is not entirely clear. In the case of the Antinomians and Quakers there were obvious candidates, and so the results of those crime-waves were not witch-hunts, although like witch-hunts they were ritualized acts of purification. No probative evidence is presented against the groups involved, just as none is against witches. Instead, they are the victims of a social fear of internal collapse. The society feels that it needs to get rid of them, even though it cannot cogently express the reason.

The real reason, as an anthropologist would see it, is rising anxiety about competition that has resulted from weakening internal integration. As Douglas notes, when ambiguity is high a society is highly competitive. People avoid their social obligations and do not pay their superiors what they owe and yet remain unpunished. Such power obviously does not come from socially accepted sources, and so must derive from the foreign, at least in the worldview of a society with strong external boundaries. When social roles and obligations are ignored, when norms and morality and institutions are threatened the power must stem from the outside, and so the outsiders concealing themselves within the social group must be found. Witch-hunts are the result, the discovery of those who wield power that comes from the foreign and threatens the social.

Since witch-hunts are a kind of ritualized act, we can see how they function, as Catherine Bell puts it, as a strategy for constructing certain

26. Douglas (*Purity and Danger*, pp. 108-10) has discovered that people in positions of power are almost never accused of witchcraft, and are quite unlikely to be prosecuted for it. The powerful can be accused of sorcery, which differs from witchcraft in the sense that it is a charge of legitimate social power that has been misused. Witchcraft, on the other hand, is power that derives from illegitimate sources.

types of power relationships.[27] In an act such as a witch-hunt, objective constructions of power are produced that are believed to derive from some ultimate source such as God or tradition. As people participate in such a drama—and in the case of the 1692 witch-hunt the participants included the girls who laid the charges, the court that prosecuted them, the witches themselves, those who believed the charges, and even those colonists who said and did nothing while the witch-craze made its way through the colony—they embody the constructions of power produced in the ritualized act.[28] Simply by agreeing that certain people are witches the participants signal their agreement that there are people within the society who wield illegitimate power, power that stems from evil and that aims at destroying the social good. They acknowledge that such power is in fact illegitimate, and that those who employ it must be removed from society or killed. In such an act, however, the veracity of social norms, obligations, roles, morality and institutions is implicitly affirmed. The affirmation of the power of the social body to order itself and the lives of its members sneaks in through a back door, as it were. Not only is social unity expressed as the society works together to purify itself from evil, but subjugation to the social is dramatized as the participants do so. They submit to the social power to classify and to command action. In witch-hunts the anthropologist sees a reaction against internal ambiguity and a strengthening of social integration. Participation implies assent to the social, and such assent, as Rappaport pointed out, is the basis of morality. We may also say with Bell that it is the basis of social power.

The situation in the divorces and expulsions of Ezra 9–10 is similar to the Massachusetts Bay Colony witch-hunt. In the texts we see an obsession with purification and an emphasis on the foreignness of and the danger posed by the women. They are seen as the source of the foreign and dangerous power that threatens the social. Insiders are blamed for allowing them through the external boundaries in the first place—not an unexpected charge in a witch-hunt, as Douglas discovered[29]—but the source of the danger is the women themselves. The society must purify itself of them if it is to survive, the thinking goes within the social body itself. The society is attempting to reduce internal ambiguity and shore up its boundaries, says the anthropologist.

27. Bell, *Ritual Theory*, p. 197.
28. Bell, *Ritual Theory*, pp. 206-207.
29. Douglas, *Natural Symbols*, p. 169.

The Witch-hunts of Sixteenth- and Seventeenth-Century Europe. The scholars of the eighteenth and nineteenth centuries who studied the witch-hunts of sixteenth- and seventeenth-century Europe commonly attributed them to a recrudescence of medieval superstition, writes Hugh Trevor-Roper, for they found it difficult to conceive of such illogical beliefs flourishing at the same time as Locke and Bacon.[30] However, Trevor-Roper found in his own study of these witch-hunts, while some people during the Middle Ages believed in the existence of witches and the power of the occult, the church and prominent theologians were at pains to discredit such views. Only in the later part of the medieval period would the denial of the existence of witchcraft, a denial that had been accepted by canonical law, be reversed.[31] While there were pagan survivals in the European Christianity of the Middle Ages, writes Trevor-Roper, belief in witches was only fragmentary and could hardly be called a systematic religion. The system was supplied by the inquisitors.[32]

The hunt for witches in Europe began, if one date can be given, in 1484 when Pope Innocent VIII issued a papal bull at the request of inquisitors in Rhineland who wished to put a stop to witchcraft there.[33] It is no coincidence that the witch-hunts were, in the beginning, focused in the Alps and Pyrenees, mountainous areas where the church had been trying to eliminate the heresies of the Albigensians and the Vaudois. By the time Innocent issued his bull the witch-craze had been in existence in those areas for almost two centuries.[34] The connection between persecution of heresy and persecution of witchcraft, writes Trevor-Roper, is not terribly difficult to make: both represent forms of social intolerance, attempts to stamp out opposition against the arbiter of the social worldview and morality, the church.[35] So it was in Spain that the persecution of Jews and that of witches reached their peaks at the same time. Witches were hunted before the formal establishment of the Inquisition, after which time the

30. H. Trevor-Roper, 'The European Witch-Craze of the Sixteenth and Seventeenth Centuries', in *idem*, *The European Witch-Craze of the Sixteenth and Seventeenth Centuries and Other Essays* (New York: Harper & Row, 1967), pp. 90-102 (97-101).

31. Trevor-Roper, 'The European Witch-Craze', pp. 91-93.

32. Trevor-Roper, 'The European Witch-Craze', p. 126.

33. Trevor-Roper, 'The European Witch-Craze', p. 101. Notably, Alexander IV had denied a similar request from the Dominicans in 1257, stating that he would not grant inquisitorial power unless heresy could be proven on the part of those subject to an inquisition (p. 103).

34. Trevor-Roper, 'The European Witch-Craze', pp. 102-105.

35. Trevor-Roper, 'The European Witch-Craze', p. 108.

inquisitors focused their energies on Jews. In Germany, however, Jews were persecuted first and witches later. Both were forms of social non-conformity, and so either could be made the focus of fears surrounding the collapse of social integration.[36]

When the craze springs up in earnest and throughout Europe in the mid-sixteenth century, claims Trevor-Roper, social integration was precisely the issue. In fact, he ascribes it directly to the conflict between Protestantism and Roman Catholicism, since every major outbreak of the craze occurred in a frontier area between the two groups.[37] In the 1560s as the witch-hunts first began to increase in intensity the Reformers were working to evangelize people in the newly Protestant states. Opposition to their gospel was described both as popery and as witchcraft. Similarly, when the Catholics began their reconquest in the 1580s, opposition was described both as Protestant heresy and as witchcraft. Yet the more control a government had over a region, concludes Trevor-Roper, the less likely were women in such areas to be charged with witchcraft.[38]

External boundaries were not threatened nor at stake here; the question lay in how much control societies had over the hearts and minds of their members. Those who were heretics could obviously be tried and executed as such, but witches were another matter. There was no need to charge heretics, those who sympathized with the other side (the foreigners), with witchcraft. The witch-craze was, as Trevor-Roper points out, a response to social non-conformity; or, we could say, the fear of it. When anxiety in a society about social integration runs high, as it surely would in newly converted areas or in those that bordered lands belonging to the other denomination, it runs high because people fear that there is no true social conformity, even though there are no true heretics in sight. Witches, after all, are accused of being witches, not of being heretics. Although they pose no real threat to social integration, people are singled out as witches when there is enough social anxiety about non-conformity and internal dis-integration and there are no other obvious candidates for the charges. And yet, as has been noted above, there are obvious benefits to such actions in their ability to extract the participants' assent to social worldview and morality. Where social control in Europe at this time was strong, witch-hunts were socially superfluous and so quite rare.

36. Trevor-Roper, 'The European Witch-Craze', pp. 110-12.
37. Trevor-Roper, 'The European Witch-Craze', pp. 139-40, 143.
38. Trevor-Roper, 'The European Witch-Craze', pp. 188-89, 191.

Witches among the Melpa. Among the Melpa of the New Guinea Highlands the term *kum* is used for witchcraft, and more generally designates non-reciprocal behavior.[39] The 'dominant ethic' of the Melpa is one of production for exchange, writes Andrew Strathern.[40] When Europeans first appeared in the region, the Melpa did not regard them as human until they showed themselves willing to engage in exchange of goods and services. When the power of *kum* takes hold of people they are said deliberately to violate this norm of exchange and production. Excessive consumption is considered suspect, and the Melpa believe that production and investment are social ideals.[41] Among the Melpa, then, witchcraft is quite obviously anti-social behavior.

Like the other societies of our case studies, the Highland communities have strong external boundaries. The clans of the area are geographically distinct,[42] and marriages are made within carefully circumscribed groups, meaning that people cannot enter other clans by marriage except those that are closely allied.[43] While some allegiance is expressed to the tribe, especially in times of war, people within the same clan (the next largest level of social organization) are all said to be descended from the same father. Exchange of marriage partners usually occurs within the allied clans of the same tribe;[44] and exchange in general, the dominant ethic of the Melpa, is mandatory among affines. Clans are open to exchange with other friendly clans, but when such exchange occurs the participants will stress that the men of the groups involved are descendants of a single person.[45] The external boundaries are not perfectly closed (no society has boundaries that are), for the clans meet others in warfare, and have co-existed with Europeans since the 1930s. It was in fact the fear of exchange with the Europeans, writes Strathern, that prompted a rumor of witchcraft among the Melpa in 1977.

39. A. Strathern, 'Witchcraft, Greed, Cannibalism and Death: Some Related Themes from the New Guinea Highlands', in M. Bloch and J. Parry (eds.), *Death and the Regeneration of Life* (Cambridge: Cambridge University Press, 1982), pp. 111-33 (112).

40. Strathern, 'Witchcraft', p. 114.

41. Strathern, 'Witchcraft', p. 115.

42. A. Strathern, *One Father, One Blood: Descent and Group Structure among the Melpa People* (London: Tavistock, 1972), p. 55.

43. Strathern, *One Father*, p. 14.

44. Strathern, *One Father*, pp. 18-19.

45. Strathern, *One Father*, p. 228.

The cargo cult of 1968–71 was an attempt to solve the problem of the Europeans' control of money and to find a way for the Melpa to produce money themselves, rather than simply exchange coffee for it. The cult collapsed after its supporters had poured a great deal of pork, food and cash into it, and all of the investments were lost. The result, writes Strathern, was that '[a] supreme engine of production was revealed as its opposite. The cult and its leaders had "eaten" all their investments and given nothing back. The wish for cargo had been an inordinately strong desire, a *kum*, and had brought its own destruction.'[46] When the rumor of witchcraft evolved in 1977, then, it manifested a fear that the society was self-destructing as greedy, individual impulses not rooted in the primary social ethic of production and investment were tearing the social body apart. At this time the price for the coffee beans produced among the Melpa had reached a peak, sparking consumer demand for imported goods.[47] What the Melpa saw, however, was not the effect of increased wealth in the community, but anti-social greed; witchcraft, in other words.

The particular rumor of 1977 focused around cannibalism. Those controlled by *kum* were said to be robbing the flesh of newly buried corpses. Cannibalism is a practice abhorred by the Melpa, notes Strathern, and the people claim that a witch's lust for human flesh is like the pleasure people express when eating the flesh of young piglets as opposed to that of grown pigs. In both cases we find the theme of the desire for incorrect consumption that contradicts the predominant ethic of production for exchange.[48] When a body dies its flesh or 'grease' is thought to contribute to the earth's fertility. When the witches ate newly buried corpses, then, they negated this exchange.[49] In short, when economic circumstances caused an increase in imports and consumption among the Melpa in 1977, the fear of witchcraft was the result. What was really at stake, from the point of view of the anthropologist, was anxiety surrounding the collapse of internal social integration. As people consumed, the thinking went, they must be disregarding their social duties of production, and so failing the moral norms of Melpa society. Attention to individual desires rather than the social good will, if widespread enough, lead to social disintegration in any society. This was the fear among the Melpa.

46. Strathern, 'Witchcraft', p. 117.
47. Strathern, 'Witchcraft', pp. 114-15.
48. Strathern, 'Witchcraft', p. 114.
49. Strathern, 'Witchcraft', pp. 117-18.

Notably, however, they did not act to place limits on consumption, nor on the exports of coffee that allowed the money to flow into the social body in the first place. The matter was, in one sense, an economic one, and yet the society undertook no economic reforms. Why? In large part because the fear surrounding social disintegration was so vague that the members of the social body could not pin down its causes. If Strathern's analysis of the cannibalism rumor is correct, it was sparked in part because of events that occurred six years prior. The Melpa had recently become hypersensitive to the issue of over-consumption, which in their worldview is also an issue of anti-social actions in its disregard of the basis of their social ethic. The Melpa word for 'mind' is *noman*, and the term designates the seat of the motivation, will and morality. Among witches *kum* replaces *noman*,[50] and so they are unable to function in the moral way that society demands. Among the Melpa, their actions will thus be viewed primarily as overly consumptive; they produce nothing and eat what they did not make, thus denying the validity of the exchange system that undergirds Melpa society.

The Melpa see witches involved in necrophagy while the anthropologist sees a reaction to fears of social collapse. There being no single group upon whom to place the blame for the recent advances in consumption in the society and the social anxiety being diffuse enough, blame falls upon witches. The situation, then, is rather like that of the 1692 witch-hunts of the Massachusetts Bay Colony. Vague and diffuse fears of social collapse within a society with strong external boundaries lead to a hunt for witches. And as the Melpa terminology makes clear, witches are people who are no longer capable of fulfilling social obligations and obeying social morality. The seat of such impulses, the *noman*, has been replaced by *kum*, an anti-social power. Notably, the Melpa most frequently suspect women to be involved in cannibalism.[51] Women are also considered to be associated with consumption among the Melpa, while males are, ideally, investors of goods.[52]

Conclusions. A number of points relevant to the case of the divorced women in Yehud may be drawn from these case studies:

1. Vague and diffuse social fears result in witch-hunts. When the source of the challenge to internal integration is clear, as it was in the case of the

50. Strathern, 'Witchcraft', p. 122.
51. Strathern, 'Witchcraft', p. 113.
52. Strathern, 'Witchcraft', p. 115.

Antinomian and Quaker controversies, then the social body will demand the expulsion or death of those people. Such people may not be charged with any crime—the Quakers were expelled and killed before the colony had a law regarding Quakers—or the charges may be extremely unclear—as was the case with Anne Hutchinson—but the social body will purify itself of them. Like witch-hunts they are ritualized acts of purification since the punishment results in expulsion or death (exit from the social body), since they are charged with no crime or are charged without probative evidence, and since the purification is a result of social anxiety about internal integration. But when there is no one clearly identifiable cause for social anxiety, then a witch-hunt will begin and witches will have to be manufactured.

2. These social fears concern weakening social integration. In a society where disintegration appears to its members to be a distinct possibility, where people are disregarding the moral codes they have been brought up with, where they ignore what they owe to their superiors and to social institutions, where they act, in short, for themselves and ignore the social good, we find competition. The society itself may compete with other social systems for the hearts and minds of its members, as was the case in post-Reformation Europe. When power relations are ambiguous and movement from one social position to another is not sure and seamless, people must compete with others in order to move up the social ladder. Commanding officers must compete for loyalty, parents must compete for obedience. In the Massachusetts Bay Colony of 1692, social leaders competed with each other for power and other citizens competed with each other for land. Given the evidence of the sermons of the time, there was a widespread feeling that social morality—adherence to social norms and roles and institutions—was collapsing. People no longer believed that others were paying the social dues that they owed. As Douglas points out, it will seem in societies with weakening internal integration that the universe is inhabited by dark forces that people may tap into in order to circumvent society's rules of behavior; and so the flimsy witness of three young girls is enough to begin a witch-hunt that puts hundreds in jail and kills almost 30 people. The colony did not find a world of demonic powers and Satanic influence (although it thought it did), it only discovered people willing to believe that such forces existed and willing to act on such beliefs based on the smallest of excuses. The population's experience of competition and failure in competition was strong enough that people were more than willing to believe that the powers of the occult were at the root

of such events. Such beliefs will be the result of weakening social integration, and witch-hunts will attempt to purify the social body of such evil forces.

In these two societies, where the people believe their morality to be based upon the commands of God, women who associate with and draw their power from Satan are poised against the social order. The Melpa have no such conceptions of a personified source of evil, and there witchcraft is the anti-social *kum* that displaces the *noman* or seat of social morality. The witches people find are predisposed to the destruction of the social order. So among the Melpa vague fears of over-consumption, fears that were fed in part by the earlier collapse of the cargo cult, lead to the manufacture of witches, mainly women. Witches among the Melpa are people who consume too much and who do not produce and invest—who are set against the social morality of the Melpa which demands the opposite. Where we find witch-hunts we find fears that social deviancy is about to destroy the society.

3. Witch-hunts occur in societies with strong external boundaries. Such was the situation in all three of the case studies. Witches, however, are thought to draw on foreign sources of power and so are, in that sense, foreigners. As Fenn puts it, the boundaries of the society must be strong, yet permeable enough so that some foreign influences may enter. Those singled out as perpetrators of anti-social activities will be branded as being under the influence of foreign power. Witches draw on the power of the devil or whatever is opposed to the social. They become rather like newly discovered foreign spies.

That they are related to the foreign and anti-social—societies with strong external boundaries obviously fear the foreign and so equate it with the anti-social—is borne out by the punishment handed out in the three case studies: execution or expulsion. In either case corporal punishment or imprisonment is not enough, and the social body must have them out of its midst. In both Massachusetts and Europe death was the punishment for witchcraft, among the Melpa it is expulsion from the village.[53] They are either destroyed or returned to the place of their true origin.

4. Witchcraft is not a charge brought against certain groups of people in order to deliberately hide social struggles about power, wealth, ethnic purity, or some other matter. Among the Melpa those charged with witchcraft could have been charged with over-consumption and told to mend

53. Strathern, 'Witchcraft', p. 113.

their ways. In Europe and Massachusetts, witches could simply have been charged with heresy. There is no sense in these case studies that witchcraft is a trumped-up charge meant to obfuscate the real reasons why such people—mainly women—are put to death or forced out of the society. In sixteenth- and seventeenth-century Europe many were killed for being heretics, but witches were killed for being witches. Or, from the point of view of the anthropologist, they were killed because of vague fears of social non-conformity that had not been quelled through the execution of known and suspected heretics. Had they really been theological dissenters they would have been executed as such. Fear of witches arises when societies with weakening internal integration and strong external boundaries believe that the foreign has entered into its midst to destroy it but have no obvious candidates—such as Quakers or Antinomians—to charge.

5. Charges of witchcraft and acts of witch-hunts and other types of purification benefit society by increasing its internal social integration. In the cases of the Quakers and Antinomians and in the cases of the Protestant and Catholic heretics in sixteenth- and seventeenth-century Europe, the purity rituals aimed at purifying the social body of people who obviously challenged the social order. In the case of the Melpa fears surrounding the influence of *kum* and the consequent hunt for those influenced by it result in a heightened awareness of the evils of over-consumption and the need to adhere to the dominant social ethic of production and investment. Regardless of the economic results of these events, the matter focuses people's attention on social morality and worldview, reminding them of the ways they should act and the ways they ought not to act. In Europe, as Trevor-Roper points out, persecution of witches was closely associated with the persecution of heretics and Jews, and the former persecution could be carried out in the presence or absence of the latter. The two were so closely linked that witch-hunts reminded people of which worldview was good and would be tolerated—that of the social body, grounded in the laws of God—and which was evil and had to be eliminated—that of the witches and stemming from the power of Satan. The same points could be made for the witch-hunts of Massachusetts.

The witch-crazes also provide a chance for community members to act in light of the bifurcation of reality to which they have been exposed. In their participation in the witch-hunts themselves they can concretely manifest their subjugation to the social order by killing or expelling those who, they have been told, stand against the social order. Only those within the society who actively work to stop the witch-hunts can be said to be non-participants. Those who believe in the existence of witches, or even those who do not and yet do not act on their beliefs, have acknowledged their subjugation to the social order. Remember, Rappaport noted that ritual acts engage assent and not necessarily belief. Participation publicly signals assent to the social order dramatized in a ritual (or here, we would say, a ritualized act), and whether or not one truly believes, one has given one's assent to the order and worldview, and this becomes the basis of morality. An 'ought' has been established from which the 'is' may be judged.

Ritualized acts such as these witch-hunts, however, do not specifically state social goods and worldviews that people should engage in or believe. What has been accomplished here is, in part, a matter of negative inference: the social body has participated and demonstrated in an act which demonstrates that the society must purify itself of those who *oppose* the social worldview. Positive social goods are emphasized in an implicit contrast with negative ones. There is also the issue of power, as Bell points out. In subjugation to the social order participants in the ritualized act implicitly acknowledge the power of the social to order their lives. In doing so, they acknowledge the power of those the social has invested with authority and they acknowledge the goods and loyalty and honor they owe to others. The social order here is established implicitly and vaguely and without specificity and systematization, but it is established nonetheless. To draw upon another point made by Rappaport, the ritual (or ritualized act) forces a yes/no response from its participants. There are no gray areas, and if there are they become private matters of indecision that cannot, ethically speaking, affect the participant's actions, since participation indicates assent and so the basis of social morality. People will be judged by whether or not they live up to their public assent to the social worldview. In participating in witch-hunts, then, people make a commitment to the social worldview, broadly defined, that they have acted to defend in killing or expelling witches, whose power is anti-social. The details of the consequences of this assent may become clear only in later rituals or ritualized acts, but the basis of assent has been assured, and so social integration has been strengthened.

3. *Women and their Place in the Social*

a. *Women, Nature and Culture: The Theory of Sherry Ortner*

One of the curious aspects of witch-hunts, including the ones examined above, is that their victims are almost universally women. The initial problem here may be stated this way: why, if a charge of witchcraft is (from the anthropologist's point of view and the point of view I am privileging here) a charge of wielding anti-social power (social deviance, as Erikson puts it, or social non-conformity, as Trevor-Roper does), are powers that challenge the integrity of the social mainly associated with women? Sherry Ortner claims that the secondary status of women—whether this be regarded as ideology that explicitly devalues women, symbolic devices that implicitly portray women as inferior, social-structural arrangements that exclude women's participation in society's highest powers, or some combination of them—is something found in every society. No study, she writes, has ever discovered a truly egalitarian society.[54] This is a matter due not to biological determinism—the belief that males are considered to be superior because they are genetically dominant, a notion that has been dismissed by anthropology—but to social factors. While no one would deny that males and females are biologically different, it is culture and not biology that attaches labels of good/bad and inferior/superior. To understand the universal secondary status of women, writes Ortner, we can only conclude that women are identified with or a symbol of something that every culture devalues.[55]

One thing that every culture does devalue, or that every culture places in opposition to its social center, is nature. In opposing culture and nature, Ortner is clear that she does not refer to the Western sense of humanity struggling to dominate a nature that is subject to certain universal laws, for that is a culturally specific worldview. The bifurcation she suggests is one of culture in confrontation with that which limits human agency.[56] Her understanding of culture is 'human consciousness, or... the products of human consciousness (i.e., systems of thought and technology), by means of which humanity attempts to assert control over nature'.[57] So nature for Ortner is, in essence, what impurity is for Douglas: the opposite of the social, that which the social must keep at bay if it is to survive and flourish.

One thing society must put keep at bay if it is to survive is decay and death. Ortner, following Simone de Beauvoir, notes that much more of

54. S.B. Ortner, *Making Gender: The Politics and Erotics of Culture* (Boston: Beacon Press, 1996), pp. 21-24.

55. Ortner, *Making Gender*, pp. 24-25.

56. Ortner, *Making Gender*, p. 179.

57. Ortner, *Making Gender*, pp. 25-26.

women's body, space, time and energy is devoted to reproduction—a matter that includes menstruation, pregnancy and nursing—than men's. Women produce humans, who are perishable, while men, by contrast, are thought to be uniquely associated with the production of culture, goods and ideas and institutions that are believed to last forever. Furthermore, women's bodily processes locate them in social situations that are, in turn, seen as closer to nature than to culture. Their association with the nursing and raising of infants is suspect, since infants are unsocialized beings, humans unaware of their social roles and obligations. Numerous anthropologists have commented on the opposition of family and culture in society, for the family is a potentially divisive unit that can draw loyalty and devotion from society. Women, writes Ortner, because of their association with infants and the home in childbirth and nursing, become associated with the un-social infants and potentially anti-social home.

Finally, since women are largely responsible for childcare they are the first socializer of boys and girls. The boys, however, build relationships with their fathers as they are socialized into the world of men and into dispositions that are considered to be more abstract, less like the nature with which their mothers and sisters are associated.[58] Of these three arguments, the basic relationship of women with the biological process of reproduction appears to stand at the root of the situation. Connected with childbirth and nursing, women are associated with the impermanent, what threatens the unity and eternity of culture. It is then not surprising that when anxiety seizes a community that it is about to disintegrate it will look to women as the root of the cause when there is no other group that may be easily located. They are the people most easily associated with the anti-social. And when a society has strong external boundaries, it will not hesitate to see women as really under the control of the foreign, that force par excellence that opposes the social.

To return to Douglas's terminology of the impure as the anti-social or disorder that threatens the social body, we can find verification for Ortner's theory in the Pentateuchal laws, at the least. In these laws the term *niddâ*, 'impurity', a term Ezra 9–10 uses to describe the foreigners, tends to be associated with menstruation and death (biological processes where the transience of life is evident), while elsewhere it is connected with what is clearly anti-social, such as images that are used in non-YHWHistic worship (Ezek. 7.19-20) and what defiles the temple (2 Chron. 29.5). It is obviously not, in this worldview, difficult to move from menstruation to

58. Ortner, *Making Gender*, pp. 28-37.

the anti-social. For example, Lev. 12.2-8 states that a woman who bears a child is *ṭāmēʼâ* and *niddâ* (both terms can be translated as 'impure', although the former is often rendered as 'polluting'). Until the time of her purification she may not approach the sanctuary or touch any holy thing. Both menstruation and idols, it seems, are offensive to YHWH because both are *niddâ*.

This is really the same point made in Chapter 1—the impure in Israelite thought, whether it be idols, food or menstrual blood, is opposed to the holy—but I should also point out that the root *ndd* means 'to flee'. What is *niddâ*, then, is what must be pushed out of the social body. Since what is *niddâ* may also be described as *ṭāmē'*, 'polluting', it appears that Douglas's analysis of pollution or impurity as foreign or anti-social holds true for ancient Israel, as does Ortner's theory. Women after childbirth or during menstruation (Lev. 15.19-24) are impure, the precise opposite of holy, and are isolated from the community for a certain period of time. It is not difficult to see, then, that when the social body was anxious that it was disintegrating and blamed foreign influences, it singled out a group of women as the dangerous foreign influence when there was no other group obviously to blame. The logic is fuzzy, as Bourdieu puts it, but it is logic nonetheless.

b. *Women and the Impurity of Death*

Ancient Israel was not the only society in which death and birth are considered to be polluting and impure. In Numbers 19, for example, *niddâ* is used to refer to the water that is used to purify those who have come into contact with a corpse. Death as well as birth would seem to be threats to the claim of the permanence of culture; and Maurice Bloch has concluded that in many cultures women are associated with the polluting aspects of death as well as those of birth.

> It is surely no accident that in nearly all the cultures we know, it is principally women who are expected to weep, whether this be the organised weeping that we find in such places as Iran, or the disorganised individual weeping of Britain and France. Similarly it is again and again the case that it is women who wear mourning in its varying manifestations... Again and again women are *given* death while the social order is reaffirmed elsewhere.[59]

59. M. Bloch, 'Death, Women and Power', in M. Bloch and J. Parry (eds.), *Death and the Regeneration of Life* (Cambridge: Cambridge University Press, 1982), pp. 211-30 (226). His emphasis.

It is not simply that women are associated with death, Bloch points out in this article, but that they are associated with death insofar as it poses a threat to the unity of the social body, insofar as it stands as the opposite of the social order. To build on Ortner's observations, we might say that because women are biologically associated with childbirth and nursing, aspects of life that run counter to social claims of permanence since they are associated with beginnings and not with the eternal, they are associated with death which has the same connotations.

Bloch examines the funeral rituals of the Merina, a people who live in central Madagascar. Divided into local kin groups that Bloch calls demes, the Merina regard all people who live in the demes as continuators of the ancestors, a present incarnation of an eternal social group. The notion of the ancestral land of the deme is merged with the notion of ancestors, and it is believed that blessing and fertility come from the ancestors. The worst crime a people can commit is to disperse the people or the land of the deme. The Merina thus enjoin endogamy, protection of the land, and the regrouping of the corpses of the dead. The ancestral blessing of fertility will not be given unless the corpses of the deme dead are placed in a common tomb, and each one of these tombs can contain a great number of corpses and so symbolizes community.[60]

In the Merina worldview women are associated with disunity. In many rituals, writes Bloch, the house stands for the individual family isolated from and in opposition to the deme, and the house is clearly marked 'as women's territory, the place of individual and individuating birth and death'.[61] When someone dies an initial funerary ceremony is held in which the corpse is buried in an individual grave close to where he or she died. This ceremony is associated with sadness and mourning, as well as with pollution. In this initial ceremony the corpse is associated with pollution linked to decomposition, of which the Merina stress that they have a particular horror. It is women who are primarily associated with both the mourning and the pollution of this part of the ceremony. They are the ones who must wash the corpse and everything in the house polluted by it, and they even throw themselves upon it to ritually take on its pollution.[62]

In the second funerary ritual, however, the corpse is exhumed once it has completely decomposed. The bones are recovered and taken to the

60. Bloch, 'Death, Women and Power', pp. 211-13.

61. Bloch, 'Death, Women and Power', p. 214. Also see my comments on Bloch's analysis of the Merina initiation rite in the introduction (pp. 27-32).

62. Bloch, 'Death, Women and Power', pp. 214-15.

central ancestral shrine where they are added to those of the ancestors. The flesh appears to act as a metaphor for the impermanence of the individual since, like the individual, it passes away, whereas the bones act as a metaphor for the social since, like the deme and its ancestors, they remain forever and are united in community. The dominant emotion expressed in such ceremonies is joy, and this return is often celebrated with singing and dancing. The contrast between this communal burial and the earlier individual one is constantly stressed, and the second burial is said to be a time of blessing, fertility, children, crops, wealth, and so on. Since actual contact with dead bodies is a frightening matter for the Merina, it is women who are forced to carry the corpse from its original burial place to its final one; and yet, once the bones of the dead person have finally been regrouped with those of the ancestors, it is the men who make speeches on top of the tomb and request blessings from the dead.[63]

The point is not, Bloch indicates simply that women are associated with death, but that they are associated with its polluting and so its anti-social aspects. The two funeral ceremonies of the Merina emphasize the goodness of the unity of the community and degrade whatever stands against it. In the end the permanence and unity of the deme is shown to overcome even the discontinuity of death. In order to dramatize this to the participants in the ritual, however, the opposite of unity and permanence must be degraded, and this is a matter associated with women, likely for the reasons that Ortner enumerated. Women are believed to be what drives a community apart, and if a social body needs to look for perpetrators when none seems readily available (such as Quakers or Antinomians), it will likely look to women.

63. Bloch, 'Death, Women and Power', pp. 215-17.

Chapter 3

THE BOUNDARIES OF THE PERSIAN PERIOD TEMPLE COMMUNITY

1. *The Political Organization of the Temple Community*

If the temple community of Persian period Yehud had strong external boundaries and weak internal integration, then we expect it to engage in purification rituals such as witch-hunts if anxiety about the erosion of internal boundaries becomes high. The purpose of this chapter is to show that it was just such a community. I begin here with a short exposition of the political organization of the province and community, a necessary prelude if the following discussion on boundaries is to be put in its proper historical context.

From a combination of bullae and jar handles discovered in Palestine we are able to fill in some of the gaps in Yehud's leadership left by the biblical text that mentions no administrative head of the province between the governors Zerubbabel in 515[1] and Nehemiah in 445.[2] A bulla published by Nahman Avigad and dated paleographically to the late sixth century bears the impression *l'lntn pḥw'*, 'belonging to Elnathan, the governor',[3] while a seal of the same period reads *lšlmyt 'mt 'lntn pḥ*[*w'*], 'belonging to Shelomit, the maidservant of Elnathan, [the] govern[or]'.[4] Since these were found within a collection of 65 bullae and two seals,

1. Zerubbabel is mentioned as the governor in Hag. 1.1, which clearly puts him in this office in 520. Ezra 1–6 places him in Jerusalem at the time of the completion of the temple construction—515, according to Ezra 6.15.

2. Nehemiah's memoirs (as they are preserved in Ezra–Nehemiah) state that he left for Jerusalem in the twentieth year of Artaxerxes I (465–424), or 445 (2.1). The Artaxerxes mentioned in the text must be Artaxerxes I, since the Sanballat who features so prominently in the text of Nehemiah is also mentioned in two papyri dated to 407 (*TAD* A4.7.29), when he is old enough to have ceded his power to his sons.

3. N. Avigad, *Bullae and Seals from a Post-Exilic Judean Archive* (Qedem Reports, 4; Jerusalem: Hebrew University, 1976), pp. 5-7, 17.

4. Avigad, *Bullae and Seals*, pp. 11, 18.

many of which bear the provincial name *yhd*, there is no doubt of which province Elnathan was the governor. The names *yhw'zr* and *'ḥzy* have been found on seals at Ramat Rahel dating to the early fifth century.[5] Thus, states Avigad, we have Elnathan, Yehoezer and Ahzay as governors of Yehud between 515 and 445, registering serious evidence against Albrecht Alt's hypothesis of Samarian control of Yehud before 445.[6] Scholarly arguments that the names mentioned on the bullae did not refer to individuals of the same rank as Nehemiah, or even that Nehemiah was not a governor, do not withstand close scrutiny.[7]

While we know of a few other administrative offices in Yehud below that of governor, let us turn to the temple assembly based in Jerusalem, known in Hebrew as the *qāhāl*. The *qāhāl*, I have argued elsewhere, is similar to the *puhru* 'assembly' found in Babylonian temples.[8] The *puhru* had charge of the temple's day-to-day administrative policy concerning temple function, personnel, fines, the assigning of temple lands, and so

5. Avigad, *Bullae and Seals*, pp. 6, 24.

6. A. Alt, 'Die Rolle Samarias bei der Entstehung des Judentums', in *idem*, *Kleine Schriften zur Geschichte des Volkes Israel*, II (Munich: C.H. Beck, 1953), pp. 316-37.

7. Robert North does not believe that Nehemiah was actually a governor ('Civil Authority in Ezra', in *idem*, *Studi in onore di Edoardo Volterra*, VI [Milan: A. Giuffre, 1971], pp. 377-404 [404], and also pp. 392-93 and 399-402). Yet Nehemiah is explicitly named as governor in Neh. 5.14 and 8.9, and he also mentions the doings of 'the previous governors who were before me' (5.15) in his memoirs. These assumedly include Zerubbabel, who is specifically mentioned as governor in Hag. 1.1, 14; 2.2, 21. As for our knowledge of governors of the province known from extra-biblical material, Joseph Naveh argues on the basis of a fifth-century papyrus from Migdol in Egypt (*TAD* A3.3) which uses the word *pḥwt'* (a word he translates as 'the governors') that the term *pḥw'* probably refers to a lesser government official, since we would hardly expect more than one provincial governor in a single location. In his opinion, then, Elnathan was not a provincial governor on the level of Nehemiah, since we expect the Aramaic *pḥt'* as the determinative singular form for the feminine noun 'governor' (Joseph Naveh, 'Gleanings of Some Pottery Inscriptions', *IEJ* 46 [1996], pp. 44-51 [44-45]). Note, however, that the determinative plural form of *peḥâ* in biblical Aramaic is not the expected **peḥātā'* or **paḥātā'* (which would give, by analogy, a hypothetical determinative singular form of **peḥ*^{a}*tā'* or **paḥ*^{a}*tā'*), but the irregular *paḥ*^{a}*watā'*. By analogy, it would give the determinative singular form **paḥ*^{a}*wtā'*, or *pḥwt'*, which may have been an allomorph of *pḥw'*. Or, the anomalous *t* could simply have been a scribal error. Since the context of the letter that Naveh cites does not demand that *pḥwt'* be read as a plural, we can read it as an allomorph of *pḥw'*. One cannot argue on the basis of this form alone that it refers to a different position than that of provincial governor.

8. Janzen, 'The "Mission" of Ezra', pp. 638-43.

forth. These temples owned vast tracts of land, extensive storage facilities, and slaves. Stores within the temple were considered to be the property of of the god. Membership in this community was considered to be roughly equivalent to the status of a fully enfranchised citizen in the city; it also conveyed the benefits of rations paid to the lower levels of temple personnel or prebend shares to the higher levels. It is no wonder, argues Blenkinsopp, that those citizens or members of the *puhru* who received prebend shares jealously guarded their ranks.[9]

The chief administrator of the temple, as I mentioned in Chapter 1, was the *šatammu* (or *šangu* or *rabû ša rēš āli*) who functioned as the head of the *puhru*. He never acted in an administrative capacity by himself, but always within the context of his position as the head of the assembly.[10] In the Ebabbar temple of Shamash at Sippar, we do find the *šangu* mentioned in some texts along with royal judges, and in a few cases he acts as judge, although apparently only for cases involving matters internal to the temple community.[11] In general, the *šatammu* presided over a wide range of matters, including daily administrative duties, the imposition of penalties, marriage and property issues, and so forth.[12] It is important to remember, then, that the temple community centered at Jerusalem, the *qāhāl*, was not the same as the population of Yehud, nor was the administration of the *qāhāl* coextensive with the administration of the Persian-controlled province. They were not, however, entirely separate. I will explain why this is so in Chapter 4; the only point that I wish readers to keep in mind here is the rather obvious one that the temple community was not an island isolated from the influence of the Persian administration. As strong as it might try to keep its external boundaries, there were always opportunities for foreign influences to move in. How influences moved in—where these external boundaries had flaws, we could say—will be the subject of the next chapter.

9. J. Blenkinsopp, 'Temple and Society in Achaemenid Judah', in P.R. Davies (ed.), *Second Temple Studies: 1. Persian Period* (JSOTSup, 117; Sheffield: JSOT Press, 1991), pp. 22-53 (29).

10. McEwan, *Priest and Temple*, p. 25.

11. A.C.V.M. Bongenaar, *The Neo-Babylonian Ebabbar Temple at Sippar: Its Administration and its Prosopography* (Uitgaven van het Nederlands Historisch-Archaeologisch Instituut te Instanbul, 80; Leiden: Nederlands Historisch-Archaeologisch Instituut te Instanbul, 1997), pp. 22-23.

12. Blenkinsopp, 'Temple and Society', p. 32.

2. *The External Boundaries*

a. *Excursus: The Historicity and Date of Ezra–Nehemiah*

One further point must be made before discussing the boundaries of this community, and that is the historicity of Ezra–Nehemiah. I have already argued for the historicity of Ezra 9–10 in Chapter 1, but much of the information that I will offer here regarding the social borders will come from the rest of this book, and if it is not historically reliable then it renders the discussion useless. David Clines argues in reference to the question of the Ezran substratum to the Ezra materials that '[o]nly historical implausibilities or impossibilities could tell strongly against the supposition of an Ezran substratum to the narrative…'[13] I am not making a claim here that concerns an Ezran substratum, but I do want to pick up on Clines's dictum and apply it to the matter of the historical validity of the the book as a whole. I will show here that there is no real reason to doubt the veracity of Ezra–Nehemiah's narrative of the major events it recounts; and we should thus consider them historical events unless someone can show that such things could not happen or were unlikely to happen at that time and in that place.

In Chapter 1 I argued that the works ascribed to Ezra in Ezra 7–10 and Nehemiah 8 are perfectly comprehensible when they are placed within his role (or roles) as temple administrator and priest. Another large section of Ezra–Nehemiah apparently originated in the writings of Nehemiah—a section that could include all of Neh. 1.1–7.5 and 11.1–13.31,[14] or perhaps only 1.1–7.5, portions of 12.27-43, and 13.4-31.[15] Not even the most skeptical scholars doubt that Nehemiah is responsible for these sections of the book, even if only as the author of its substratum. Quite a number of proposals have been suggested as to the form and purpose of this memoir,[16] but it seems clear that the material has received little editing.[17]

We may conclude, then, that historicity of the activities of the administrator Ezra and the governor Nehemiah are not to be doubted. Now Clines has made the useful observation that Nehemiah is not what we would call a disinterested party, and that at times he patently misrepresents

13. Clines, *Ezra, Nehemiah, Esther*, p. 7.

14. So Blenkinsopp, *Ezra–Nehemiah*, pp. 46-47.

15. So L.L. Grabbe, *Ezra–Nehemiah* (London: Routledge, 1998), p. 155.

16. For a brief summary see Clines, *Ezra, Nehemiah, Esther*, pp. 4-6.

17. See, e.g., Blenkinsopp, *Ezra–Nehemiah*, pp. 46-47; Rudolph, *Esra und Nehemia*, pp. xxiv; or Williamson, *Ezra, Nehemiah*, pp. xxiv-xxviii.

his own intentions and feelings and those of others, and has placed some events out of chronological order.[18] Nehemiah, like other writers, has his own agenda to promote; but the point I mean to make here is that there is no reason to doubt that he was appointed by the crown to be governor of Yehud, or that he led the program to rebuild the walls of Jerusalem. This means that we can speak with confidence about the major events related in Ezra 7–10 and Nehemiah 1–8 and 11–13. This is not to say that every word these chapters narrate was actually spoken, or that feelings and motivations attributed to certain characters are accurate, but it is to say that people really did return from Babylon to Yehud, that they did divorce and expel foreign women, that Ezra led the community in learning Torah, that Nehemiah was a governor and rebuilt the walls of Jerusalem.

Readers will notice, however, that for the most part I will focus on the ideology of Ezra–Nehemiah, arguing that the book presents a picture of a temple community that has and needs to maintain strong external boundaries, but that is concerned about deteriorating social integration. The best way to argue that this book does indeed reflect the ideology, worldview and concerns of the Persian period community—that it reflects the social structure of a community likely to engage in an act of purification—is to show that it was written in the Persian period. Inevitably, any attempt to date the book must deal with the dating of the career of Ezra. Ezra 7.7 states that its eponymous character left for Yehud in the seventh year of the reign of Artaxerxes, but there is no consensus as to whether this refers to Artaxerxes I (putting Ezra's journey in 458) or Artaxerxes II (putting it in 398).[19] This means that the final form of the book must either post-date 398 or, if Ezra arrived earlier, 433, the earliest date on which Nehemiah could have returned to Jerusalem from the service of Artaxerxes.[20] Scholarly attempts to date the book by relying on the date of the Chronicler should be regarded with suspicion since the collapse of the consensus of Chronistic authorship of Ezra–Nehemiah that I noted in Chapter 1. There are some chronological markers in the book itself: the list of high priests in

18. D.J.A. Clines, 'The Nehemiah Memoir: The Perils of Autobiography', in *idem*, *What Does Eve Do to Help? And Other Readerly Questions to the Old Testament* (JSOTSup, 94; Sheffield: JSOT Press, 1990), pp. 124-64.

19. For a summary of the relevant scholarly views and helpful bibliographies, see Blenkinsopp, *Ezra–Nehemiah*, pp. 139-44; and Grabbe, *Judaism*, I, pp. 88-93.

20. Neh. 13.6 states that Nehemiah returned to Artaxerxes's service in the thirty-second year of that king's reign (433), and only reappeared in Jerusalem *lqṣ ymym*, 'at the end of a certain time'.

Neh. 12.10-11 ends with Jaddua, whose father was still high priest in 407;[21] and the latest Persian king mentioned in the book is Darius II (424–405) in Neh. 12.22, unless one accepts the later date for Ezra.

If the earlier date for Ezra is accepted, there is no reason why the compilation of the book could not be placed around 400; if the later date, then perhaps the early fourth century. As Frank Cross points out, there is no reference to Alexander, or even to the Phoenician rebellion of the mid-fourth century.[22] Of late, only Williamson has maintained that the final form of the book comes from a period as late as the early Hellenistic period, and then he assigns such a late date only to Ezra 1–6. He puts the composition of the rest of Ezra–Nehemiah around 400. His rationale for the later date for the opening of the book, however, rests on the assertion that the parallels these chapters draw between the first and second temples act as a polemic against the illegitimacy of the sectarian group at Gerizim.[23] The idea is an interesting one, but very speculative. It works *if* priests from Jerusalem were in fact leaving for Gerizim as Williamson suggests, *if* the major split between Jerusalem and Gerizim occurred around 300, and *if* there were no compelling theological grounds in the Persian period to draw comparisons between the first and second temples. In fact, a distinct Samaritan sect probably emerged in the Persian period.[24] But what Williamson's reconstruction really depends upon is Josephus's narrative of the construction of the temple at Gerizim which, Josephus claims, occurred when Alexander first appeared in Palestine (*Ant.* 11.8.4). Furthermore, Josephus writes that many of the priests and Levites left Jerusalem for Samaria (*Ant.* 11.8.2), and Williamson assumes that Ezra 1–6 was an attempt to show that the Jerusalem sanctuary was the only legitimate place of worship. Excavations at Gerizim, however, show that the city and sacred precinct there were not established until around 200,[25] considerably weakening arguments that assert Ezra 1–6 was promoting one sanctuary over another and that one should rely on Josephus's account

21. His father Jonathan is mentioned as high priest in *TAD* A4.7.

22. F.M. Cross, 'A Reconstruction of the Judean Restoration', *JBL* 94 (1975), pp. 4-18 (12).

23. H.G.M. Williamson, 'The Composition of Ezra i-vi', *JTS* NS 34 (1983), pp. 1-30 (26-29).

24. J.D. Purvis, *The Samaritan Pentateuch and the Origin of the Samaritan Sect* (Cambridge, MA: Harvard University Press, 1968), p. 98.

25. I. Magen, 'Gerizim, Mount', in *NEAEHL*, II, pp. 484-92 (487).

of this story. There is no reason not to date Ezra–Nehemiah around 400 or soon after, and so no reason to assume that the ideology it presents and communal anxiety it reflects do not come from the Persian period temple community.

b. *Ideology*

As I noted in the introduction, a society with strong external boundaries is one that is able to distinguish itself from other societies with extreme clarity. It can point to things such as culture, systems of morality, ways of treating women, ways of greeting elders, the worldview communicated by its teachers, and so forth, and make the claim that in this society these things differ from those of all other cultures. The issues I mention here are all a result of what I have referred to as worldview, the way in which a culture looks at the universe that is taken to be common sense. Ideology, as pointed out in the introduction, is a manner of veiling the assumptions of the social worldview, a way of making them seem like everyday notions that universally lie beyond questioning. Ideology employs aspects of the worldview in order to make a particular argument. One of the more interesting aspects of the ideology found in the literature of the postexilic period (and even slightly before) is the notion that the temple community, those descended from the Babylonian exiles, is ontologically different from every other people, and is alone the recipient of God's work. We find here, in short, ideology drawing from a worldview that draws strong external boundaries around this social group.

The picture of the assembly as by nature ontologically different and exclusive of all who were not descended from the Babylonian exiles is, in some sense, the theme of Ezra–Nehemiah. I think that we can trace the genesis of this thought to something I will call remnant theology, which is apparent in biblical works from the exile and in the Persian period. Remnant theology is marked by a common vocabulary used to describe the postexilic assembly and, before that, the Judeans taken into exile in Babylonia. They are described as the *š'ryt*, 'remnant' (Isa. 46.3; Ezek. 11.13; Jer. 31.7; Hag. 1.12; Zech. 8.13; Ezra 9.14; etc.) or the *nš'r* 'remainder' (Ezra 1.2; Neh. 1.2) or the *plyṭh*, 'surviving group' (Ezra 9.8; Neh. 1.2; etc.). Remnant theology insists that YHWH dwelt with the group in exile in Babylon and not those left behind in Judea, and that the land really belongs to the remnant and no one else. In the postexilic period it asserts that only the remnant belongs in the temple assembly, and only they are responsible for the temple. The latter point is made as clearly in Haggai, a work composed at the outset of the Persian period, as it is in Ezra–Nehemiah.

During the exilic period, Ezekiel receives a vision deriding the claims of those who remained in Judah during the exile that the land was theirs. YHWH denies their claim because they have worshipped idols and shed blood, and promises to destroy them (33.23-29). The same such claim is recounted in Ezek. 11.14-21, where those remaining in Jerusalem say: 'the inhabitants of Jerusalem are far from YHWH; to us is the land given as a possession' (11.15). God's reply is that the exiles will be gathered from the nations and return to the land where they will purge it of its religious abominations (11.17-21). In this context, Ezekiel refers to the exiles as *š'ryt yśr'l*, 'the remnant of Israel' (11.13). Notably, this prophecy has been placed within Ezekiel's vision of YHWH abandoning the temple to dwell with the exiles (10.1-22; 11.22-25). If we claim the existence of such a thing as remnant theology, it would appear to state that the true Israelites were the exiles, not those who remained behind, and that the land belongs to those who went into exile as their inheritance from YHWH. They are the only group of Israelites with whom God will interact. Jeremiah 29.16-20, an editorial insertion into the letter from Jeremiah to the exiles in Babylon, also distinguishes between the exiles in Babylon—who in the letter receive the assurance that God will restore them to the land (29.10-14)—and those who remain in the land, whom God destines for destruction because of their disobedience (29.17-19). The following chapters (30–31) are further words of assurance of restoration to the exiles, reminiscent of the message of Deutero-Isaiah, and Jeremiah exhorts the exiles to sing to YHWH to 'save your people, the remnant of Israel [*š'ryt yśr'l*]' (31.7).

Deutero-Isaiah itself refers to *byt y'qb*, 'the house of Jacob', as *kl š'ryt byt yśr'l*, 'all of the remnant of the house of Israel' (46.3). Whether we refer to the exiles as the remainder (my translation of the niphal participle of the root *š'r*) or the remnant (my translation of the nominal form *š'ryt* based on the same root), this theology envisions two groups of Judeans: those who went into exile and with whom God dwells and to whom the land rightfully belongs and which will be restored to them, and those who remained behind during the exile, who worship idols and who engage in abominations and whom God will banish from the land. Thus Haggai refers to *kl š'ryt h'm*, 'all of the remnant of the people' (1.12; cf. also 1.14 and 2.2) when he wants to specify those who belong to the community of the returned exiles who are rebuilding the temple. First Zechariah, another work of the early Persian period, also refers to a *š'ryt* (8.6, 11) that is equated with the houses of Judah and Israel (8.13) and that will receive the divine beneficence of eschatological blessing (8.1-13). And in Ezra–Nehemiah, as we shall see below, the identification of the people of Israel with the exilic community, the remnant, is clear enough. As I noted in Chapter 1, Ezra continually refers to the threat the women pose to the *š'ryt* and *plṭh* in Ezra 9.

This ideology of the remnant's exclusive claim to the land, then, is something that predates the events of Ezra–Nehemiah. It reflects the worldview of a community obsessed with separateness, with the idea that it constituted the holy people who belong to the holy place. That God would one day return the people to the land and annul the claims of all others who lived there would have been comforting news to the exiles in Babylonia. What this apparently implied, however, is that no one else should live there and that no one else should become part of the community that did. The community's exclusive claim to the land is thus paralleled by a concern for the purity of the community. By the time of the events recorded in Ezra–Nehemiah, remnant theology would be infused with the notion that God can also remove the community from the land and send it back into a final exile for its sins.

Obviously, then, one demand of remnant theology is that one be able to trace one's lineage to the returned exiles. This matter will be considered in more detail in the section on genealogies, but I want to continue here by pointing to the effects of remnant theology on the ideological boundaries that separated the temple community from other groups. Being *y^ehûdî*, 'a Judean, Jew', to this community had everything to do with descent from the exiles and little to do with worship of YHWH or geographical location. Tobiah, a denizen of Aram, and Sanballat, the governor of Samaria, while YHWHists, were not part of the assembly, and were in fact named by Nehemiah as its enemies (Neh. 3.33-4.17 [ET 4.1-23]; 6.1-19; 13.4-9).[26] The YHWHists who remained in the land during the exile were also refused entry into the assembly (Ezra 4.1-3). To the remnant they were foreigners, and so foreigners, insofar as the temple assembly would define them, lived even within the province. When, in the story of Nehemiah 5, the poor appeal *'l 'ḥyhm hyhwdym*, 'to their kin, the Yehudim' (5.1), for relief from economic hardship, the argument they make to the Yehudim is one of non-differentiation—'our flesh is like their flesh, their children like our children' (5.5)—that has not been recognized as valid by the temple

26. The name Tobiah is YHWHistic, and Sanballat's two sons had YHWHistic names (*TAD* A4.7.29).

community. That is, although these people live within Yehud, they are not considered Yehudim even though they claim them as kin, nor are they considered to be part of the temple assembly.

Moreover, there appear to be members of the temple community who lived outside of the province of Yehud. Nehemiah mentions *hyhwdym hyšbym 'ṣlm*, 'the Yehudim living near them (Jerusalem's enemies)' (Neh. 4.6 [ET 4.12]), who were apparently assembly members who lived outside of the province. Beyond this biblical evidence of Yehudim living among the community's enemies, we have epigraphical evidence of YHWHists living in Palestine but outside of the borders of Yehud who may well have belonged to the temple assembly.[27] This may lend some credence to the statement that 'they [the assembly] camped from Beersheba to the valley of Hinnom' (Neh. 11.30). While the province of Yehud certainly did not extend as far south as Beersheba which was part of Arabia at the time, members of the assembly likely lived there. That is, in this list of geographical sites of Neh. 11.25-36 that designates some places where the community lived, the mention of towns south of the actual province corresponds to the epigraphical evidence placing YHWHists there, as well. The understanding of Yehudim was clearly not a geographical one associated with the province of Yehud.

On the other hand, some citizens of the military colony in Elephantine in Egypt had emigrated from Judea and were YHWHists. They could refer to themselves as *yhwdy'*, 'the Yehudi'; and while this term may simply

27. The fourth-century Aramaic ostraca from Arad attest the presence of Arabs, Ammonites, Babylonians, Egyptians, Phoenicians, Edomites and Arameans near the city (J. Naveh, 'The Aramaic Ostraca from Tel Arad', in Yohanan Aharoni (ed.), *Arad Inscriptions* [Judean Desert Studies; trans. Judith Ben-Or; Jerusalem: Israel Exploration Society, 1981], pp. 153-76), but a full 50 percent of the names on these sherds are Hebrew (G.A. Klingbeil, 'The Aramaic Ostraca from Lachish: A New Reading and Interpretation', *AUSS* 33 [1995], pp. 77-84 [83 n. 22]). Ostraca from a site which can be defined no more exactly than somewhere just south of Yehud (published in I. Eph'al and J. Naveh, *Aramaic Ostraca of the Fourth Century B.C. from Idumaea* [Jerusalem: Magnes Press, 1996]; and A. Lemaire, *Nouvelles inscriptions araméenes d'Idumée au Mušee d'Israel* [TransSup, 3; Paris: J. Gabalda, 1996]) also attest the presence of Jewish names south of Yehud, albeit as a minority among those of Edomite and Phoenician origin. Two names with YHWHistic elements have been found at late Persian period Jemmeh on the Wadi Besor, also in southern Palestine (J. Naveh, 'Aramaic Ostraca and Jar Inscriptions from Tell Jemmeh', *Atiqot* [Eng] 21 [1992], pp. 49-53 [49]). The extant finds as a whole show the presence of Jews in the south as a minority among Edomites, Arabs and Phoenicians.

have designated place of origin, they obviously saw themselves as religious compatriots of the community centered at Jerusalem. When the YHW temple in Egypt was destroyed they wrote to the high priest and nobles in Jerusalem, but the Elephantine community reported in 407 that *'grt ḥdh l' šlḥw*, 'they did not send us one letter' (*TAD* A4.7.19). Only their appeal to Bagohi, the governor of Yehud, and Delaiah, the son of Sanballat and the governor of Samaria receives a positive response (A4.9). To the assembly at Jerusalem, the community in Elephantine lay far outside the borders of the legitimate Yehudim, a term used to refer to those descended from the returned exiles *and no one else*. It is obviously not simply the worship of YHWH by which one is accounted a Yehudi by the community, nor is it geographical location. For this reason both 'Judean' and 'Jew' are misleading translations of *y^{e}hûdî* as Ezra–Nehemiah uses the term.

Ezra–Nehemiah gives us more information as to the exclusivity of this remnant community, and very clearly contrasts it with the peoples that surround it. It appeals, in short, to the remnant theology's ideology of exclusivity that acts to guard the community from other people and promote its separateness. And such ideology, as Geertz points out, is effective only when grounded in the social worldview, the way of looking at things that everyone takes for granted. Ezra 2 gives a list of returned exiles that functions, as the introduction to its repetition in Nehemiah 7 makes clear, as a 'genealogy' (7.5). As I will point out in the next section on genealogies, it, too, functions to maintain strong external boundaries, as the text explains that one may only be considered a member of the temple community if one can trace one's lineage to the people enumerated there.

After this initial definition of the community at the beginning of the story of Ezra–Nehemiah, the assembly is defined in opposition to the people of the land. It is not just genealogies that draw a strong boundary between the temple community and all other peoples—whether they live in Yehud or not—but the ideology of the community as a whole. The central section of Ezra consists of the community's travails in rebuilding the temple. No sooner have plans been made for its construction (Ezra 3) then opposition from *ṣry yhwd wbnymyn*, 'the enemies of Judah and Benjamin', is launched against *bny hgwlh*, 'the children of the exile' (4.1). At no point in the narrative is any mention made of why they are enemies; it is a matter the text assumes. Ezra 4–6.12 is the story of the opposition and its final defeat through a decree of Darius. The builders are *bny yśr'l*, 'the children of Israel', defined as 'the priests and the Levites and the rest of the children of the exile' (6.16), who celebrate the completion of the temple construction with a dedication of the temple. This celebration is immediately followed by observance of the Passover (6.19-22), commemorated on the fourteenth day of the following month and connected in the narrative to the celebration of the completion of the temple (6.22). Just as *bny glwth* (Aramaic), 'the children of the exile', dedicated the temple (6.16), *bny hgwlh* (Hebrew), 'the children of the exile', are the ones who observe the Passover (6.19). They are also described as 'the community of Israel, the captives from the exile [*mhgwlh*]' and 'the group which separated itself [*hnbdl*] from the impurity of [*mṭm'*t] the nations of the land, in order to seek YHWH, the God of Israel' (6.21).

At the end of the temple construction, in other words, the narrator has presented the readers with a complex set of interrelated terms to express the relationships between God, temple, people and adversaries. The exilic community or remnant alone is Israel, and it alone is worthy to build the temple and to worship YHWH, the God who belongs uniquely to Israel, or the exilic community. If the community is to worship YHWH, it must separate itself from the impurity of the nations. The need for separation from the impure foreigners is stressed as strongly here as it is in the case of the divorces in Ezra 9–10. This gap of impurity separates God, temple and Israel from the nations or the peoples of the land. The impure is diametrically opposed to God and the temple, and in Ezra–Nehemiah, to the exilic community. This community may be defined as the group separated from the polluting influences of the impurity of the people of the lands. Those within the community are protected by boundaries of purity, and no one outside of these boundaries should be permitted to transgress them. So it is that the narrative of Ezra 1–6 begins with the list of the exiles entering the land and ends with a cultic celebration invoking this identity through its assurance of the purity of the participants. Participation in the worship of YHWH at Jerusalem is yet another way to define the community.

As I noted in my discussions of the language of impurity in Chapter 1, however, impurity is highly contagious. So it is no wonder, then, that both the leaders of the community and Ezra appear so shocked when they discover that 'the people of Israel and the priests and the Levites have not been separated from the peoples of the lands' (9.1). Instead, 'the holy seed' has mixed itself with them (9.2). The holy people—the descendants of the exiles—are not to mix with foreigners since, as we saw in Chapter 1, the collision of *qōdeš* and *ṭum'â* results in destruction. Ezra's consequent concern about the impending demise of the community that he then goes on to express in the prayer of 9.6-15 is understandable only once the whole story of Ezra–Nehemiah up to that point has been properly considered. The remnant, established by means of God's righteousness, is threatened through its own inattention to its purity. The simple presence of impurity, the presence of foreign women and their children who have no claim to the pedigree of the remnant community, is enough to endanger its existence. In the ideology of the text, the nature of the community is to be separate (*bdl*) from all impure influences. The women are expelled from the community not because of what they have done, but because of who they are (impure) and who they are not (members of the exile community). The charge that Ezra lays before the assembled *qāhāl* is, as I showed in Chapter 1, that simply bringing the foreign women into the community increases the guilt of Israel and so threatens the exercise of God's wrath (10.10). The women are simply in a place where they should not be. The point appears to be that despite boundaries established by ideology and genealogy, foreigners have crept in. Their presence endangers the community, and so they must go. After the women are expelled, the list of those men who sent away their wives is given in Ezra 10.18-43, a kind of parallel to the opening genealogy of Ezra 2. This is the newly purified *qāhāl* and *bny hgwlh*.

Nehemiah 1–6 has somewhat the same format as Ezra 1–6: after a return to the land (Neh. 1–2.10, corresponding to the first wave of returnees in Ezra 1), the rebuilding of Jerusalem's walls begins (2.11–3.32, corresponding to the temple construction in Ezra 3), the participants in the community and the building project are listed (Neh. 3, corresponding to Ezra 2), and enemies and problems beset the work (Neh. 4–6.14, corresponding to Ezra 4–6.12), followed by an announcement of the completion of the work (Neh. 6.15-16, corresponding to Ezra 6.13-15). In the story in Ezra of the construction of the temple, the triumphal announcement of its completion is followed by the cultic celebration of Passover, which reemphasizes that the cultic community is limited to those who trace their ancestry to the returned exiles (6.19-22). The Nehemiah narrative also follows its building tale with a cultic celebration (Sukkoth, in this case), and notes that 'all the assembly, the captives from the captivity [*kl hqhl hšbym mn hšby*], made booths and they dwelt in the booths' (8.17), emphasizing both that the community consists specifically of those who descended from returned exiles, and that only these people participated in the cultic celebration. One can belong to the assembly if and only if one is descended from a particular group of returned exiles. Like Ezra 1–6, a building project that specifically involves the temple assembly and no one else is followed by a cultic celebration involving the temple assembly and no one else. I delay an investigation of its use of genealogies to the section below and its focus on weak internal integration and communal responses to it to the section on the community's internal boundaries.

In Nehemiah 8, Ezra reads the law to the people, while certain others 'were teaching [*mbynym*] the people the Torah' (8.7). At the end of the day, the people celebrate and rejoice 'because they understood [*hbynw*] the words that had they had made known to them' (8.12). After the people agree to keep the law, they are described as *kl hnbdl m'my h'rṣwt 'l twrt h'lhym… kl ywd' mbyn*, 'all the group separated from the peoples of the lands to the law of God…everyone knowing (and) understanding (it)' (10.29 [ET 10.28]). As in Ezra's prayer in Ezra 9, the law functions to separate the community from all other people. And if the assembly may be defined in part as those who worship YHWH (Ezra 6; Neh. 8), then to be part of the assembly is also to be separated *from* the peoples *to* the law of God, and to understand (*byn*) the law. To be separated (*bdl*) from the peoples is to keep the law, the basis of social morality, that holds the community together. Should assembly members fail to keep the law, the society stands in danger of falling apart. The problem that Ezra identified was assembly members abandoning God by ignoring the law or social morality, and precisely the same point is made in Nehemiah 9, as we shall see in the section on the community's internal boundaries below.

The point, however, is that the stories of Ezra–Nehemiah describe a community that is threatened by the peoples around them and needs, due to reasons expressed theologically, to be separate from them. The book uses ideology that taps into a worldview where such a situation is simply taken for granted. In Nehemiah, surrounding peoples threaten the construction of the city walls, and Ezra 4 describes the native YHWHists as 'enemies' without feeling the need to supply an explanation for this appellation. The ideology expressed in this book and in remnant theology as a whole describes and enforces a communal worldview that keeps the community separate from all others, often employing the theological bifurcation of holy and impure. It is this remnant community that is holy, pure, and that strives for dedication to its social basis of morality, the law of God.

c. *Genealogies*

The themes of the peoples of the lands as impure and the temple community as the group that exists as a remnant because of God's grace stand, as we have seen, as polar opposites throughout the story of Ezra–Nehemiah. Those who belong in God's 'holy place' (Ezra 9.8) and 'the holy city' (Neh. 11.1) are 'the holy seed' (Ezra 9.2); and while Ezra is in large part the story of the construction of the temple and Nehemiah is in large part the story of the construction of the city walls, the book as a whole also narrates the construction of the identity of the remnant who belongs in Jerusalem and its temple. As Tamara Eskenazi shows, it is the people, not Ezra or Nehemiah, who are the main character of the book.[28] The story of Ezra–Nehemiah itself begins with Edict of Cyrus directing *kl hnš'r*, 'all of the remainder', to return to Jerusalem to rebuild the temple (Ezra 1.2-4). The remnant is then introduced more specifically in Ezra 2, where a long list of the returned exiles is given by their families of descent. This list is introduced with the statement, 'Now these are the children of the province [*bny hmdynh*] who went up from the captivity of the exile [*mšby hgwlh*] whom Nebuchadnezzar, king of Babylon, exiled to Babylon' (2.1). A list of the leaders of the 'going up' is given, and then the list proper begins with the superscription, 'The number of the men of the people of Israel [*'m yśr'l*]' (2.2). The children of the province, or the Yehudites, or the people of Israel—all of these are terms denoting the same group—are the descendants of those who went into exile. The *bny hmdynh* are the sum of the descendants of the *bny* PNN found in 2.3-64—where, in fact, the group as a whole is given yet another title: *kl hqhl*, 'all of the assembly' (2.64). The boundaries of the assembly are very explicitly detailed, and much of Ezra–Nehemiah is devoted to describing the defense of these boundaries against impurities. We have seen how these terms appear again and again in the book in order to distinguish the holy people from the impure foreigners, and their clustering at the beginning of the narrative makes the point that the assembly, the community with which Ezra–Nehemiah is concerned, consists specifically of those who have descended from the Babylonian exiles. (As I mentioned earlier, when this list is repeated in Neh. 7, it is specifically called a genealogy.)

Ezra 2.59-63 provides us with an interesting case which can help narrow down the exilic community even farther. Here we have a number of agnatic groups returning from exile who 'were not able to make known the

28. T.C. Eskenazi, *In an Age of Prose: A Literary Approach to Ezra–Nehemiah* (SBLMS, 36; Atlanta: Scholars Press, 1988), pp. 48-53.

house of their father nor their seed, if they were from Israel' (2.59). These people 'searched their genealogical records, but were not found, and they were desecrated [*wyg'lw*] from the priests' and told by the governor not to eat from the holiest food (2.62-63). The use of the root *g'l* II to describe those who have no written genealogical record to attest to their inclusion within the community proves striking. Those 'defiled [*ng'lw*] with blood' in Lamentations are called *ṭāmē'*, 'impure' (4.14-15). Malachi proclaims that those who offer *lḥm mg'l*, 'polluting food', on YHWH's altar despise God (1.6-7). Those priests excluded from the community because of their failure to produce written evidence of their ancestry are simply ontologically different from those who are included: they are impure, outside of the true community which belongs within the holy precincts of the temple. The genealogy acts as a written boundary between the remnant and the pollution outside of it.

In at least the view of the narrator of Ezra–Nehemiah, to be part of this exilic community is to have a written record of descent that is a guarantor of one's worthiness and ontological capability to exist within the precincts of the temple. The (written) remnant, and only it, belongs to the holy place of YHWH, and all others, as the narrator makes clear later in the story, are actually a danger to the true community. The redactor's concern to define precisely the community reflects, as Fenn's work should lead us to suspect, a community obsessed with the notion of who belongs inside of it and who does not; a purity concern, in other words. Those who, like the priests of 2.59-63, cannot prove their right to inclusion are described with the language of impurity. They belong to the foreign and so are described with terms of impurity the way foreigners are.

This emphasis on the exclusiveness of the community is highlighted by the repetition of the list of returnees that first appeared in Ezra 2 in Nehemiah 7. When God tells Nehemiah to enroll the people by genealogy, he writes, 'I found the book of the genealogy of the ones who went up at the first' (7.5). The book has become a kind of genealogy, in the sense that all those who are part of the community and can participate in the cultus must trace their lineage through it. Above, I noted the similar structure of Nehemiah 1–6 and Ezra 1–6, but mentioned that while this first section of Ezra ends with a cultic celebration, a similar event in Nehemiah does not occur until after the genealogy of Nehemiah 7. The readers who expect the cultic celebration to follow immediately upon the completion of the building project just as was the case in Ezra 1–6 are jarringly reminded of the limits of the community when the genealogy precedes the celebration of

Sukkoth. And by repeating the list found at the beginning of the story, which was there linked very specifically to the captives from exile, the redactor makes the point that this remains the basis of the community. The community remains exclusive of all those who are not descended from the Babylonian exiles. The genealogy of Nehemiah 7 and the worship and dedication to the social morality in Nehemiah 8 are all different ways of defining who does and who does not belong in this community.

It is difficult to think of biblical genealogies without turning one's attention to 1 Chronicles 1–9, a set of genealogies that lead from Adam in ch. 1 to the complete tribes of Israel in chs. 2 through 8, followed by a postexilic updating of the list in ch. 9. It is true that much of the interest in these genealogies (or, in this genealogy) is antiquarian, but that is hardly the point of the construction of these chapters. At points the genealogy enters the Persian period and, in a sense, makes the same point as the genealogies of Ezra–Nehemiah: one must trace one's pedigree to this list to be considered a Yehudi.

Chronicles is dated variously to 400,[29] 300,[30] and even as late as the first half of the third century.[31] If we can rely on the genealogy of Davidides in 1 Chronicles 3 for help, it ends, as Cross points out, at the end of the fifth century, suggesting a date of composition around 400. While the matter is not an easy one to decide, Kenneth Hoglund has pointed to the genealogies themselves as indicative of the history-writing in the Hellenistic world in the fifth century,[32] which not only argues against those who claim the genealogies are a later addition,[33] but suggests another bit of evidence for the dating of Chronicles near the end of or just after the fifth century.

The genealogies serve a number of functions. In the genealogy of 1 Chronicles 1, notes Manfred Oeming, the Chronicler begins with Adam and traces the lineages of the various nations around Israel, only to begin once again with Adam and move to Abraham in 1.24-27. The point here

29. Cross, 'A Reconstruction', p. 12; and P. Hanson, *The Dawn of Apocalyptic* (Philadelphia: Fortress Press, 1975), p. 270.

30. S. Japhet, *I and II Chronicles* (OTL; Louisville, KY: Westminster/John Knox Press, 1993), pp. 27-28.

31. P. Welten, *Geschichte und Geschichtsdarstellung in den Chronikbuchern* (WMANT, 42; Neukirchen–Vluyn: Neukirchener Verlag, 1973), p. 200.

32. K.G. Hoglund, 'The Chronicler as a Historian: A Comparativist Perspective', in M.P. Graham, K.G. Hoglund and S.L. McKenzie (eds.), *The Chronicler as Historian* (JSOTSup, 238; Sheffield: Sheffield Academic Press, 1997), pp. 54-72 (21-22).

33. For example, Noth, *The Chronicler's History*, pp. 36-42.

appears to illustrate Israel's election out of all the nations of the world.[34] The point is made that the special relationship between God and Israel has existed since the beginning, not since a historical event such as God's call of Abraham.[35] Joel Weinberg has noted that the construction of chs. 2 through 8, with the tribe of Judah (combined with Simeon) at the beginning, the Levites in the middle, and the tribe of Benjamin at the end emphasizes that the postexilic community's territory belongs primarily to Judah and Benjamin, and implies that everyone else listed in 1 Chronicles 2–8 are really members of those tribes.[36] Jonathan Dyck has argued that these genealogies are actually inclusive, rather than acting to enforce external boundaries of the community. The Chronicler, he claims, wants to assert that the Israel of the 12 tribes that appears in chs. 2 through 8 is still alive and well in the postexilic period. To this end, when the exile is briefly mentioned in 9.1, the Chronicler states that people from Judah, Benjamin, Ephraim and Manasseh—two northern and two southern tribes, representing all of pre-exilic Israel—resettled the land, a picture consonant with the Chronicler's attempt to show the North as a legitimate part of the people elsewhere in the work.[37]

I believe such an interpretation misconstrues the Chronicler's intention here, however. The Chronicler does pass over the exile in just one verse here, stating tersely in 9.1 that 'all of Israel was enrolled by genealogies' and that 'Judah was taken into exile'; and then continues on immediately to note that the land was resettled. The (assumedly intended) conclusion of those who read the book of Chronicles in the Persian period would then be that their community constituted the entirety of Israel that resettled the land. I believe, in short, that Weinberg has it right when he states that the use of the term 'Israel' by the postexilic community—both here and elsewhere—indicates an attempt on its part to present itself as the only legitimate representative of the 12 tribes.[38] The opening genealogies of Chronicles, then, serve the same purpose as that of Ezra 2/Nehemiah 7: they draw a boundary around the postexilic community. This community

34. M. Oeming, *Das wahre Israel: Die 'genealogische Vorhalle' 1 Chronik 1–9* (BWANT; Stuttgart: W. Kohlhammer, 1990), pp. 89-91.

35. Japhet, *I and II Chronicles*, p. 44.

36. J. Weinberg, 'Das Wesen und die funktionelle Bestimmung der Listen in I Chr 1-9', *ZAW* 93 (1981), pp. 91-114 (111).

37. J.E. Dyck, *The Theocratic Ideology of the Chronicler* (BIS, 33; Leiden: E.J. Brill, 1998), pp. 120-21.

38. Weinberg, 'Das Wesen', p. 112.

alone is the one favored by God, and those associated with the community centered around Jerusalem are its only true representatives. These genealogies thus appeal to the same worldview as the issues mentioned in the previous section, and it is a worldview that assumes that the community is and should remain distinct from all other peoples.

d. *Physical Separation*

Despite the fact that temple community members appear to have resided outside of Yehud, we find a curious clustering of sites around Jerusalem in Persian period Yehud, as can be seen from Moshe Kochavi's archaeological survey of Judea, Benjamin and Manasseh.[39] In the Judean hill country, an area extending south of Jerusalem to the northern Negev, there were 28 sites at the end of the Iron Age, and 33 in the Persian period. Notably, only seven Iron II sites were resettled in the Persian period, while 17 of the Persian period sites were resettled in the Hellenistic period, showing discontinuity before the Persian period, likely due in part to the Babylonian invasion, but continuity in settlements during and after.[40] The Persian period settlements were, unlike their Iron II counterparts, closely clustered around Jerusalem; and whereas in Iron Age II the mean distance of a site in the Judean hill country to Jerusalem was 34 kilometers, in the Persian period it was just 13 kilometers.[41] A similar picture emerges from the survey of Benjamin and the hill country of Ephraim, the mountainous area between the cities of Jerusalem and Samaria, which witnessed a precipitous decline in settlements from 51 in Iron II to 15 in the Persian period. Only three of the sites in the later period had been settled in Iron II.[42] Israel Finkelstein and Yitzhak Magen's survey of Benjamin found that of the 75 Persian period sites in Benjamin (a decline from 180 in Iron II), 49 (65 percent) were within 14 kilometers of Jerusalem.[43] This

39. M. Kochavi (ed.), *Judaea, Samaria and the Golan: Archaeological Survey 1967–1968* (Publications of the Archaeological Survey of Israel, 1; Jerusalem: Carta, 1972).

40. Kochavi (ed.), *Judaea*, pp. 83-84.

41. In the Persian period, the farther south one gets from Jerusalem in the Persian period, the sparser the sites become, while in Iron II they are fairly evenly spread throughout Judea. In the southern third of the survey (098-083), the third at the farthest remove from the capital, there were 12 Iron II sites but only one from the Persian period.

42. Kochavi (ed.), *Judaea*, p. 155.

43. I. Finkelstein and Y. Magen, *Archaeological Survey of the Hill Country of Benjamin* (Jerusalem: Israel Antiquities Authority, 1993), pp. 450-53.

indicates that settlement in northern Yehud, just as in the south of the Persian period province, generally abandoned Iron Age II settlement patterns for a pattern in which sites clustered closely around the capital.

The surveys just mentioned do not limit themselves to Persian period Yehud, but were conducted along larger geographical and earlier tribal boundaries. As we turn to the political boundaries of the Persian period province, however, I accept the borders of the province of Yehud as drawn by Charles Carter, a reconstruction based upon site surveys as well as a consideration of the geographical structure of the area.[44] He excludes the Shephelah in the west, arguing that it was traditionally a homogeneous area; in the south he draws the border north-west from En-Gedi just south of Hebron up to the Shephelah; in the north he follows the traditional Benjamin/Ephraim border to include Jericho on the Jordan River. Carter also distinguishes between a Persian Period I (538–450) and a Persian Period II (450–332), and I am dealing with the settlement and population figures that fall in the latter period, since Ezra's career would have occurred at that time. Carter's Yehud during Persian II contains 132 sites with an estimated population of around 20,000.[45]

One useful aspect of the division of sites in the province into two separate periods during the Persian period is that we can track how settlement patterns changed in the fifth century. Overall, the population of the province grew by 55 percent from Persian I to Persian II, while the number of sites increased by 45 percent.[46] Of somewhat more interest is to track where, precisely, the new settlements arose, and three-quarters of the settlements new to Persian II remained within 15 kilometers of the capital. It is difficult to know exactly how to interpret these figures, although they may shed some light on the extent of the province. The sites in the Persian period are clustered much closer to Jerusalem than at any time in Iron II. In fact, writes Avi Ofer, while the population of the Judean hills doubled every century from the mid-eleventh through the eighth centuries to a maximum population of about 23,000, the settled area there began to decline after the time of Sennacherib's invasion at the beginning of the seventh century. Yet it is not until the Persian period that we witness the concentration of population in the area north of Hebron and the relative paucity of settlements to the south of it that I noted above. So while the

44. For Carter's borders and his rationale for drawing them, see his *The Emergence of Yehud*, pp. 82-100.

45. Carter, *The Emergence of Yehud*, pp. 185, 201-202.

46. Carter, *The Emergence of Yehud*, p. 225.

population density north of Hebron and Beth Zur might have actually increased somewhat at this time, the population in the hill country south of Hebron declined to less than half its Iron II size.[47] Was this clustering of sites in any way related to the establishment of the new Persian province? Since most of the sites were newly settled following the exile, there may be some significance in the deliberate positioning of them near Jerusalem when the returned exiles could have settled anywhere.

Hoglund has argued that settlement patterns to be found in Persian period Yehud were a result of imperial policy, since the empire was likely interested in settling people where they could supply a steady flow of goods to imperial centers.[48] He does not, however, specify precisely what kinds of goods the empire would want, or what type of land would be good for producing them. To reiterate, it is difficult to imply intention from archaeological surveys. The clustering of sites may have had to do with imperial policy (although Hoglund does not offer much evidence for this suggestion), or it may have had to do with strong external boundaries, or it may have had to do with establishing sites in order to maximize possibilities for the production of goods for trade, or it may have to do with some combination of these. Whatever the intention, there was certainly a noticeably larger physical gap between the sites of Yehud and those of surrounding areas than in Iron II, and this would hardly have promoted interaction with foreigners. However, as I will point out in Chapter 4, an argument can be made that settlement in Yehud gravitated toward areas that produced products for export and to areas close to important trading regions, and this would have promoted interaction with foreigners. In sum, it is difficult to explain the rationale for the clustering of sites in Yehud—and there may well have been more than one—but at least one of the effects of this situation was to separate the Yehudim from the foreigners.

e. *Conclusion*

The sense one gets, then, is of a community with a worldview that stresses the importance of separation between the social and everything else. The ideology employed by remnant theology and of the Persian period writings suggest as much. This group—the temple assembly which, a century after its return, refers to itself as 'the captives from the captivity'—is alone favored by God and is alone authorized to worship at Jerusalem. This

47. A. Ofer, 'Judean Hills Survey', in *NEAEHL*, III, pp. 815-16 (816).

48. Hoglund, 'The Achaemenid Context', pp. 58-59.

group is the Yehudim alone, and it is a term that refers neither, strictly speaking, to religion, nor to geographical location, but to pedigree. The worldview as expressed in the ideology of this group's texts, in its dependence upon genealogies, and possibly in the way it chose to settle the land upon return all suggests a community obsessed with separateness. Boundaries, however, cannot be absolutely closed in any society; and here we find members who lived outside of Yehud, far from the capital and in the midst of foreigners, and a community subservient to the wishes of the Persians who ran the country. This permeability of the external boundaries, what allows the entrance of foreign influences, will be the focus of Chapter 4. Here I will note only, to reiterate the point made by Fenn, that there will be some permeability that will throw off internal integration which is why, as we have seen, there are ritualized acts of purification in the first place. The situation that creates the particular type of act of purification that I have been calling a witch-hunt is one where the sources of this foreign influence are so diffuse, so difficult to pin down, that a generalized hunt for the easiest suspects is launched.

3. *Internal Integration*

a. *The Evidence of Ezra–Nehemiah*

Having seen the strong external boundaries of the Persian period temple community, we know that we should also expect to see weak internal integration here if the expulsion of the foreign women in Ezra 9–10 was truly an example of a witch-hunt. We will search, in short, for instances of anxiety about social cohesion. Is there widespread doubt that citizens are fulfilling their social roles? Paying their dues? Observing the moral codes of the society? Assenting in ritual to social demands? People in this society, as we shall see, were in fact concerned about precisely these issues, and this is why they engaged in the witch-hunt as narrated in Ezra 9–10, for that was an attempt to strengthen social integration.

There are two main passages in Ezra–Nehemiah that reflect weak internal integration in the temple community, and we have already examined one of them. Ezra's prayer in Ezra 9 was, as I mentioned, filled with references to the community's own guilt that was to lead to its destruction. The people, according to the text, had 'abandoned' God's law (9.10), an indication of failure to follow social codes of morality. The same fear is found in Nehemiah 9–10, a section that follows the Ezra material of ch. 8 where the remnant dedicates itself to adherence to social morality in explicit distinction from the surrounding cultures. The recitation of Nehemiah 9 may be divided into six sections. The first, 9.6-15, recounts the salvation history of Israel from creation to the giving of the law. 9.16-25, the second section, states that God gave the land to Israel, even though it disobeyed the law. In 9.16 we find the first verbs in the recitation with Israel as subject (except for *wy'brw* in 9.11 to describe the crossing of the Reed Sea), and they are verbs of rebellion: 'and our ancestors acted insolently and they stiffened their necks and did not listen to your commandments'. The emphasis throughout, however, is one of God's grace in overlooking these transgressions, no matter how grave. But in 9.26-27, 28-29a and 29b-31 we find a cycle of episodes in which Israel is disobedient and God punishes Israel by giving the nation to its enemies, only to relent and save it after listening to its pleas. No particular times or incidents are mentioned in sections three to five; the verbs of disobedience remain disturbing but vague: 'they rebelled' (9.26); 'they returned to doing evil' (9.28); and so on. The author, it would seem, is simply trying to point out how Israel continually tried God's patience, how disobedience lies in the nature of who Israel is.

The final section, 9.32-37, provides a summation of Israel's history and brings the community to their present time. Rather like Ezra's juxtaposition of the community's abandonment of God and God's refusal to abandon Israel in Ezra 9, this recitation states that 'you are righteous… for you have acted faithfully, but we have acted evilly' (9.33). Because the ancestors did not obey the laws (9.34-35) 'behold, we are slaves today' (9.36) and 'we are in great distress' (9.37). The outcome of this narrative of Israel's salvation history appears to be in doubt, for the community is no longer the kingdom of Israel, but slaves, a point Ezra also made in his prayer (Ezra 9.9). This is clearly a community anxious about its future. Given Israel's history and present situation, it seems obvious that God has not seen fit to restore the community to its former position. While the ancestors enjoyed the goodness of the land (9.25 and 36), now 'its great yield belongs to the kings whom you established over us because of our sins' (9.37). The point seems to be that a fine line stands between the community and utter destruction. They are charged not only with their own sins, but those of their ancestors, and any mistake will put an end to their line of credit extended by God's grace. Both Ezra 9 and Nehemiah 9 regard the present as a kind of probationary period, the last chance the community has to live rightly. Adherence to social morality—to turn from evil and toward the law—is being urged, with the acute sense that if repentance does not occur immediately, God will destroy the community.

Both the repeated cycles of Israel's disobedience and the vague verbs used to describe it are significant, I believe. The cycles and the final summation warn that God could once again punish the community by destroying it by means of the nations. This is indicative of the level of anxiety in the community, as is the choice of verbs. While Israel sins continually, it is difficult to pinpoint exactly *how* they have done so. In the discourse, sinning is part of Israel's nature, the manifestation of its great guilt in opposition to God's righteousness, to use the language of Ezra 9. There is really no indication as to specifically what Israel has done in the past that warranted punishment, and the point seems to be that Israel's very nature is disobedience, met at times with divine punishment and at times with divine grace, precisely the same point made in the prayer of Ezra 9. The picture is of a community that assumes it is prone to disobedience and punishment, but cannot exactly put its finger on precisely what it has done to merit the punishment. It is, in short, a community consumed with the fear of punishment and the belief both that it has deserved it and continues to deserve it. This belief is so firm that no specific illustrations need be offered in explanation. The fear of social collapse is very present, but not distinct. And like Ezra's prayer, the recitation of Nehemiah 9 highlights the community's perilous current situation. Just as the repetitive use of the word 'now' in Ezra 9.6-15 emphasizes that time is of the essence because the community has violated the terms of its probationary period, Neh. 9.36-37 contrasts Israel's dire present with its past experience of God's grace. Although the community's pre-exilic ancestors experienced the good of the land that God gave to them, because of Israel's sinful essence the members of the present community 'are slaves today', and God currently gives the land's produce 'to the kings whom you gave over us in our sin'.

In the narrative, Nehemiah 9 follows upon the teaching of the law in ch. 8 that separates the community from the peoples who surround it. The negative mood that pervades Nehemiah 9, however, is far different than the optimism surrounding the acceptance of the law in the preceding chapter. We see here an anxiety that the people stand close to destruction; or, an anthropologist might say, a fear that social integration is extremely weak. The people's failure to adhere to social norms and obligations—expressed here as rebellion against God, the one who gave the law that enforces social obligations to the people—is inherent in who they are and even now threatens to destroy the social body.

'But despite this',[49] the oration continues (apparently referring to Israel's propensity to disobey the law), the community is binding itself to a written agreement (10.1 [ET 9.38]). Like the written genealogies that deny outsiders access to the community, the written compact to obey the law also acts as a boundary between the assembly and pollution. To be in the community is to obey the law—or, we could say, to admit the validity of social norms, morality and obligations. The implication from both the recitation of sins in Nehemiah 9 and the compact in Nehemiah 10 is that this is a society anxious that once again disobedience will lead to God's punishment. Today they are slaves in great distress; who knows what will happen tomorrow? The contract states that the separated community will abide by the law (10.30 [ET 10.29]), and this is spelled out in three particular stipulations. First, they will not enter into marriages with 'the peoples of the land' (10.31); second, they will not buy from these peoples on the Sabbath and agree to observe the Jubilee (10.32); and third, they agree to tithe, pay an annual fee and bring their first fruits to the temple; and the latter portion ends with the assertion that 'we will not abandon the temple of our God' (10.33-40). To make sure that they do not irrevocably break the terms of their probation, they have agreed to exclude foreigners from their community, to erect the Sabbath and Jubilee as a wall between themselves and foreigners, and to dedicate themselves to the upkeep of the temple, the center of their purity. All of these stipulations act as boundaries to isolate the community from impurities, and in this way the community is 'separated from the peoples to the law of God' (10.29 [ET 10.28]). Only now is Jerusalem, 'the holy city', ready to be filled by the people (11.1). The assembly has already been called 'the holy seed', and it was these people, separated from foreigners, rededicated to the Torah, and descended from returned exiles who are authorized to live in the holy city.

The agreement addresses itself to external boundaries in banning foreigners from the community and to internal integration in demanding loyalty to the temple cult. The latter point is especially important insofar as anxiety about weakening internal integration in Ezra–Nehemiah is expressed as abandonment of or disobedience to the God of Israel and the laws that come from that God. Notably, the verb *'zb*, 'to abandon', appears with God's law as its object in both Ezra 9 and Nehemiah 9. Adherence to the morality of the social body—the core of internal integration, broadly

49. For 'despite this' as a translation of *bkl z't* see Isa. 5.25; 9.11, 16, 20; 10.4; Ps. 78.32.

speaking—can be judged by the litmus test of enthusiasm about loyalty to the cultus, manifested in adherence to its festivals and in providing for its material needs. It is participation in cultic and social ritual, as Rappaport pointed out, that demonstrates assent to the social order.

In ch. 10 a certain level of sanguinity has replaced the pessimism of Nehemiah 9, but anxiety about weak integration comes to the fore again at the end of the book. Despite the community's written pledge to adhere to the religion of Israel, to observe its demands for loyalty and its material needs—and so demonstrate its adherence to the social order—Nehemiah 13 suggests that the community was not intent on paying what it owed to the temple cultus and, by extension, to the social body. The narrative reports that when Nehemiah returns to Jerusalem after a stint of personal service to the Persian monarch, he is forced to remove a foreigner from the temple and restore neglected tithes for the Levites (13.4-14), cleanse the city of Tyrian merchants who bartered in Jerusalem on the Sabbath and put a stop to all trade on that day (13.15-22), and cleanse the people and the priesthood of foreign marriages (13.23-29).

Even though the priests and Levites purified [*wyṭhrw*] the people and the city after the wall of Jerusalem had been constructed (Neh. 12.30), the community has allowed impurity to creep back in. Despite all the precautions taken to enforce social integration, says Ezra–Nehemiah, it breaks down all too quickly. Despite the severity of the danger that threatens the community—the punishments mentioned in Nehemiah 9—the text gives the impression of a community's anxiety about extreme indifference to the loyalty pledged to the temple cult in Nehemiah 10 and so the social order as a whole.

So despite the strong external boundaries we see a community that believes it has not kept them strong enough. Through its own guilt it has allowed foreign influences to creep in and these will destroy it. When anxiety rises high enough, as we have seen, a witch-hunt ensues if there is no specific foreign group upon which to place the guilt. In a society with strong external boundaries, witches are those who are discovered to be foreigners polluting the society—or, from an anthropological view, introducing foreign worldviews that reduce social cohesion. This, I have suspected, is the root cause of the divorces and expulsions of Ezra 9–10; but I will comment on the matter further after examining two more Persian period texts.

b. *The Evidence of Malachi and Third Isaiah*

The chief concern of Malachi, a work that should be dated to the period between the construction of the temple and the mid-fifth century[50] is the neglect of the temple cult by both priests and laity, one of the same manifestations of a lack of internal integration that Nehemiah addressed. This neglect has apparently resulted from the community's disappointment with its lot. The people describe the cult as 'a weariness' (1.13), and believe that it is vain to serve a God who rewards the wicked rather than the righteous. The community members, according to Malachi, have said, 'all who do evil are good in the eyes of YHWH' (2.17), and have complained about the uselessness of serving God while the evil prosper (3.14-15). Malachi is, in large part, a response to the communal belief that the social order no longer recognizes the difference between good and evil. If there is no public confidence in the social morality, no belief that one's adherence to social norms and obligations will render the proper benefits, then the moral order will command little loyalty and internal integration will weaken. This was simply a matter that the ancient Israelites would have phrased in the terms of the presence or lack of divine justice, especially as the law was believed to be divinely ordained. Malachi is arguing, however, that the social morality holds—that God truly is just, in other words—and that people should adhere to social norms and obligations.

One of the main foci of the book is the divine response to the lax attitude exhibited toward the cult by priests, Levites and laypersons. Such an attitude is also encountered in Nehemiah 10 where the people pledge to

50. This dating is almost universally accepted by contemporary scholars, and for good reason. The context of the book suggests a fully functioning temple cult, indicating that the temple is already in working order. The prophet mentions *pḥtk*, 'your governor' (1.8), an official title in the area that appears only during the Persian period. Many scholars point to the issues that both Malachi and Ezra–Nehemiah address: the neglect of the temple cult (the chief concern of the book); an interest in the role of the Levites; the lack of economic support for the clergy; and concern over intermarriage (although I believe that David Petersen is correct when he states that this passage [2.10-16] has nothing to do with human marriage but simply employs metaphorical language to decry the deteriorating relationship between YHWH and the people [*Zechariah 9–14 and Malachi: A Commentary* (OTL; Louisville, KY: Westminster/John Knox Press, 1995), pp. 195-206]). Moreover, Andrew Hill's use of Robert Polzin's linguistic typology also dates Malachi to the period between Haggai and the mid-fifth century (A. Hill, 'Dating the Book of Malachi: A Linguistic Reexamination', in C.L. Meyers and M. O'Connor [eds.], *The Word of the Lord Shall Go Forth* [Festschrift D.N. Freedman; Winona Lake, IN: Eisenbrauns, 1983], pp. 77-89).

renew their obligations to the cult and in Neh. 13.4-14 where Nehemiah discovers that the people had not been tithing to the temple and, as a result, the Levites and hierodules had left Jerusalem. Malachi states that the cultic offerings are inadequate (1.6-14) and that tithes are not being brought to the temple (3.8-12). Neglect of the temple cult, as I mentioned, acts as a kind of litmus test of social cohesion for the community. Failure to express in public loyalty to one's God appears to reflect failure to adhere to—or at least to indicate a widespread questioning of—social morality. Malachi makes this point as fervently as Ezra–Nehemiah for, as we have seen, its main concern is the suspicion within the community that God is unrighteous and therefore God's laws, the basis of social morality, are unjust.

Like Ezra–Nehemiah, Malachi warns of divine punishment should obedience to the divine law and loyalty to the divine cult—the former a manifestation of adherence to social norms and obligations, the latter a public promise to do so—not increase. YHWH promises to send an eschatological precursor who will rectify the temple cult, followed by a divine judgment of the wicked (3.1-5). The future judgment of the unrighteous on the Day of YHWH is repeated in 3.19-21 [ET 4.1-3], and we should note that both prophecies of wrath are directed in response to the community's belief that God favors the wicked. The divine eschatological acts prophesied in Malachi are directed against the community that has begun to neglect God's cult and disobey God's laws. We do not find the anxiety that we do in Ezra–Nehemiah in which the existence of the entire assembly is threatened, but Malachi does believe that many in the community have neglected the cult through their anti-social behavior and so are liable for the consequences of divine wrath. Still, the punishment that it envisions is not directed at the entire community, only at the unrighteous within it, and there is no mention of the presence of foreigners endangering the community. What we do find in Malachi, however, is anxiety about weakening social boundaries, an anxiety that apparently built through the Persian period.

Lester Grabbe has stated in regard to Third Isaiah (Isa. 56–66) that 'there has been useful [scholarly] agreement: most of these chapters probably originate in the early part of the Persian period'.[51] This is not entirely true, if Grabbe means to imply complete scholarly agreement, although it is almost true. Some scholars do argue that there is no definitive evidence

51. Grabbe, *Judaism*, I, p. 47.

for a break between Isaiah 55 and 56, and certainly not one so definitive as to argue for different authorship in the sections traditionally called Second and Third Isaiah.[52] In general the position of which Grabbe writes still holds, however, and for good reason. Chapters 60–62, often thought to be the oldest part and the core of Third Isaiah, seem to refer to a city that still lies in ruins but that will be rebuilt with glory, and 66.1-2 suggests that plans have been made for work on the temple but have not yet been carried out. Beyond chs. 60–62, suggests Claus Westermann, the specific times of composition of the other strands of Third Isaiah cannot be determined with any precision, but do not seem to be much later.[53] R.N. Whybray generally agrees, arguing that the whole work appears to have been composed within a generation or two of the first return, although he concedes that a date as late as that of Nehemiah cannot be ruled out.[54]

One aspect upon which all scholarly interpreters of these chapters agree, however, is that they point to a community in turmoil. One of the most intriguing and widely followed interpretations of the work is that of Paul Hanson, who argues that these chapters were produced by a group that was ostracized by the temple hierarchy. While the earlier oracles of the group (e.g. Isa. 60–62) express the same enthusiastic belief in God's imminent world rule from Jerusalem,[55] as the group was removed from the center of power, it began to accuse the assembly of false worship that would be punished by God (65.1-7). It seems clear that this group was excluded by

52. C. Seitz ('On the Question of Divisions Internal to the Book of Isaiah', in E.H. Lovering, Jr [ed.], *Society of Biblical Literature 1993 Seminar Papers* [Atlanta: Scholars Press, 1993], pp. 260-66) argues that there is no good evidence that Second and Third Isaiah were composed in separate geographical locations, and can both be considered to be composed at the same time in Jerusalem, at the very end of the exilic or beginning of the postexilic period. J.D.W. Watts (*Isaiah 34–66* [WBC, 25; Waco, TX: Word Books, 1987], p. 368) believes that the entire book of Isaiah was continually being added on to, bit by bit, from the eighth-century prophet through to the time of Nehemiah. In his opinion, all of chs. 56–66 may be dated to the Persian period, but at different points. The problem with this approach, however, is that there are few good chronological markers in Third Isaiah as a whole, let alone in the blocks of five or six chapters that he isolates as the various 'acts' and attempts to date to various parts of the Persian period.

53. C. Westermann, *Isaiah 40–66* (OTL; Philadelphia: Westminster Press, 1969), pp. 295-96.

54. R.N. Whybray, *Isaiah 40–66* (NCBC, 23.2; Grand Rapids: Eerdmans, 1975), p. 42.

55. Hanson, *The Dawn of Apocalyptic*, pp. 59-77.

the assembly—'Abraham does not know us and Israel does not recognize us' (63.16), it says—and it is equally clear that it does not believe that it will share the eschatological punishment that it prophesies for the assembly, but will instead participate in God's new eschatological creation (Isa. 65; cf. esp. 65.8-25). Berquist's rather more elaborate analysis of these chapters points to its 'key dynamic' as one of a struggle for control for the society.[56] Whybray also points to the divisions within the community.[57]

Even if Hanson or any of these other scholars are not correct in all the details of their explanations, we still find the same issues that we saw in Ezra–Nehemiah and Malachi: there are charges against the assembly of failure to follow the divinely ordained social order, specifically as such behavior manifests itself in neglect of the cult; and the text claims that this behavior will lead to the destruction of the assembly through the wrath of God. Like Ezra–Nehemiah but unlike Malachi, the text states that the entire assembly has earned God's wrath, although the group in which it originated claims that it will be exempt from this catastrophe.

The anxiety as expressed in Ezra–Nehemiah is that the assembly members' refusal to obey the law would result in divine wrath and the destruction of the assembly and temple. By that time the community's internal integration is so weak—or at least many within the community believe it to be weak—that it attributes its anxiety about the possible collapse of the social body to God's wrath. Malachi's earlier expression of anxiety surrounding social disintegration is not as extreme, or perhaps merely expressed differently, since it projects divine punishment against only one part of the community. Nonetheless, it clearly reflects a situation where assembly members have questioned the social order and have seriously considered (or have even begun) abandoning it. Third Isaiah mirrors the same anxiety, but appears to reflect it from a point outside of the assembly. In all three works, neglect of the temple cult is cited as evidence for threats of divine wrath directed against either a portion of or the whole of the assembly since, as we have seen, professions of loyalty to God in the temple cult are equated by the texts with professions of loyalty to social norms and obligations. It is in public ritual, as I pointed out in the introduction, that members of a society indicate their obeisance to the social order. By the time of the events narrated in Ezra 9–10, however, this fear that social integration has collapsed is so pervasive that the community engages in an act of purification to alleviate it.

56. Berquist, *Judaism in Persia's Shadow*, p. 79 (and see pp. 73-79).

57. Whybray, *Isaiah 40–66*, p. 41.

c. *Conclusion*

The assembly centered at Jerusalem was, if the writings it produced may be considered as any evidence at all, a community with strong external boundaries that remained in some anxiety over whether they were truly strong enough. The blame for the problem of this lack of social cohesion is, in one sense, laid upon the community itself, and rightly so. If members of a society refuse to adhere to social norms and obligations then surely that is their decision. Malachi states that the assembly itself has angered God because of its questioning of the goodness of the divine law and validity of divine justice. Even in Ezra 9–10 the text is quite clear that while the presence of the foreign women endangers the community, it is the men who married them, who caused them to dwell where they should not, who are to blame.

So why the divorces and expulsions? As we saw in Chapter 2, acts of purification have particular social benefits, and will be employed when social cohesion needs to be reinforced. Such acts draw the community together as it works as a unit in order to expel the offending body, and force it to choose for the social order, redirecting social attention to the demands of this order's norms and obligations and institutions. This, at any rate, is the anthropologist's explanation for the social benefits to an act such as a witch-hunt. To a community with strong external boundaries and fears that internal ones are quickly eroding, there is a clear understanding that its own members are ignoring social mandates for action and belief; this, obviously, is the definition of weakening internal integration. Acts of purification result from the anxiety that surrounds the dissolving of internal boundaries, and such acts depend on the worldview of the society. As Fenn noted, it is easier ultimately to blame the foreign for this state of affairs. From the point of view of the society involved, the witch-hunt or other act of purification is simply the influence that results from the foreign, the source of all anti-social forces in the understanding of a society with strong external boundaries, seeping into the bounds of the social. At times there may be an obvious candidate within the society for purification, as was the case with Quakers or Antinomians; but when there is not, when the causes of anti-social behavior are so many and diffuse or so vague that one source alone cannot be pinpointed, the society will look for the obvious candidates, where obvious is defined by social worldview. These candidates, as we know, are likely to be primarily women.

It would appear, then, that the use of the language of purity in Ezra 9–10 that we noticed in Chapter 1 is no coincidence, but accurately reflects the worldview of the Jerusalem temple community. It was the type of society likely to engage in an act of purification, and so drew upon the theological language it had at its disposal in an attempt to convey the significance of its actions. This is not to suggest that these chapters are a verbatim account of events, but it is to say that they have captured the spirit and worldview of the proceedings. One does not have to attempt to reconstruct the 'real' causes behind the expulsions, for the community expresses its rationale in the text itself. The language of purity in this society points, as it does in many societies, to fears of foreign anti-social forces that have crept inside the external boundaries. Such influences must be the real cause of the community members' failure to adhere to the social morality, and so they must be found and expelled. A witch-hunt, of course, is a particular kind of ritualized act of purification, one that occurs when there is not a single definable foreign group to blame. Such was the case in Yehud, I shall show in the next chapter, for there were many sources of foreign influences that would have made their way into the province in the Persian period. It was impossible to name simply one source as the culprit, and so a suitable group—the foreign women—was located.

Chapter 4

The Genesis of the Witch-craze Anxiety

1. *Introduction*

We have already seen the high level of anxiety present in the text of Ezra–Nehemiah and the Persian period temple assembly, the community's desire for purification and separation in general, and we have found that these anxieties and desires appear to have stemmed from fears of social collapse due to weak internal social integration. In this chapter I wish to examine the sources of the anxiety that led to the purification of the witch-hunt. The community's belief that foreigners and their influence were stealing the hearts of members of the social body—weakening internal integration, in other words—had, I believe, some basis in fact. Such fears do not arise from nowhere. There were foreign influences in Yehud, and members of the temple assembly itself lived among foreigners and would have presumably interacted with them on a daily basis. If some in the community believed that other members were turning away from their social obligations in order to follow other religions or sources of teaching and healing, neglecting their duties to their God and their temple and their parents and their teachers, it may well be that some members were doing precisely that. We have already seen the anxiety about the community's neglect of the temple cult, and we know that failure to participate in a culture's public rituals is an obvious sign of unwillingness to subjugate oneself to the social morality. The situation within the temple community may not have been as dire as the community of Ezra–Nehemiah makes it out to be, but that does not mean that there were no foreign influences present in the province at all. The point of this chapter is to show that there were.

It focuses on two main issues: the extensive trade in Persian period Palestine, and the presence of the Persian central government in and its control over Yehud and the temple assembly. The vast amounts of trade in the region—the issue discussed mainly in section 2—would have meant that foreign traders and goods found their way into Yehud in the same manner that they moved all over Palestine. Nehemiah's displeasure with the Tyrian merchants trading in Jerusalem on the Sabbath (Neh. 13.16) makes it clear that Yehud and Jerusalem were not immune from the unprecedented levels of trade in the region during the Persian period. With foreign trade comes, naturally, foreign traders along with the goods, and with foreigners come foreign ideas and foreign religions. We will see that in this period foreigners were spread throughout Palestine, and much of the reason for this appears to be due to the vast amounts of trade. There would have been many opportunities for members of the temple community to come into contact with foreigners and their ideas, cultures and religion.

Section 3 focuses on Persian control of Yehud and the temple assembly. Not only did the Persians allow the flow of trade and guard and maintain its routes, but their military and administrative presence in Palestine was yet another source of foreign influence in the region. Persian presence in the region had another effect on the level of anxiety in the assembly than raising it simply because it was another source of foreign cultures and religions. To a community whose worldview has been shaped by destruction, exile and return, Persian control made it very clear that the central government could institute another exile on a whim. To a group who saw exile as a very real experience, foreign control and military presence could only have increased anxiety. We have seen that in both Ezra 9 and Nehemiah 9 the community members are described as 'slaves', and their tenure in the land a probationary period, one that God could quickly end by means of the Persians. In a worldview where foreign domination is seen as divine punishment for sin, Persian control would only have increased the community's feeling of guilt and so its anxiety that its sin (or disregard of social morality, to put it another way) was responsible for its situation. This would have raised levels of anxiety and pushed the community to look for a way to strengthen internal integration.

All of these factors put together are the root causes of the lack of social integration and the anxiety it provoked that prompted the witch-hunt of Ezra 9–10. Further, the fact that there were many causes—foreign traders, a foreign administration, the presence of foreign soldiers and tax collectors, and all the cultural accoutrements that came along with such people—means that the community would have been unable to explain the weakening integration that manifested itself in neglect of the temple cult by blaming it on simply one source. This is why we see a witch-hunt and not some other kind of ritualized act of purification.

2. *Foreigners and Trade in Palestine*

In this section I will offer evidence to support the thesis that Palestine witnessed a vast growth in trade during the Persian period, and that this and other factors resulted in the mixing of peoples and cultures as goods and their traders crossed borders. There is plenty of evidence for this thesis from the rest of Palestine, and the evidence produced by archaeology suggests the same situation existed in Yehud. It is true, as we have seen, that this appears to have been a community devoted to separateness, but, as I show in section 3, the Persians had constructed an infrastructure to protect the roads over which this trade passed. The community may have had little say in preventing such trade, as appears to be the case with Nehemiah's rancor toward the foreign merchants in Jerusalem. He can only stop them from trading on the Sabbath, not from trading altogether. So I turn now to demonstrate both the ubiquity of trade in Palestine and the mixing of cultures there during the Persian period. I hope that readers will indulge me if I seem to devote an inordinate amount of space to the trade and mixing of populations in the areas around Yehud, but I feel that it is necessary to do so in order to provide an economic and demographic context in which the archaeological evidence from Yehud may be understood.

a. *Samaria*

The distribution of Persian period settlements in Samaria appears to reflect the importance of trade and exports in that province. First of all, Israel Finkelstein observed that in sparsely settled Benjamin, specifically in the area just to the north of Yehud, the Persian period is marked by a slight movement of settlements to the west of the area—59 percent of all the Persian period sites were in the western half of the surveyed area, as opposed to 51 percent of all the Iron II sites.[1] He connects this move to the vibrant activity on the coastal plain in the Persian period,[2] a viable explanation for this phenomenon, as we shall see. Second, Adam Zertal's

1. I. Finkelstein, 'The Land of Ephraim Survey 1980-1987: Preliminary Report', *TA* 15–16 (1988/1989), pp. 117-83 (155). It is true that the extreme south-eastern section of this survey area would fall into the borders of Persian period Yehud, but the vast bulk of it is in an area north of the province, in what would have been the southern portion of Samaria. See Finkelstein's map of the survey area on p. 118.

2. Finkelstein, 'The Land of Ephraim Survey', p. 155. On the other hand, since the number of settlements in the Persian period is so small (only 92, a sharp drop from the 190 of Iron II), the shift may not be terribly significant.

analysis of the settlement patterns in Samaria demonstrated that they focus around urban centers but tend to concentrate in the areas traditionally known for olive and grape production. Fully 70 percent of all of the Persian period sites were found in such regions, rather than those known and suitable for grazing and raising grain crops, suggesting, as Zertal avers, that the region's economic structure appears to have relied almost entirely on oil and wine production.[3] Finally, of all the Persian period Samarian sites, 96 (41 percent) were small, mainly farms.[4] Shimon Dar notes that the Iron Age farms were mainly quite large, about 100 to 150 dunams, and mainly without clear demarcations between properties, more suited to an agrarian kinship structure. Those of the Persian and Hellenistic periods, however, were smaller—about 25 to 45 dunams[5]—and witness the appearance of defined territories and boundaries.[6] This likely points to changes in the social and economic structure of the peasantry, but at best we can only speculate as to the significance of this information. All of this information considered together does suggest, though, that this may have been a result of a movement to an economy based on the export of oil and wine, meaning that settlements grew up in land that could produce these goods.[7] If the field tower system, apparently constructed throughout Samaria for the purpose of wine production,[8] helps us decide the matter, it

3. A. Zertal, 'The Pahwah of Samaria (Northern Israel) during the Persian Period: Types of Settlement, Economy, History and New Discoveries', *Trans* 3 (1990), pp. 9-30 (13).

4. Zertal, 'The Pahwah of Samaria', p. 13.

5. S. Dar, *Landscape and Pattern: An Archaeological Survey of Samaria 800 BCE-636 CE* (BAR International Series, 308; Oxford: BAR, 1986), p. 253.

6. Dar, *Landscape and Pattern*, pp. 7-8.

7. This option is echoed by the speculation of Hans G. Kippenberg, who argues that Achaemenid Judea turned to export products in order to obtain the silver necessary to fulfill the annual tribute to the central government. See his *Religion und Klassenbildung im antiken Judaea* (Göttingen: Vandenhoeck & Ruprecht, 1978), pp. 42-53.

8. The field towers were massive stone structures useless for defense, but perfectly suited for wine production. They were not built to withstand a siege, could not be defended, few possessed an enviable line of sight, and few had even enough physical space for human habitation. On the other hand, they provided darkness, protection from ultra-red radiation, and a cool and steady temperature during summer days. The tower phenomenon is, as far as we know, apparent mainly in western Samaria, beginning in the Persian period and flourishing in the Hellenistic era. It coincides, furthermore, with the transformation of agriculture in the region from the large farms noted above to smaller areas more suited to the individual family. See Dar, *Landscape and Pattern*, pp. 88-125, especially pp. 109-11.

would seem that sophisticated wine production employing these artifices was just beginning in the Persian period, and, notably, in the western portion of it.

I noted above Finkelstein's suggestion that the movement of settlements in Benjamin to the West in the Persian period may have been related to the burgeoning activity in Phoenician Palestine. There is evidence to support the claim that this region as a whole from Benjamin to Galilee engaged in trade with the Phoenicians and were influenced by their culture. Shulamit Geva, for example, has examined jars from late Iron II found at Tyre and determined through neutron analysis that they came from Galilee.[9] Some of her conclusions regarding the neutron analysis were rightly challenged by Patricia Bikai, but even the latter argued for trade from Tyre to Israel.[10] This, of course, is only evidence for economic ties between Galilee and Tyre in the Iron Age, but I have already mentioned the possibility that exports such as oil and wine formed an extremely important part of the economic life of Samaria in the Persian period. André Lemaire has even gone so far as to suggest a Phoenician colony near Shechem.[11] We do know that art work in the Phoenician tradition was produced in the Sebaste region through the fifth century, and that a tomb of the second quarter of the fifth century found on the southern slope of Mount Ebal contained locally produced bronze objects in Phoenician and Eastern Greek traditions, as well as bronzes produced in Babylonia and Persia.[12] This may be evidence for Phoenician occupation in the area, or could simply indicate a vibrant Phoenician cultural influence there, perhaps strengthened through trade. Josephus even mentions a group of people living around Shechem at the end of the Persian period who referred to themselves as 'the Sidonians (living) in Shechem' (*Ant.* 11.344). The implication, as Lemaire points out, is that there was a Phoenician colony in Samaria, and one located in a city close to Yehud.

9. S. Geva, 'Archaeological Evidence for the Trade between Israel and Tyre?', *BASOR* 248 (1982), pp. 69-72.

10. P.M. Bikai, 'Observations on Archaeological Evidence for the Trade between Israel and Tyre', *BASOR* 258 (1985), pp. 71-72.

11. A. Lemaire, 'Populations et territoires de la Palestine', in E.-M. Laperrousat and A. Lemaire (eds.), *La Palestine à l'époque perse* (Paris: Cerf, 1994), pp. 31-74 (67).

12. E. Stern, 'A Phoenician Art Centre in Post-Exilic Samaria', in Piero Bartolini *et al.* (eds.), *Atti del I Congresso Internazionale di Studi Fenici e Punici*, I (Collezione di Studi Fenici, 16; Rome: Consiglio Nazionale delle Richerche, 1983), pp. 211-12.

The Samaria papyri found at Wadi ed-Daliyeh in Samaria contain legal documents executed 'before PN the governor of Samaria',[13] and although the governors appear to be YHWHists in the main, Samarian coins[14] produced in the last 45 years of the Persian period bear names—or parts of names—of non-YHWHists who were apparently officials in the province. Some are known from the Samaria papyri, such as *ḥnnyh*, *sn* (short for Sanballat), and *dl* (possibly short for Delaiah, the son of Sanballat I, known from two Aramaic documents from Elephantine [*TAD* A4.7, 9] written in 407). However, we also find the names *yrb'm*, 'Jeroboam' (on five coins), *bg* and *bgbt* in Aramaic and *bagabatas* in Greek, *bdyḥbl*, *hym*, *yhw'nh*, *bdyh*, and *mz* (probably short for Mazday, the satrap of the area after 345 whose name also appears on coins of Sidon after that time).[15] Not all of these people were necessarily governors of Samaria, but we should at least expect them to have held positions of authority there. Bagabatas is evidently a Persian name, and *bdyḥbl* seems to be a construct of Phoenician and Aramean elements. *bd* appears frequently in Phoenician names, while *yḥbl* might be read 'let Bel grant life'. Whether or not these persons held the rank of governor, there were certainly officials in the province who were not YHWHists.

At least some were likely officials appointed by the Persian government to administer the satrapy of Across-the-River, of which Palestine was a part. A number of officials from Across-the-River, the satrapy to which Palestine belonged, besides those local to Yehud are known to us from Babylonian and classical sources. Among these are two people mentioned on a cuneiform tablet of 486 given the title *sepīru*, 'Aramaic scribe' (in contrast to the title *ṭupšarru*, a cuneiform scribe), who are also both called *bēl ṭēmi*.[16] This corresponds to the two Aramaic titles found in Ezra 4.8-

13. F.M. Cross, 'Samaria Papyrus 1: An Aramaic Slave Conveyance of 335 B.C.E. Found in the Wadi ed-Daliyeh', *EI* 18 (1985), pp. 7*-17* (7*, 15*). One of the papyri is sealed with the bulla of *[yš?]yhw bn [sn']blṭ pḥt šmrn*, another with that of *[ḥ]nnyh pḥt šmryn*. For one reconstruction of the governors of Samaria in the Persian period, see Cross, 'A Reconstruction', pp. 5-6.

14. Some marked variously as *šmryn, šm, šn* and *š* (Y. Meshorer and S. Qedar, *The Coinage of Samaria in the Fourth Century B.C.E.* [Jerusalem: Numismatic Fine Arts, 1991], p. 13). The coins were all found in two hoards in Samaria, but only 18 demonstrate the name of the province on the die. The rest can be conceived as Samarian by analogy based mainly on design and iconography.

15. Meshorer and Qedar, *The Coinage of Samaria*, pp. 14-17.

16. M. Heltzer, 'A Recently Published Babylonian Tablet and the Province of Judah after 516 B.C.E', *Trans* 5 (1992), pp. 57-61.

17, denoting one Rehum as *b'l ṭ'm* and one Shimshai as *spr'*, terms that apparently refer to royal functionaries in the foreign province. In the case of the cuneiform letter, the two men carry out the satrap's order concerning an amount of barley; in the text from Ezra, the two officials monitor the reconstruction of Jerusalem's defenses under Nehemiah and inform Artaxerxes of the situation, urging him to put a stop to the matter.[17] Since we know that Yehud had a governor at the time (Nehemiah), then this office (and that of the *spr*, 'scribe') must fall under the satrap but above the local governors in reference to scope of power.[18] Ezra 4.17 states that these bureaucrats lived in Samaria, which may explain some of the foreign names that we find on the coins produced there. That is, like the Persian generals in fourth-century Tarsus who minted their own coinage to pay for military expenses,[19] they might have produced money to underwrite administrative costs. The Persian, Phoenician and Aramean names found on the coinage may then refer not only to foreign administrators of Samaria, but also to administrators of Across-the-River who happened to be stationed in Samaria. So along with the numismatic evidence from Samaria and the biblical texts, we find cuneiform evidence of Persian officials in Samaria who had the power to oversee and interfere in Jerusalem's affairs.

Samaria is obviously a testament to the movement of people, the focus on international trade, and the ubiquity of the Persian administration in the period. These are themes that we will encounter throughout this chapter. Borders throughout Palestine and, indeed, the whole empire, were extremely porous. Goods and people and the Persian administration transgressed them regularly, and the situation in Yehud appears to be similar, as we shall see. The Samarians appear to have an economy driven by exports and trade, there appears to have been a colony of Phoenicians living in the province. Notably, this was in the southern portion of the

17. The king heeds the advice, and authorizes them to carry out his orders (Ezra 4.17-23). The king is the one who gives an order (*wmny śym ṭ'm*, 'and an order was given by me' [4.19]), while Rehum and Shimshai and those under their command are authorized to convey the royal command (*k'n śymw ṭ'm*, 'Now, give an order' [4.21]); hence, Rehum is the *b'l ṭ'm*.

18. Or perhaps such offices existed in some other more ambiguous relationship to each other. Ezra is also called a scribe (Ezra 7.6, 12, 21; Neh. 8.4, 9, 13), although in every case except the letter of Artaxerxes (Ezra 7.12-26) this title appears to refer specifically to his authority to interpret and transmit the Jewish law.

19. A. Lemaire and H. Lozachmeur, 'La Cilicie à l'époque perse, recherches sur les pouvoirs locaux et l'organisation du territoire', *Trans* 3 (1990), pp. 143-55 (147-48).

province where Finkelstein noted a movement of settlements in the Persian period toward Phoenicia, an important trading region in the period. There were, furthermore, officials representing the Persian government living in the capital at the time. Moreover, while most of the names from the papyri found in Persian period Samaria are YHWHistic, 'there is also a sizable number of foreign names reflecting the mixed character of the Samaritan population'.[20]

b. *The Phoenician Territories*

As we shall see, a great deal of evidence points to Phoenicia as an important center for trade during the Persian period. The Phoenician areas in Palestine themselves display a rapid growth throughout this period, and trade flourished all along the Palestinian coast in the Persian period to a greater extent than at any other time in antiquity. There were 35 Persian period settlements on the coast of the Sharon Plain alone, and the vast majority of them witnessed unprecedented levels of activity,[21] especially in the area of trade as indicated by the vast amounts of East Greek and Attic ware found at many of the sites. The Phoenician cities began to produce their own coinage in the mid-fifth century,[22] likely in order to facilitate trade with other regions of the empire and with Greece, and to simplify trade in the local marketplaces.[23] The area clearly experienced an economic renaissance in the Persian period.

20. F.M. Cross, 'The Papyri and their Historical Implications', in P.W. Lapp and N.L. Lapp (eds.), *Discoveries in the Wadi ed-Daliyeh* (AASOR, 41; Cambridge: ASOR, 1974), pp. 17-29 (20). Theophoric elements alert us to the presence of Edomites, Moabites, Babylonians, Phoenicians and Syrians in Samaria.

21. E. Stern, *Excavations at Tel Mevorakh (1973–1976): Part One* (Qedem Reports, 9; Jerusalem: Hebrew University, 1978), p. 79.

22. J. Elayi, 'La diffusion des monnaies phéniciennes en Palestine', in E.-M. Laperrousaz and A. Lemaire (eds.), *La Palestine à l'époque perse* (Paris: Cerf, 1994), pp. 289-315 (289).

23. J. Elayi ('Le phénomène monétaire dans les cites phéniciennes à l'époque perse', in T. Hackens and G. Mouchante (eds.), *Numismatique et histoire économique phéniciennes et puniques* [Studia Phoenicia, 9; Louvain-la-Neuve: Université Catholique de Louvain, 1992], pp. 21-31 [25]) notes also that from 480 to 450 the Phoenician navies were devastated in battles with the Greeks on behalf of their Persian overlords. Given the expense of the upkeep of the fleet, she suggests that the cities may have hoped to profit from the difference between the actual value of the natural silver and its value when minted.

The Phoenician territories in Palestine appear to have maintained greater and more significant contacts with the hinterland than the cities farther north on the Syrian coastline.[24] These two areas were also economically distinct insofar as the northern cities witness an economic decline in the last half of the fifth century and a recovery beginning about the second quarter of the fourth,[25] while in Palestine the Phoenician cities flourished until the beginning of the fourth century, when they became the center of a power struggle between the Persian empire and the rebellious pharaohs of the twenty-ninth dynasty and their allies. Tyre and other cities were seized by Evagoras of Salamis by 386 (Diodorus 15.2.3-4), and other parts of Phoenicia and Palestine as a whole reveal the remnants of Egyptian control in the first quarter of the fourth century.[26] After the Persians wrested the area from the Egyptians, the Phoenician cities united in a short-lived revolt (351–345) under the leadership of Tennes of Sidon. Once the Persian army arrived, the revolt was quickly crushed and Sidon destroyed (Diodorus 16.40-45),[27] but there is little archaeological evidence that the rebellion and its after-effects did much to stifle the economic life of the area, a situation that appears to be paradigmatic of Palestine's economy during the Persian period.

The Territories of Sidon. Sidon, although far north of Yehud, potentially exercised great influence there because of its control of the coastal Sharon Plain that bordered the Jewish province. The sarcophagus inscription of

24. J. Lund argues (in 'The Northern Coastline of Syria in the Persian Period: A Survey of the Archaeological Evidence', *Trans* 2 [1990], pp. 13-36) that the northern cities were all within a few kilometers of the coast (p. 26), and that while agriculture may have been important in these regions (p. 28), it does not seem that they maintained the intensity of contact that Tyre did with Galilee, say, or Sidon did with the Sharon.

25. Lund, 'The Northern Coastline of Syria', pp. 31-32.

26. An inscription giving the titles of Nepherites I (399–93) was discovered at Gezer (R.A.S. Macalister, *The Excavation of Gezer*, II [London: Palestine Exploration Fund, 1912], p. 313 and fig. 452), and the upper part of a column base from an altar stand was found in Akko with an inscription that mentions the Pharaoh Achoris. Part of another monument of Achoris was discovered in Sidon at the Eshmun temple (A. Rowe, *A Catalogue of Egyptian Scarabs* [Jerusalem: Palestine Archaeological Museum, 1936], pp. 295-96).

27. Diodorus notes that the Phoenician cities began their revolt during the consulship of Marcus Fabius (351). A fragment of Artaxerxes III's Chronicles states that Sidon was captured in the fourteenth year of the king's reign (345) (A.K. Grayson, *Assyrian and Babylonian Chronicles* [Texts from Cuneiform Sources, 5; Locust Valley, NY: J.J. Augustin, 1975], no. 9.1-8).

the Sidonian king Eshmunezer makes this control of the Sharon clear: 'Moreover, the lord of kings [the Persian monarch] gave to us Dor and Jaffa, the great lands of grain that are in the Sharon Plain, in accordance with the great deeds that I did; and we added them to the border of Sidon, our land, forev[er]' (*KAI* 14.18-20). The fourth-century *Periplus* of Pseudo-Scylax supports this claim, referring to Dor as a Sidonian city.[28] Other evidence from Dor and Jaffa[29] and the Sharon Plain[30] verifies this claim. A survey of the Sharon shows that during the Persian period there was a sharp increase in settlement in the region. Port cities and small towns sprang up along the coast, while other sites were enlarged during this period.[31] In all, there were 35 towns and villages along the coast between Dor and Jaffa in the Persian period, and we find settlements near

28. Text in Menahem Stern, *Greek and Latin Authors on Jews and Judaism*, III (Jerusalem: Israel Academy of Sciences and Humanities, 1984), p. 10.

29. A building inscription from fourth-century Jaffa indicates the existence there of a temple to Eshmun, the god of Sidon (C.R. Conder, 'The Prayer of Ben Abdas on the Dedication of the Temple of Joppa', *PEQ* [1892], pp. 170-74), while a fourth-century inscription from Dor suggests the presence of a person there with a name including the theophoric element Eshmun (the text reads *mlkn*[ ]/*n'r 'š*[*mn*], 'Milkn[ ], the servant of Esh[mun]'; found in J. Naveh, 'A Phoenician Inscription from Area C', in E. Stern [ed.], *Excavations at Dor, Final Report*, IB [Qedem Reports, 2; Jerusalem: Hebrew University, 1995], p. 489).

30. A group of Phoenician and Aramaic inscriptions from the Persian period were discovered at Eliachin (143/202) in the north central Sharon (published in R. Deutsch and M. Heltzer, *Forty New Ancient West Semitic Inscriptions* [Tel Aviv: Archaeological Center, 1994], pp. 69-89). The Phoenician text on one bronze votive bowl includes the names *'šmnytn wmgn wb'lpls*, 'Eshmunyaton and Magon and Baalpilles', all Phoenician, and the first Sidonian. Another inscription from this find mentions the Sharon Plain, indicating, as does Eshmunezer's inscription, that the whole plain was thought of as a single geographic (and perhaps administrative) area. A coin hoard found at the same site contains five Sidonian coins that date between the end of the fifth century to the reign of Tennes (d. 345) (published in R. Deutsch and M. Heltzer, 'Numismatic Evidence from the Persian Period from the Sharon Plain', *Trans* 13 [1996], pp. 17-20). Excavations at Appolonia, a town on the coast between Dor and Jaffa, produced a Phoenician inscription mentioning Eshmun, as well as a hoard of 20 coins, almost all of them Sidonian (I. Rolli and E. Ayalon, 'Appolonia-Arsuf', in *NEAEHL*, I, pp. 72-75 (73). A coin discovered in the early fourth-century stratum of Tel Michmal, four kilometers south of Appolonia, bears the name *'bd'štrt*, 'Abdashtart', the king of Sidon known to the Greeks as Straton (Z. Herzog, 'Michmal, Tel', in *NEAEHL*, III, pp. 1036-41 [1038]).

31. R. Gophna and M. Kochavi, 'An Archaeological Survey of the Plain of Sharon', *IEJ* 16 (1966), pp. 143-44 (144).

the estuaries of all the rivers and wadis in this region, apparently for the purposes of anchorage.[32]

The archaeological remnants of the Sharon sites demonstrate the high level of economic activity in the area. Dor (142/224) has two main Persian period strata,[33] and the remains from the southern slope of the tell included many long, narrow rooms that were once filled with storage jars. These were apparently storehouses for commercial activity, and the large quantities of Attic and East Greek ware found there indicate that a good deal of this activity was connected with imports and exports.[34] The impressive range of imports of Athenian pottery there show 'a complete repertoire of shapes and sizes', and were imported throughout the Persian period.[35] Without mentioning every one of the many settled sites along the coast of the Sharon in detail, we may simply say that the situation at most of them was much like that of Dor: the mass of East Greek and Attic ware discovered there is testament not only to the commercial activity along the Phoenician coast, but also to the trade with the Greeks, or at least areas to the north-west of Palestine that traded with them.[36] Notably, a jar found in

32. Stern, *Excavations at Tel Mevorakh*, p. 79.

33. There were, strictly speaking, three Persian period strata (VI, V A, and V B), but V A is really just a repair and rebuilding of V B, which was damaged by the Persian suppression of the Tennes Rebellion. So E. Stern, *Excavations at Dor, Final Report.* IA. *Areas A and C* (Qedem Reports, 1; Jerusalem: Hebrew University, 1995), p. 34.

34. E. Stern, 'Dor', in *NEAEHL*, I, pp. 357-68 (361).

35. R. Marchese, 'Athenian Imports in the Persian Period', in E. Stern (ed.), *Excavations at Dor, Final Report.* IB. *Areas A and C: The Finds* (Qedem Reports, 2; Jerusalem: Hebrew University, 1995), pp. 127-33 (127).

36. Just south of Dor was Tel Mikhmoret (138/201), where a Persian period settlement was established in the late fifth century and destroyed at the end of the Tennes rebellion. This was a site founded in the Persian period, and the large quantity of Attic ware and the Persian period storehouses discovered there shows the site was used extensively for trade (Y. Porath *et al.*, 'Mikhmoret, Tel', in *NEAEHL*, III, pp. 1043-46 [1044-45]). A similar scene is found at Appolonia (132/178), a site never settled prior to the Persian period, in which there were four phases of settlement. The finds there of 'numerous imported Greek vessels' caused the excavators to conclude that this was a trading station (Rolli and Ayalon, 'Appolonia-Arsuf', p. 73). Nearby Tel Michmal (131/174) had witnessed previous habitation, but had been abandoned for 150 years until the late sixth century, the beginning of its prosperous existence in the Persian period. While the first Persian period level (stratum XI; late sixth to early fifth centuries) consisted only of a fort with silos, the pottery there was dominated by East Greek imports. Stratum IX (second half of the fifth century) contained 'an extremely

Jaffa in a Persian period burial cave bore the Phoenician inscription *kd hrms*, 'the jar of Hermes'. The name 'Hermes' is Greek and quite common in the Eastern Mediterranean.[37] This may suggest that a Greek with the name Hermes lived there, or it may simply mean that the name was taken by a Phoenician. In either case, it indicates Greek influence there. One bronze bowl found at Eliachin, a Sharon settlement, bears an inscription with the names *'tḥ*, known only in Arabic, and *bgwy*, an Iranian name known also from the Elephantine papyri as *bgwhy*, the governor of Yehud (*TAD* A4.7, 9), and from Ezra and Nehemiah as *bigway* (Ezra 2.2, 14; 8.14; Neh. 7.7, 19; 10.17).[38] This is testament not only to the ethnic mix in the area, but also perhaps to the presence of a Persian administrator. Many of the Sharon sites had never been previously settled, or had been abandoned for centuries before the Persian period. And from Dor to Jaffa we see the results of an environment that was apparently kind to economic expansion through international trade. The vessels from the Greek areas, whether imported for their own sakes or for that of their contents surely indicate that something was being traded for them, most likely agricultural products. Eshmunezer's inscription, after all, prizes the region because of its 'great grain lands'. But whatever the products at stake, this bustling commercial activity was being enacted next door to the province of Yehud.

Since Sidon controlled the Sharon, this may make it unlikely that the cities of Lod and Ono, located on the plain, were actually part of the province of Yehud, even though the lists of geographical sites in Ezra 2.21-35 (= Neh. 7.25-38) and Neh. 11.25-36 seem to suggest otherwise. Yet there is some doubt as to exactly when the Persians gave this area to

large quantity of black-figure Attic ware'. So this settlement, too, was likely a trading center (Herzog, 'Michmal', p. 1038). Stratum VI (fifth to fourth centuries) of Tell Qasile (131/168) includes some Attic ware, although not to the extent of the other tells mentioned here. Still, many locally produced trading vessels were found there, such as the basket-handled jars, indicating that trade played some role in the settlement's economic life (A. Mazar, 'Qasile, Tel', in *NEAEHL*, IV, pp. 1204-212 [1206-1207]). Jaffa (127/162), on the other hand, was more typical of its Sharon counterparts, with its large quantities of imported Attic ware. The remains there also demonstrate economic prosperity and expansion from the second half of the fifth century on (J. Kaplan, 'The Archaeology and History of Tel Aviv-Jaffa', *BA* 35 [1972], pp. 66-95 [87-88]).

37. R. Avner and E. Eshel, 'A Juglet with a Phoenician Inscription from a Recent Excavation in Jaffa, Israel', *Trans* 12 (1996), pp. 59-63.

38. The Eliachin inscriptions are in Deutsch and Heltzer, *West Semitic Inscriptions*, pp. 69-89.

the Sidonian crown. Depending on the date of the reign of Eshmunezer in whose reign the area was given to Sidon by the Persian monarch, it may be possible that these cities were actually a part of Yehud until as late as the mid-fifth century, the majority opinion for the beginning of his reign.[39] It is, of course, possible to place the entire Eshmunezer dynasty before Tetramnestos (d. 479), as Thomas Kelly[40] and some others do. If, for example, we assume that Eshmunezer's 'great deeds' that won him the Sharon relate to the involvement of the Sidonian fleet on the Persian side during the Ionian Revolt of 499–493 (Herodotus 6.14), that would date him to the beginning of the fifth century. I am, however, not interested in resolving this debate here, but raise the issue only to note that the Sharon was a gift to Sidon no earlier than the beginning of the fifth century, and was most likely a mid-fifth-century gift. It is certainly not outside the realm of possibility, then, that towns such as Lod and Ono on the Sharon were originally within the jurisdiction of Yehud for nearly a century, only to be transferred to Sidonian control. This means that if members of the temple assembly lived there, a conclusion supported by the biblical lists mentioned above, they would have resided in foreign territory and may have borne allegiance to a foreign government. They certainly would have been exposed to a greater degree of foreign influence than those who lived closer to Jerusalem.

That there was Greek influence in the Persian period in the areas controlled by Sidon is beyond dispute; what does come under question is whether this amounted to actual occupation—Greek quarters within the boundaries of Phoenician towns, say—or simply consisted of cultural and economic influence. Ephraim Stern has argued strenuously for the former

39. Typical of the dating of the Eshmunezer dynasty is Everett Mullen's presentation: Eshmunezer I (479–470), Tabnit (470–465), Eshmunezer II (465–451), Bodashtart (451–?), where Eshmunezer II is the king to whom the Persian monarch gave the Sharon ('A New Royal Sidonian Inscription', *BASOR* 216 [1974], pp. 25-30 [26]). The dating of Mullen and others follows a popular argument by J.B. Peckham (*The Development of the Late Phoenician Scripts* [HSS, 20; Cambridge, MA: Harvard University Press, 1968], p. 86 n. 81), who believes that Eshmunezer II must be placed near the middle of the fifth century, as his claim to have done 'mighty deeds' for the Persians would make no sense if he lived earlier in the century. Herodotus's account of the Phoenician performance at Salamis (480) and at Mycale (479), after all, is hardly glowing. In this school of thought, the Eshmunezer dynasty followed that of Tetramnestos, mentioned by Herodotus as king in 479.

40. T. Kelly, 'Herodotus and the Chronology of the Kings of Sidon', *BASOR* 268 (1987), pp. 39-56.

position in regard to Dor. He points to the finds of two favissae in an area of the city filled with votive figurines in the Greek style, as well as Attic and East Greek pottery. This is evidence, in his opinion, of a Greek temple in Dor—for how else to explain Greek votive objects?—and a Greek settlement in the city.[41] Dor, he writes, in fact contained the largest assemblage of Greek pottery (both East Greek and Attic) found in Israel.[42] In Stern's opinion, it seems likely that the Greeks settled as merchants among the larger population in places such as Al-Mina, Sukas, Akko and Jaffa, or as mercenaries in Egyptian forts such as Migdol, Daphnae and Naukratis.[43] At Makmish, only a few kilometers south of Dor, Nahman Avigad discovered a Persian period temple with figurines and stone statuettes of Phoenician, Egyptian, Cypriot and Greek styles, and since a similar assemblage was also found at Dor, Stern accepts this as evidence for a Greek settlement at Machmish, as well.[44] It is certainly possible that foreigners, Greeks among them, lived in the area, for Arrian reports that after Alexander captured Tyre he sold many Tyrians and foreigners whom he found there into slavery (*Anab*. 2.24.5),[45] although he does not mention the origin of the foreigners.

As Josette Elayi notes, however, the votive finds that Stern cites alone cannot support his claim of Greek occupation.[46] The Phoenicians may have worshipped Greek deities, and they certainly may have produced votive figurines in Greek style locally. This objection to Stern's hypothesis is reinforced by the finds at Mikmash, which show a broad mix of cultural influences at the same site in the same period. There was undoubtedly both

41. E. Stern, 'Two *Favissae* from Tel Dor', in C. Bonnett *et al.* (eds.), *Religio Phoenicia* (Studia Phoenicia, 4; Namur: Societe des études classiques, 1986), pp. 277-87.

42. Stern, 'Dor', p. 361.

43. E. Stern, 'The Beginning of the Greek Settlement in Palestine in Light of the Excavations of Tel Dor', in S. Gitin and W.G. Dever (eds.), *Recent Excavations in Israel: Studies in Iron Age Archaeology* (AASOR, 49; Winona Lake, IN: Eisenbrauns, 1989), pp. 107-24 (116).

44. Stern, 'The Beginning of the Greek Settlement', p. 107.

45. Specifically, Arrian says, 'Tyrians and the foreigners who were caught (there) were brought into slavery'. Diodorus 17.46.4 states that Alexander sold the women and children in the city into slavery and hung all the young men, but mentions no foreigners among the populace.

46. J. Elayi, 'Presence grecque sur la côte palestinienne', in E.-M. Laperrousaz and A. Lemaire (eds.), *La Palestine à l'époque perse* (Paris: Cerf, 1994), pp. 245-60 (257-58).

direct and indirect trade between Athens and the Palestinian coastal settlements, as well as with the East Greek cities as we have seen. The more important lesson to draw from this evidence, I believe, is its proof of the existence of a vigorous environment of trade with Greece, and the reach of these economic ties to the interior of Palestine, to which the spread of Greek pottery manifests a vibrant witness. We should note as well the cultural influences which accompany such trade, whether they take the form of Phoenicians worshipping Greek deities, or whether they may actually have included the presence of Greek communities in Phoenician cities.

The Territories of Tyre. Tyre stands about 35 kilometers south of Sidon on the coast, and so these two cities shared a border during the Persian period. Tyre appears to have controlled the Akko Plain during this era, and quite likely all the area from Tyre south to the northern border of Sidon's prosperous Sharon province that included Dor and Jaffa. Pseudo-Scylax stated that Akko was a Tyrian city,[47] and this is supported by archaeological evidence as well.[48] The entire Akko plain was densely settled during this period.[49]

47. In Stern, *Greek and Latin Authors*, III, p. 10.

48. The two Persian period coin hoards discovered at Akko contain only Tyrian coins, as does the one discovered at nearby Tell Abu Hawam (J. Elayi and A.G. Elayi, *Trésors de monnaies phéniciennes et circulation monétaire [Ve–IVe siècles avant J.-C.]* [TransSup, 1; Paris: J. Gabalda, 1993], pp. 163-85 [hoards 33, 34 and 35]). A Tyrian coin was also found among the imported Greek ware in Akko Stratum 5, which apparently lasted through the duration of the fifth century (M. Dothan, 'Akko: Interim Excavation Report First Season, 1973/4', *BASOR* 224 [1976], pp. 1-48 [26-27]). The seals discovered at Persian period Akko display Tyrian iconography (Lemaire, 'Populations et territoires', p. 60), and a graffito found there (*KAI* 49.34) was written by someone who described himself as *ḥṣry*, 'the Tyrian'. A coin hoard discovered at Tell Nahariya, about ten kilometers north of Akko on the coast, contained ten coins that predated Alexander, and of these, all but one was Tyrian (D.T. Ariel, 'Coins from Excavations at Tel Nahariya, 1982', *Atiqot* [Eng] 22 [1993], pp. 125-32). A group of Phoenician seals from the fourth century contain at least three geographical names, two of which appear to indicate settlements south of Tyre (J.C. Greenfield, 'A Group of Phoenician City Seals', *IEJ* 35 [1985], pp. 129-34 [129-32]). The third is Sarepta, 16 kilometers south of Sidon, a city that Esarhaddon says he took from a rebellious Sidon and gave to Tyre in the early seventh century (text in R. Borger, *Die Inschriften Asarhaddons Königs von Assyrien* [*AfO*, 9; Osnabrueck: Biblio, 1967], p. 49). The presence of this geographical name among the seals from within the Tyrian sphere of influence suggests that Sarepta was still a Tyrian city in the Persian period.

49. E. Stern, *Material Culture of the Land of the Bible in the Persian Period 538–*

South of Shiqmona and the Akko Plain lies the Sharon, controlled by Sidon. The two largest urban centers on the coast between Jaffa at the south end of the Sharon and Gaza were Ashdod and Ashkelon, and Pseudo-Scylax claims that '[Ashke]lon is a city of the Tyrians'. There is no doubt that this was a Phoenician city in the Persian period, and an inscription from Athens during this period shows the presence of Phoenicians in Ashkelon and, in the case of this inscription, of an Ashkelonite traveler to Greece.[50] The city produced its own coinage of the type generally called Philisto-Arabian,[51] although this is no reason to argue for its independence. The Tyrians may have permitted a mint there in order to supply the coinage demand necessitated through the trade in the region. The city of Ashdod, about 15 kilometers north of Ashkelon and south of Sidon's Sharon province, may also have been part of Tyre's territory. Lemaire claims that Ashdod was a separate province on the basis of the appearance of the gentilic form of the city's name in Neh. 4.1 (ET 4.7), 13.23 and 24,[52] but we should treat this argument with caution. Ashdod may well have been a separate province in the Persian period, but it could also simply have been a city in a Tyrian area that also included Ashkelon. While we can make no certain conclusions I will treat Ashdod in this section of Palestinian areas controlled by Tyre, if only for ease of organization.

The Tyrian possessions in Palestine shared in the prosperity and trade enjoyed by the Sidonian settlements on the Sharon. The towns on the Akko Plain were, like those on the Sharon, marked by large finds of East Greek and Attic pottery, indicating a significant volume of trade during the Persian period.[53] Akko is, furthermore, mentioned as the destination of a

332 B.C. (Jerusalem: Israel Exploration Society, 1982), p. 241.

50. A bilingual funerary inscription from Athens (*CIS* 1.115) reads in part in the Phoenician section 'I am Shamai, son of Abdashtart, the Ashkelonite' and in part in the Greek section, 'having left Phoenicia, here in the ground my body remains'. The unfortunate Phoenician was killed by a lion. Phoenician text emended with C. Bonnet, 'Antipatros l'Ascalonite dévoré par un lion: Commentaire de *CIS* I, 115', *Sem* 38 (1990), pp. 39-47 (40).

51. Y. Meshorer, 'The Mints of Ashdod and Ashkelon during the Late Persian Period', *EI* 20 (1989), pp. 287-91, 205* (205*). By the fourth century, the coins of Ashkelon were labeled *'n*, while those of Ashdod were marked *'š*.

52. A. Lemaire, 'Histoire et administration de la Palestine à l'époque perse', in E.-M. Laperrousaz and A. Lemaire (eds.), *La Palestine à l'époque perse* (Paris: Cerf, 1994), pp. 11-53 (31).

53. Achzib (159/273), likely on or near Tyre's northern border with Sidon, is

business trip on the part of an Athenian citizen in a fourth-century civil case that Demosthenes argued (*Against Callippus* 20). Moreover, an ostracon found in the Persian period levels uses three Greek loan words, the

marked in the Persian period by a large building. Several of the rooms apparently served as storehouses, to judge from the numerous jars found *in situ* (J. Briend, 'L'occupation de la Galilee occidentale à l'époque perse', *Trans* 2 [1990], pp. 109-23 [110]). This may have been used for trade or merely storage. Tel Nahariya (159/267) was a Tyrian possession near the Sidonian border. Its Persian period settlement (strata II and III) was the first occupation of the tell since the Late Bronze. In the later part of the period there appears to have been a great deal of activity there, as is evident by a number of large buildings described by the excavators as having a public character. There was a great deal of pottery found at the site, including imported Attic ware (O. Yogev, 'Tel Nahariya', *ESI* 2 [1983], pp. 75-76 [75]). Akko (158/258) shows a stable development from its Iron Age strata to its Persian period strata (VI-IV). In part of the city, in even the earliest Persian stratum (VI; late sixth to early fifth centuries) Attic ware forms a high percentage of the pottery finds (Briend, 'L'occupation de la Galilee', pp. 112-13). In most of the city, Attic ware is prevalent beginning in stratum V (fifth century), and there were some buildings there from the sixth to fourth centuries with a high percentage of Attic ware that appear to have been storehouses for the Greek imports (M. Dothan, 'An Attic Red-Figured Bell-Krater from Tel 'Akko', *IEJ* 29 [1979], pp. 148-51 [148]). Tell Abu Hawam (152/245) was abandoned for two centuries before being resettled in the Persian period at the beginning of the fifth century. Destroyed in the Egyptian occupation of 400–380 (level II), it was immediately rebuilt, first as a series of silos, then by a new construction of the city. Historically, the tell served as an important trading center, occupying land adjacent both to a good harbor and to a significant east-west road, and this situation does not appear to change in the Persian period. Attic ware was prevalent there, with an average of four to nine Greek jars per cubic meter of Persian period level (J. Balensi *et al.*, 'Le niveau perse à Tell Abu Hawam, résultats récents et signification dans le contexte regional cotier', *Trans* 2 [1990], pp. 125-36). At Shiqmona (146/248), the Persian period town (stratum P) lasted only from the end of the sixth century to the first third of the fifth, yet here we find at least one storeroom with 53 intact vessels on the floor (J. Elgavish, 'Shiqmona', in *NEAEHL*, IV, pp. 1373-78 [1375-76]), evidence of at least local trade. At Tel Megadim (145/237), stratum II was the main Persian period level, and it flourished in the fifth century. The tell itself was quite large—about 22 dunams—and was protected by a casemate wall, although this was more for protection from pirates than to offer any real defense against a powerful army. The inhabitants abruptly deserted the town at the beginning of the fifth century, perhaps in response to violence surrounding the Egyptian incursion, leaving behind a vast assemblage of almost the entire repertoire of pottery types found in Western Palestine in the Persian period. In the opinion of the excavators, the large amounts of foreign pottery there 'testify to an intensive overseas trade' (M. Broshi, 'Megadim, Tel', in *NEAEHL*, III, pp. 1001-1003).

earliest examples known of Greek entering Phoenician.[54] There was enough Greek pottery at the tell to lead the excavators to surmise that there may have been a Greek settlement within the walls of Akko, at least in the mid-fifth century.[55] Greek trade and cultural influence here are obvious. At Atlit (144/234), a harbor was formed sometime in the late sixth or early fifth centuries by the construction of two moles, one jutting out from the mainland, the other from an offshore island. The moles not only acted as breakwaters to shelter the anchored ships, but also functioned as docks: cargo ships could anchor on either side of the two jetties and unload or take on cargo. The construction of the harbor itself is quite a marvel, for part of the harbor's seafloor itself was quarried and leveled with foundation courses. Modern archaeologists are unsure as to precisely how such a feat was accomplished in water that was over two meters in depth. Two shipwrecks by the moles contain amphorae from Tyre and Sidon dating to the end of the fifth century. A third wreck contains the basket-handled amphorae used for trade throughout the Palestine and the Mediterranean in the Persian period, and these were constructed in Cyprus or Syria in the mid-fifth century. A fourth wreck contained fifth-century wine amphorae from Asia Minor.[56]

South of the Sharon at Ashdod (118/129), the Persian period city (stratum V) contained both local pottery and Attic ware. The city also produced its own coinage, marked *'šdd* at first,[57] and later *'š*.[58] Ashkelon (107/119) also had its own coinage, as I mentioned above, and Tyre may well have allowed this to facilitate the trade that produced one of the richest towns at the site in antiquity. Persian period Ashkelon saw five different phases of settlement, with monumental ashlar buildings constructed in the Phoenician style. The town had a series of warehouses, the earliest one unearthed by archaeologists with one room still full of the Phoenician amphorae and Attic ware that the others likely contained at one

54. M. Dothan, 'A Phoenician Inscription from 'Akko', *IEJ* 35 (1985), pp. 81-94.

55. Dothan, 'An Attic Red-Figured Bell-Krater'; and A. Raban, 'A Group of Imported "East Greek" Pottery from Locus 46 at Area F on Tel Akko', in M. Heltzer *et al.* (eds.), *Studies in the Archaeology and History of Ancient Israel* (Festschrift Mothe Dothan; Haifa: Haifa University, 1993), pp. 73-98 (98).

56. A. Raban and E. Linder, ''Atlit: Maritime 'Atlit', in *NEAEHL*, I, pp. 117-20 (118-20).

57. A. Lemaire, 'Le trésor d'Abu Shusheh et le monnyage d'Ashdod avant Alexandre', *Revue Numismatique* [6th series] 32 (1990), pp. 257-63 (259).

58. Meshorer, 'The Mints of Ashdod', p. 205*.

time, as well. While Phoenician amphorae and thc basket-handled jars used for trade dominated the ceramic assemblage, a great deal of Attic ware was found there, especially from the fifth century.[59]

So we see a situation in the Tyrian dominated regions much like that in the Sharon. The Persian period was a time of economic expansion as sites abandoned for centuries were refounded, and all areas seemed to participate in the thriving economy of the region. It seems that we may attribute much of this to trade, not only with Athens and the Greek cities of Asia Minor, but also with areas such as Cyprus and the Syrian coast. Whatever designs the Persian kings may have had on Greece, they did not stop the economic and cultural interaction between those sometime enemies of the empire and Phoenicia. The coastal cities, apparently, made the most of their location and access to trade routes, and this is reflected by the burgeoning settlements in the region we have just sampled.

Tyre also had strong ties with Galilee, although we cannot know if these extended beyond the normal influence exerted by trade to political control. An early fourth-century ostracon from Tell Yoqne'am on the western border of the Jezreel Valley gives a list of names, two of which are Phoenician.[60] I mentioned earlier (section 2a) Geva's thesis that jars found in ninth- to seventh-century Tyre seemed to have originated in Israel, based on neutron analysis and similar jar types in Israel.[61] J. Briend's survey of excavations in Western Galilee demonstrated that there was Attic pottery at almost all of those sites, as well as Tyrian money. At Tel Qishon, for example, a site about nine kilometers southeast of Akko, the first Persian period level (3b; about 580–480) contained a mix of local, Attic and East Greek pottery that we might expect to find in a contemporary settlement on the coast.[62] The shaft tombs in the area provide further evidence of Phoenician cultural influence.[63] We should note, moreover, that Galilee seems to have undergone the same renaissance that affected the coastal

59. L. Stager, 'Ashkelon', in *NEAEHL*, I, pp. 103-12 (107-109).

60. J. Naveh, 'Published and Unpublished Aramaic Ostraca', *Atiqot* (Eng) 17 (1985), pp. 114-21 (119-20).

61. Bikai responded that the sherds sampled by the neutron analysis were far too narrow to produce accurate results, and, furthermore, that it appeared that these jars were actually manufactured in Tyre, and that it is more likely that such jars were produced in Tyre and exported to Israel, since similar ones were produced in Sarepta. While this is evidence for trade during Iron II, the finds show no reason to believe this trade was discontinued in the Persian period.

62. Briend, 'L'occupation de la Galilee', pp. 113-22.

63. Briend, 'L'occupation de la Galilee', p. 119.

areas under Phoenician control. The region was almost totally abandoned following the destruction of Samaria in 732 until the Persian period, when a dense network of rural sites sprung up that formed the hinterland of the coastal areas.[64] This fact certainly lends some credence to Finkelstein's suggestion that the westward movement of sites in Persian period Samaria was influenced by the Phoenician economic expansion.

Gaza. Herodotus writes that Gaza (or Kadutios, as he calls it) 'is a city, so it seems to me, not smaller than Sardis' (3.5), and as Sardis was the most important city in Asia Minor at the time, this is no faint praise. He remarks in the same section that it is the northernmost of the seaports belonging to the Arabs, who controlled the coast to Ienysus on the border with Egypt. Assumedly, then, this marks the southern border of the land controlled by Tyre. Gaza was an important way station for the Persians on their way to conquer Egypt (Herodotus 3.7), and likely remained so through the duration of the empire as Egypt struggled for independence and the Persians fought to maintain their colonial hold on the region. The city was eventually destroyed by Alexander (Arrian, *Anab.* 2.26-27), and Strabo, writing his *Geography* at the end of the first century BCE, says that even by that time it had not been repopulated (16.2.30).[65]

Gaza played an enormously important role in the trade of the area. It lay at the end of the Spice Road that ran from Eilat on the Red Sea to the Mediterranean. While Herodotus mentions Gaza as part of Arabian territory, he writes earlier in the *History* that 'the coastal areas of Arabia are held by the Syrians' (2.12). This makes the question of who exactly controlled the city somewhat difficult to discern, but whatever the answer, it played an important role in facilitating the spice trade that was the foundation of its economy.[66] As we shall see, the Spice Road proved another vehicle not just for the flow of goods through the region and beyond, but also for the interaction of peoples and cultures. At Eilat in the far southeast of the Negev, for example, a late fifth-century or early fourth-century

64. Z. Gal, 'Galilee: Chalcolithic to Persian Periods', in *NEAEHL*, I, pp. 448-51 (451).

65. These two accounts do not quite match, for Arrian writes that after all the defenders had been killed and the women and children sold into slavery, Alexander populated the town with people from the neighboring areas, and used it as a fortress (*Anab.* 2.27.7).

66. L. Mildenberg, 'Petra on the Frankincense Road?', *Trans* 10 (1995), pp. 69-72 (69).

Phoenician ostracon was discovered bearing Phoenician names.[67] We should not be surprised, then, to find an Arabian inscription mentioning an Arab who lived at Gaza.[68]

The importance of Gaza as a trading center can be made most plain through an examination of its coinage. The coins of Gaza were originally described by the early twentieth-century numismatist G.F. Hill as 'Philisto-Arabian'. They are generally copies of Attic coins, created and used by rulers along the caravan routes.[69] Philisto-Arabian coins generally adapted Attic standards for weight, and the earlier Philisto-Arabian drachms weighed four grams, like those of Athens. Gaza also minted its coins on the Attic weight standard, and was the first Palestinian city to do so.[70] Attic coins, widespread and widely available, provided the most widely recognized medium for international trade.[71] Imitating this coinage, then, is simply a way to facilitate trade with the Greeks and other peoples. Leo Mildenberg, noting the similarity between the coins of Gaza and the Philisto-Arabian coins that circulated in Arabia, suggests that both groups originated in Gaza.[72] Whether or not both were actually produced at a mint in Gaza, the similarity between the two types does suggest a coordinated effort to facilitate trade between Gaza and the caravans, as well as between Gaza and the foreigners from the West who purchased the spices.

67. J. Naveh, 'The Scripts of Two Ostraca from Elath', *BASOR* 183 (1966), pp. 27-30.

68. A Minean inscription mentions an Arabic *'b'*, 'Abba', from Gaza (*ANET*, p. 666).

69. L. Mildenberg, 'The Philisto-Arabian Coins—A Preview: Preliminary Studies of Local Coinage in the 5th Persian Satrapy. Part 3', in T. Hackens and G. Monchante (eds.), *Numismatique et histoire economique phénicienne et puniques* (Studia Phoenicia, 9; Louvain-la-Neuve: Université Catholique de Louvain, 1992), pp. 33-40. One coin bears the image of a rider on a camel (plate 9.10), an indication of the type of trade this coinage facilitated.

70. H.J. Katzenstein, 'Gaza in the Persian Period', *Trans* 1 (1989), pp. 67-86 (78). The coins even displayed the head of Athena.

71. U. Rappaport, 'Gaza and Ascalon in the Persian and Hellenistic Periods in Relation to their Coins', *IEJ* 20 (1970), pp. 75-80 (76).

72. L. Mildenberg, 'Gaza Mint Authorities in Persian Time: Preliminary Studies of the Local Coinage in the 5th Persian Satrapy. Part 4', *Trans* 2 (1990), pp. 137-46 (143). He writes that the two groups of coins 'have the same fabric, weight standard and denomination and are very similar in type and engraving. Thus, they must be contemporary and certainly come from the same milieu.'

Conclusion. The Phoenician territories, it would appear, blossomed during the Persian period, witnessing the founding of new territories and re-establishing old ones that had not been settled for centuries. Much of this appears to be thanks to the vibrant trading patterns that we noted in the region that extended north to the surrounding coastal regions in Palestine, west to the Greek territories in Asia Minor and Greece itself, and inland to Galilee, Samaria and Arabia. That it extended to Yehud is made clear in the mention of Tyrian merchants in Jerusalem during the time of Nehemiah. It appears equally obvious that this trade led to international travel and likely immigration, as we have seen. Perhaps the vast amount of trade during the Persian period is best chronicled not so much by the finds of Greek pottery *in situ* in Palestine, but by the pottery finds off the coast. Avshalom Zemer has noted that variants of one type of storage jar produced from the sixth to fourth centuries have been found in the waters of the Eastern Mediterranean from Palestine as far as Carthage. This jar type alone accounts for one half of all the pottery finds from *every* period off the coast of Palestine,[73] and when we consider the many other jars that found their way to coastal floor of the Levant in the Persian period, we get some idea of the vast amount of sea trade that allowed the expansion of the Phoenician settlements and the flourishing of their economies. We can also understand why Samaria might move to an export-driven economy, for the infrastructure and international trading partners were certainly present to make such a shift attractive. Darius even went so far as to construct a canal from the Nile to the Arabian Gulf to permit easy sea access from Persia to Egypt and the Mediterranean.[74] Borders, it would appear, were falling throughout the empire and beyond, allowing a free flow of goods and individuals. Nowhere is this more evident than in the Phoenician territories that benefited from their location which allowed them to take advantage of the rich opportunities in international trade, causing their settlements to flourish to a degree not seen in centuries, and we have every reason to believe that large volumes of this international trade made its way into Yehud from Phoenicia, just as it did into Samaria and Galilee.

73. A. Zemer, *Storage Jars in Ancient Israel* (Haifa: National Maritime Museum Foundation, 1977), p. 25 (jars nos. 19-21).

74. Text and translation of the Darius Suez inscription from R.G. Kent, *Old Persian: Grammar, Texts, Lexicon* (AOS, 33; New Haven: American Oriental Society, 1953), p. 147.

c. *Arabia*

While Herodotus claims that the fifth Persian satrapy excluded 'the Arab part' (3.91), and that the Arabs were exempt from the annual taxes paid by the lands subject to the crown, the Persians appear to have viewed the situation in a somewhat different light. When, for example, on an inscription found at Persepolis, Darius I writes 'these are the countries that I held with this Persian people, that were afraid of me (and) bore tribute', he includes in the list of countries 'Arabia'.[75] It is difficult to decide between the two sources, but we do have enough evidence to vouch confidently for Persian administrative presence in Arabia alongside the local monarchy.[76] The Persians appear to have been interested in the tax income that could be derived from the Spice Road that ran from Eilat to Gaza, and to have organized institutions to extract it.[77] As we shall see below, a series of royal fortifications were constructed in part to guard it, and the Persians may have also used them to draw taxes from the cargo.

The area in question is quite large. Herodotus refers to the entire area east of the Nile Delta, from the Mediterranean to the Red Sea, as 'Arabia'

75. Text of the Darius Persepolis E inscription from Kent, *Old Persian*, p. 136.

76. In Aramaic inscriptions of the Persian period from the region of Teima, an important urban center in Arabia, we find two officials present in the same area at the same time, one bearing the title *mlk*, 'king', the other the title of *pḥ'*, 'governor' (F.M. Cross, 'A New Aramaic Stele from Tayma', *CBQ* 48 [1986], pp. 387-94). A Lihyanite inscription from Dedan mentions both *gšm bn šhr w'bd fḥt ddn*, 'Gashmu the son Shahru and Abd, the governor of Dedan' (A. Jaussen and R. Savignac, *Missions archéologique en Arabie II* [Paris: Paul Geuthner, 1914], pp. 524-25; following the universally accepted emendation of this text by F.V. Winnett), and we know from both the Nehemiah narrative and the Tell el-Maskhouta inscription (see n. 78) that Gashmu was a local monarch. Xenophon also mentions a Persian satrap in the region (*Cyr.* 8.6.7). It is not unlikely, then, that local dynasties and bureaucrats of the central administration coexisted in the same region. This does not necessarily tell us much about the specifics of the administration of the region; the area is specifically excluded by Herodotus from the fifth satrapy (3.91), and it may have had neither a unified political structure (so I. Eph'al, *The Ancient Arabs: Nomads on the Borders of the Fertile Crescent 9th–5th Centuries B.C.* [Leiden: E.J. Brill, 1982], p. 193) nor any firm control over the nomads who wandered the countryside (so E.A. Knauf, 'The Persian Administration in Arabia', *Trans* 2 [1990], pp. 201-17 [204]).

77. An ostracon from Eilat, found with those that mention the Phoenician names, refers to *qrplgs*, apparently a loanword from the Greek *karpologos*, meaning 'tax gatherer (in kind)' (N. Glueck, 'Ostraca from Elath', *BASOR* 80 [1940], pp. 3-10 [8-9]).

(2.8, 15, 19), which may be close to what was actually the case.[78] Arabia may also have extended as far north as the southern border of Yehud as the inscriptional evidence of an Arabian monarch at Lachish demonstrates (see n. 78). Northern Arabian names, often identified by the orthographic indication of the nominative singular ending *w*, can be found in inscriptions at Beersheba,[79] at Yatta, ten kilometers south of Hebron,[80] at Arad,[81] at Lachish,[82] and possibly from an area near Hebron.[83] Exactly what can be said about political boundaries given this evidence is uncertain. For example, only 11.9 percent of the names from the Arad ostraca are Aramaic, while 50 percent are Hebrew. The names from these ostraca actually display quite a mix of ethnic groups, including Ammonites, Edomites, Egyptians, Phoenicians and Babylonians.[84] The Yatta ostracon contains

78. In a cache of silver bowls discovered at Tell el-Maskhouta in the Eastern Nile Delta, objects dedicated to the goddess Han-'Ilat, one bowl bears the Aramaic inscription *zy qynw br gšm mlk qdr qrb lhn'lt*, 'that which Qaynu, the son of Gashmu, the king of Qedar, dedicated to Han-'Ilat'. Since the script on the bowls is dated to about 400, this makes it likely that the Gashmu mentioned on the inscription is the *gšmw h'rby*, 'Gashmu the Arab', mentioned in Nehemiah's memoirs. Notably, his name is vocalized in the biblical story both as *gešem* (Neh. 2.19; 6.1), the expected Hebrew development of the *qatl* pattern, and as *gašmû* (Neh. 6.6). A late fifth-century inscription from Dedan, almost 300 kilometers south of Eilat and more than 100 kilometers south of Teima, also mentions a Gashmu son of Sharu, suggesting that all of the area between Dedan and the Nile fell within the control of this dynasty (W.J. Dumbrell, 'The Tell el-Maskhouta Bowls and the "Kingdom" of Qedar in the Persian Period', *BASOR* 203 [1973], pp. 33-44, esp. p. 36). An Arabian monarch is also mentioned in an inscription found at Lachish, only about 15 kilometers southwest of the border of Yehud (A. Lemaire, 'Un nouveau roi arabe en Qedar dans l'inscription de l'autel à encens de Lachish', *RB* 81 [1974], pp. 63-72). This suggests that Arabia stretched from Teima and Dedan in the south to the eastern Nile Delta in the west to Lachish in the north.

79. J. Naveh, 'The Aramaic Ostraca', in Yohanan Aharoni (ed.), *Beer-Sheba I: Excavations at Tel Beer-Sheba (1969–1971 Seasons)* (Tel Aviv: Tel Aviv University, 1973), pp. 79-82; and J. Naveh, 'The Aramaic Ostraca from Tel Beer-Sheba (Seasons 1971–1976)', *TA* 6 (1979), pp. 182-98.

80. Naveh, 'Published and Unpublished Aramaic Ostraca', pp. 117-18.

81. Naveh, 'The Aramaic Ostraca from Tel Arad', pp. 153-76.

82. Lemaire, 'Un nouveau roi arabe'.

83. These are inscriptions purchased on the antiquities market and published in Eph'al and Naveh, *Aramaic Ostraca*; and in Lemaire, *Nouvelles inscriptions*. Because they were purchased and not found *in situ* by archaeologists, Lemaire's suggestion that they originated west of Hebron (p. 139) should be considered speculative.

84. Klingbeil, 'The Aramaic Ostraca from Lachish', p. 83 n. 22.

only three names, but all of them are Arabic. The names at Beersheba are mainly Aramaic and Edomite, but here we see personal names that contain both the Edomite theophoric element *qws* and Arabic verbal roots,[85] suggesting intermarriage or, at the very least, a thorough mixing of cultures. Through the vagaries of war, trade, intermarriage and the passing of empires, Arabs seem to have moved into this region and mixed with its native population.

I have already mentioned the Spice Road that ran through Arabia from Eilat to Gaza and the coinage produced in the area to facilitate trade. Trade appears to have been an important part of the Arabian economy. Herodotus notes that Arabia was the only place in his known world that produced frankincense, myrrh, cassia, cinnamon and ledanon (3.107), and for this reason alone the produce of Arabia would have been in high demand. With a near monopoly on the supply of some of these spices, we should not be surprised to find that Arabian trade was spread throughout the Persian empire. One Minean inscription dated to the late fifth century mentions an individual who *rtkl ddn wmṣr wṣr wṣ[dn]*, 'traded with[86] Dedan and Egypt and Tyre and Si[don]',[87] while another from the fourth

85. The most likely explanation for this state of affairs in my opinion is that the area south of Beth Zur was controlled by Arabs, although its mixed population in the Persian period reflected its history. 2 Kgs 24.1-7 says that Jehoiakim revolted against Nebuchadnezzar about 601/600, and that the Babylonian responded by attacking with a combined army of Babylonians and local allies: Arameans, Moabites and Ammonites. At the time, Arad appears to have been under Judean control. A Hebrew ostracon from Arad mentions soldiers from Arad and Qinah being sent to Ramat-Negeb in order to defend the city. The author writes, 'Behold, I have sent to inform you this day (concerning) the men of Elyasha, lest Edom come there' (cf. A. Lemaire, 'L'ostracon "Ramat-Negeb" et la topographie historique du Negeb', *Sem* 23 [1973], pp. 11-26). This tells us not only that the MT of 2 Kgs 24.2 has likely read *gdwdy 'rm*, 'troops of Aram', for an original *gdwdy 'dm*, 'troops of Edom', since Aram was no longer a state and the Hebrew *d* and *r* are easily confused (A. Lemaire, 'Les transformations politiques et culturelles de la Transjordanie au VIe siècle av. J.-C', *Trans* 8 [1994], pp. 9-27 [11]), but also that it was Edom that likely took and held Southern Judea. Ps. 137.7 attests that the Edomites participated in the 586 invasion of Judah. In the exilic period, it seems that even Dedan and Teima were under Edomite control (Ezek. 25.12), yet by the Persian period the officials mentioned here are Arabic.

86. The root *rkl* is used in Hebrew to describe Solomon's international commerce (1 Kgs 10.15) and that of Tyre (Ezek. 27), especially with Arabia.

87. A. Lemaire, 'Les Minéens et la Transeuphratène à l'époque perse: Une première approche', *Trans* 13 (1997), pp. 123-39 (130).

century[88] mentions a man who *rtkl* [ ]*mṣr w''šr w'br nhrn*, 'traded with [ ] Egypt and Assyria and Across-the-River' (*RES* 3022).

Not only did this result in the flow of trade, development of coinage, and mix of ethnicities already mentioned, but we see a melange of peoples and their divinities in cosmopolitan cities such as Teima. This city gained its mixed population and important status both from trade—it sat at an oasis at the intersection of the Egypt–Syria road, the route to Mesopotamia and the route to Yemen,[89] and this fact alone would bring both different ethnicities and money to the city—and from the fact that it was the residence of Nabonidus for much of his rule. We find inscriptions that refer to temples of Mesopotamian and Syrian deities in the city.[90] These foreign gods are so well established in the fifth century as to be called *'lhy tym'*, 'the gods of Teima'.

We can see, then, that Southern Palestine was likely controlled by the Arabs, although the local monarchy ruled in coordination with Persian administrators. The northern portion of Arabia was a part of Palestine where Yehudim also lived, as the epigraphic material and the list of Neh. 11.25-36 makes clear (see Chapter 3). The inscriptions make clear, moreover, that the movement of Arabs into this formerly Edomite region resulted in a mix of cultures and intermarriage, and this movement of ethnicities may have been augmented by the trade along the Spice Road and other routes, as was the case in Phoenicia. Borders and social structures may well have been rather ambiguous in this area, given its mix of administrative structures, ethnicities and volume of trade. If temple assembly members lived among this variable mix of ethnicities, exposed to all sorts of foreign goods, gods and merchandise, we can see how they would have been an important medium for the flow of foreign influences in Yehud and Jerusalem. The inhabitants of Persian period Palestine certainly seemed amenable to accepting new gods, intermarriage, or at the very least a mix of cultures, and an export-oriented economy. Arabia is a fine example of the mixing of cultures and religions through trade and other influences in Persian period Palestine, and it was an example immediately present to members of the temple assembly.

88. So Lemaire, 'Les Minéens', p. 129.

89. J.C.L. Gibson, *Textbook of Syrian Semitic Inscriptions*. II. *Aramaic Inscriptions* (Oxford: Clarendon Press, 1975), p. 148.

90. Cross, 'A New Aramaic Stele'; and *CIS* 2.113.

d. *Yehud*

Beyond the presence of temple assembly members in foreign areas, I will point, in the next part of the chapter, to the presence and authority of the Persian administration in the area, another source of foreign influence. In this section, however, I will limit my comments to the presence of foreigners in Yehud due to reasons of trade. In this regard, we should first note first the amounts of East Greek and Attic ware found within the borders of Persian period Yehud. As Carter has pointed out, several of the major sites within the province give evidence of trade with Greece and other areas. In Jerusalem archaeologists have discovered Greek coins, Rhodian glass vessels and various types of Greek ware. Attic pottery has been discovered at Tel Goren and Jericho, and foreign coins at Beth Zur. Foreign pottery and material culture have been found in the most concentrated manner at the major centers of commerce: En Gedi, Jericho, Tell en-Nasbeh and Jerusalem.[91]

It is also worth pointing out that the most heavily settled area in Persian period Yehud was between Hebron and Jerusalem.[92] This area included only seven percent of the province's area, but had 30 percent of Yehud's population in Persian period II. It is perhaps no coincidence that this area is especially well known for grape-growing.[93] Were these grapes used to create wine for export? Something had to be traded for the content of the foreign jars that have been found in the province; and this solution would also explain the presence of the wine-presses discovered in Jerusalem.[94] This particular area of the province (what Carter calls environmental niche 5) had by far the most settlements of all the various parts of the province in the Persian I period (26), and site distribution still increased by 38 percent in Persian II, to 36.[95] One area of the province that saw a dramatic increase in settlements between Persian I and II was the far western part of the province (Carter's environmental niches 1 and 4), which witnessed a growth in sites from 19 in the former period to 32 in the latter, an increase

91. Carter, *The Emergence of Yehud*, pp. 256-57. See also the bibliography of the finds of Attic pottery in Yehud and elsewhere in Palestine in R. Wenning, 'Attische Keramik in Palastina: Ein Zwischenbericht', *Trans* 2 (1990), pp. 157-67.

92. Carter, *The Emergence of Yehud*, p. 187 fig. 17.

93. Department of Surveys, Ministry of Labour, *Atlas of Israel* (Jerusalem: Survey of Israel, 1970), map XII/3 C.

94. Carter, *The Emergence of Yehud*, p. 250.

95. Carter, *The Emergence of Yehud*, p. 228.

of 68 percent.[96] While all but five of these sites are within 14 kilometers of Jerusalem, it is notable that such a large increase in settlement would occur in the Western part of the province, the area close to Phoenicia, the part of Palestine most intensely involved in foreign trade. As Finkelstein noted, the same pattern is visible in the areas north of Yehud in the Persian period.

In short, the areas most heavily settled in the Persian period and the ones that grew heavily throughout this time appear to have been situated in order to produce crops for export and to be close to the Phoenicians, where trade exploded during the Persian period. This particular settlement trend—and it was an intentional trend, as the majority of sites that were either initially settled at this time or re-established in the Persian period were located in the western hills (close to Phoenicia) or in the central hills (the prime area for vineyards)[97]—seems to stand in some tension with the attempt to establish sites close to Jerusalem in order to distance assembly members from foreigners. Nonetheless, the inhabitants of the province must have exchanged something for the goods they imported, and the situation of sites in areas that produced goods for export and in some proximity to the great traders of the region suggests that the province was involved in trade. So when Nehemiah reports that Tyrians lived in Jerusalem and sold merchandise there on the Sabbath (13.16), we may be sure that this was not an isolated event. There is no reason to believe that Yehud's contact with foreigners because of trade deviated from the pattern that we see in the rest of Palestine and Arabia. And as contact with foreigners means contact with their culture and religious ideas, we can begin to see why people might have neglected the temple cult and their society's morality as reported in Ezra–Nehemiah and Malachi.

3. *The Persian Administration in Across-the-River*

a. *Introduction*

The larger Persian satrapy in which the provinces I have just discussed lay was called Across-the-River, *'ēber hannāhār* in Hebrew (Ezra 8.36; Neh. 2.7, 9; 3.7), *ᵃbar nᵃharâ* in Aramaic (numerous times in Ezra), and *ebir nāri* in Akkadian. Herodotus provides us with a list of the satrapies and their annual tribute that made up the Persian empire and that he says were first organized by Darius I (3.90-94). He describes the fifth satrapy as

96. Carter, *The Emergence of Yehud*, p. 225.
97. Carter, *The Emergence of Yehud*, p. 243.

including 'all of Phoenicia and the part of Syria called Palestine and Cyprus'. While we may agree with the size of the satrapy, Herodotus has anachronistically ascribed its creation to the time of Darius, when the satrapal system was initiated. A neo-Assyrian text of 486, however, refers to a certain person (the text is broken at the name, but it begins with Huta-) as the governor of Babylon and Across-the-River.[98] It appears, then, as if Babylonia and Across-the-River were originally a single satrapy, separated some time after 486. After the Tennes Rebellion of 351–345, it seems that the satrapy was annexed to the satrapy of Cilicia until the end of the empire.[99]

We have already seen how trade led to an explosion of sites in Phoenicia. The skills of the Phoenician sailors were well known, and Herodotus speaks highly of their contributions to the Persian navy. This allowed the Phoenicians access to trade with Egypt, Asia Minor and even Greece, and may well have been the stimulus for Samaria's and Yehud's export-oriented economies. As a center for international trade, that is, Phoenicia may well have influenced the economies of inland Palestine, as appears to be the case with Galilee, and it also led to the presence of Greeks in Phoenicia, Phoenicians in Greece, Phoenicians in Samaria and Arabia, and so on. When Nehemiah mentions the problem of the presence of foreign women in Nehemiah 13 he states that half of the children borne by these women could only speak the language of Ashdod (13.24), which may indicate that Phoenicians also lived in Yehud, or that members of the assembly had trading ties with Ashdod. YHWHistic names have been attested at this time even as far south as Tell Jemmeh, six kilometers south of Gaza.[100] But there was another source of foreign influence in Yehud that could have contributed to the level of anxiety there, and that was the presence of the Persian military, administration and tax system there, the subject of this section. Not only did this account for the presence of yet

98. M.W. Stolper, 'The Governor of Babylonia and Across-the-River in 486 B.C.', *JNES* 48 (1989), pp. 283-305 (288).

99. Mazday, the satrap of the new region, minted coins in Tarsus that bore the Aramaic legend *mzdy zy 'l 'brnhr wḥlk*, 'Mazday, who is over Across-the-River and Cilicia' (L. Mildenberg, 'Notes on the Coin Issues of Mazday', *Israel Numismatic Journal* 11 [1990/1991], pp. 9-17 [11]). For a picture of a representative coin see Lemaire and Lozachmeur, 'La Cilicie', pl. 9.9.

100. See Naveh, 'Aramaic Ostraca and Jar Inscriptions', p. 49. The ostraca date to the end of the Persian period, and list two YHWHistic names, along with a Phoenician and Arabic name.

more foreigners, but it also would have aroused fears in other ways. The assembly was, as we have already seen, founded on the experience of exile, and the presence of the Persian administration and military would have made it perfectly clear that the Persians could institute another exile at their will—or, as the community understood it, at God's will. Such a presence combined with the role of exile in the remnant theology would have made the threat seem even more real to the community than it actually was. And once anxiety arose that prompted a desire for the community to purify itself, to separate itself from foreign things and people, the constant awareness of Persian control through institutions such as the tax system and the military would have made it perfectly clear to the assembly that this might never happen. Overt Persian control of the economy, politics and even religion of the province made disaster seem like that much more of a looming reality. Those within the temple community frightened that society might collapse could point to the Persians as God's tool for the manifestation of this disaster.

In the section on Samaria, I noted the presence of Persian administrators there who interfered in and oversaw events in Yehud. Such officials could transgress Yehud's political boundaries almost at will—in the narrative of Ezra 5.1–6.15, for example, only a direct order from Darius is sufficient to allow the reconstruction of the temple to continue over the objections of the governor of Across-the-River. Religious boundaries are also at stake here, for it is quite possible that the Persians oversaw and approved even rituals and personnel in the Jerusalem temple. Such control could not make it more plain that foreign elements pervaded and controlled the community and, interpreted theologically, such foreign control was evidence of God's punishment for Israel's sin for failing to observe social morality (Ezra 9 and, especially, Neh. 9), and of the ease with which God could put an end to the society.

b. *Persian Military Presence in Palestine*

Military Organization and Supply. In the late fifth-century Aramaic papyri from Elephantine at the southern edge of Egypt, we find frequent mention of the *dgl*, apparently as a division of the Persian army units there. The etymology of the term is uncertain, although it is likely cognate to the Hebrew term *degel*, which is used a number of times to refer to military units (Num. 1.52; 10.14, 18, etc.).[101] The degel appears as the basic

101. The term is often seen as cognate with Akkadian *diglu*, since the 3ms suffixival form in Hebrew is *diglô*, but the Akkadian term means 'eyesight, gaze'. It is at least

military unit in Elephantine, where the parties identified in the legal documents are named by their membership in a particular degel.[102] While we cannot be certain how many troops such degels contained, it was at least 1000 soldiers, and may have been much larger,[103] although since we know of four separate degels at Elephantine and Syene,[104] it would mean an astounding number of soldiers in a small area if these were larger than 1000 soldiers each.

As soldiers, members of degels drew rations from the central government. So we find a text at Elephantine recording a disbursement of barley as *ptp lhyl*, 'a ration to the garrison' (*TAD* C3.14), and an acknowledgment of a loan of wheat by a soldier who agrees to reimburse the creditor *mn ptp' zy ytntn ly mn 'wṣr mlk'*, 'from the ration that will be given to me from the storehouse of the king' (*TAD* B3.13). There also appears to be some sort of system of feudal landholdings among the Egyptian degels, similar to the situation we find in Persian period Babylonia. From the Murashu documents at Nippur we know that soldiers were granted an unalienable piece of land, for which they owed military service. The elementary fief was called 'bow land', and was about 10 kur or 13.3 hectares in size.[105] Darius says in the Behistun inscription that he restored

possible that it may be related to the Arabic root *dgl*, that means 'to cover' or 'to speak falsely'. Note in this context the Arabic word *daggalātu*, 'a great company of men (who cover the ground with their multitude)'. In Ethiopic, the same root means 'to shackle', so it could be used in Aramaic and Hebrew in the sense of people joined together.

102. So we see representative examples such as *qwnyh br ṣdq' rmy zy swn ldgl wryzt*, 'Koniah son of Sedeq, the Aramean of Syene, of the degel of Varyazata' (*TAD* B2.1), or *mḥsyh br ydnyh yhw*[*dy z*]*y yb ldgl hwmdt*, 'Mahseiah son of Jedaniah, the Judean of Elephantine, of the degel of Haumadata' (*TAD* B2.4), etc.

103. Herodotus, while describing the troops who embarked on Xerxes's invasion of Greece, notes of the Persian commanders whom he has just mentioned that 'these were the ones who arranged and numbered (the troops) and who appointed the captains of the thousands and the ten thousands' (7.81). All of the names of the degel leaders that we find both in the papyri from Elephantine and in those from Arad are either Persian or Babylonian, and this resonates with Herodotus's list of the troops in Xerxes army, for no matter from what part of the empire the troops came, the commander Herodotus mentions is invariably Persian. Since we know that the degel was larger than a century (from *TAD* A5.5 we have the phrase 'their degel and the heads of their hundreds'), it could well have been what Herodotus called a 'thousand'.

104. B. Porten, *Archives from Elephantine: The Life of an Ancient Jewish Military Colony* (Berkeley: University of California Press, 1968), p. 30.

105. M. Stolper, *Entrepreneurs and Empire: The Murašu Archive, the Murašu Firm,*

such plots of land after quelling a number of insurrections,[106] which suggests that this semi-feudal system had been established almost at the beginning of Persian rule in Babylonia.[107] Herodotus claims that the Egyptians before Persian rule had a similar system of land tenure for their warrior class, each member receiving a plot of land (2.168).[108]

As for the appearance of the degel in Palestine, we know of its existence there as a military unit from the Arad ostraca. These texts are principally orders for the disbursement of foodstuffs to military units and their animals. The presence of the degel is seen in inscriptions 12 and 18 in the context of identifying a particular individual.[109] In general, these are concerned with much smaller units, such as tens, or even individuals. We

and Persian Rule in Babylonia (Nederlands Historisch-Archaeologisch Instituut te Instanbul, 54; Leiden: Uitgaven van Het, 1985), pp. 25 and 26 n. 100.

106. The Akkadian version of the inscription states that Darius restored *É qa-šá-a-tú*, 'the bow lands' that Gaumata had taken away (see F. Malbran-Labat, *La version akkadienne de l'inscription trilingue de Darius à Behistun* [Documenta Asiana, 1; Rome: Gruppo editoriale internazionale, 1994], sec. 13). The Old Persian version here uses the word *viθbiš*, 'households' (1.65), a rather vague term that usually refers to the royal house in Old Persian inscriptions.

107. The inscription records his struggle for the throne in 522 and the subsequent revolts throughout the empire that he was forced to quell. In the section of the inscription in question, Darius says that Gaumata had taken away the bow lands, suggesting that they had existed as a status quo system of land tenure for some time before.

108. The situation in Persian period Egypt, however, was not exactly like that of Babylonia. The Elephantine texts speak of people who are *mhḥsn*, 'property holders', in the area, and another (*TAD* A5.5) refers to a military troop as *mhḥsn*, 'holding property'. One of the texts most helpful in determining the meaning of the verb *ḥsn* here is a letter from the satrap Arsames to one of his officials regarding the case of a man who claims that the land that belonged to his now deceased father has not been given to him (A6.11). He asks Arsames, *yntnw ly 'hḥsn*, 'let them give it to me, let me hold it as heir'. Arsames agrees, so long as it has not already been made over to his estate or given to another of his servants. So a *mhḥsn* in Egypt, be it an individual or a military division, is one who holds land belonging to the government or a high official, and is land that does not automatically pass from parent to child without authorization. Like the bow land of Babylonia, *hlk'*, a particular kind of tax, was charged to such holdings. On one cuneiform tablet we find a short summary of the contents in Aramaic, which represents the Akkadian *ilku* with *hlk'* (BE 10.78). So while this is not precisely the semi-feudal system that existed in Babylonia, we do see both individuals and whole troops as holders of land over which the central authority has the ultimate control.

109. So *ḥmr 10* [ ] *mn mdynt š* [ ] *ldgl 'bdnny*, '10 donkeys [ ] from the province of *š* [ ] of the degel of Abdnanay' (12.1-2).

have already established that Arad was not part of the province of Yehud, but half of the names that appear in these ostraca are YHWHistic,[110] and all of the officials mentioned in them are, as well (with the exception of the Babylonian degel commander Abdnanay).[111]

Nor should we discount the possibility that such military units existed inside of the province of Yehud, as well, and that foreigners were a part of them. A fifth-century Aramaic ostracon from Jericho lists 13 names, three of which are found in the Elephantine papyri and designated there as 'Caspian'. Three others appear to be of Iranian origin. Given that some of the same names may be found at the Persian period military colony at Elephantine, Andre Lemaire suggests that this may well be a list of the members of a small garrison, especially given Jericho's strategic placement at a ford of the Jordan.[112] Troops also moved in and out of the area, likely dependent upon the degree of military risk a particular region suffered. Vessels manufactured in Southern Palestine during the Persian period were found near Carchemesh in Syria at a military cemetery for Persian soldiers, and contained a great number of artifacts similar to Syro-Palestinian ones. In the excavators' opinion, they likely came to Syria with soldiers stationed on the border with Egypt during the 465–456 Egyptian revolt. After the suppression of this revolt, it seems this troop of soldiers was transferred 700 kilometers north.[113] While these particular soldiers were likely stationed south of Yehud, the province itself likely saw its share of troops move in and out, given the unstable Persian control of Egypt. Again, when we think of the borders of Yehud, we can see how porous they were. Not only did large Persian forces move in and out of the region in response to the continuing threat of Egyptian revolt, but foreigners were likely stationed in the garrisons throughout Palestine and Yehud. (The presence of Persian forts in Yehud will be addressed in the section below.) It would not be terribly surprising, moreover, if temple assembly members were part of the military, drawing sustenance from military stores, taking orders from Persian or Babylonian officers, and perhaps even living on feudal or semi-feudal plots of land that belonged to the Persian government. Their allegiance to their officers may have conflicted

110. Klingbeil, 'The Aramaic Ostraca from Lachish', p. 83 n. 22.

111. Naveh, 'The Aramaic Ostraca from Tel Arad', p. 176.

112. A. Lemaire, 'Un nouvel ostracon araméen du Ve siècle av. J.-C.', *Sem* 25 (1978), pp. 87-96.

113. J.A. Blakely and F.L. Horton, Jr, 'South Palestinian Bes Vessels of the Persian Period', *Levant* 18 (1986), pp. 111-19.

with their allegiance to the temple community, and would obviously have been a medium of foreign influence in the community. The presence of the Persian military, moreover, would have been a constant reminder to the community that it was under Persian rule, and that its continued existence was subject to Persian approval.

Persian Fortresses in Palestine. If there is any doubt about Persian military presence in Palestine, there is enough evidence from the fortresses found there to allay it. These fortresses were built (or reused) in order to guard roads, protect trade and act as ration stations. Xenophon, who from his participation in the revolt of Cyrus the Younger in 401 knew firsthand of the military organization of the Persians, claims that at the inception of the empire Cyrus established a network of 'commanders in the citadels and chiliarchs commanding the guards throughout the countryside' (*Cyr.* 8.6.1). These officers, he writes, were appointed by the king and responsible to the king, not to the satrap, 'and just as Cyrus then organized it, so it still is' (8.6.9). Maintenance of these garrisons was to be provided by the local governor (*Oec.* 4.5-6). A number of garrisons were found in the countryside of Palestine in the Persian period, some constructed at that time on a recognizably similar plan, others built earlier, but reused.

Kenneth Hoglund has argued that we can see a pattern of fortresses of the open-court type[114] constructed in the mid-fifth century in Palestine. Since, he claims, some of these were abandoned within a few decades, he concludes they were built in response to the Egyptian revolt of 465–456. In his opinion, the Persians constructed them to secure their troops and supply lines against not only the Egyptians, but also against the threat from Greece.[115] Much of Hoglund's study is illuminating and groundbreaking, especially his observation that a number of fortresses could not be positioned to guard Yehud's southern border, but must have been used to guard the roads. Herodotus tells us that the Persians maintained a road from Asia Minor to Susa guarded by fortresses (5.52-54). The published reports of these fortresses show the outer casemate to be one meter thick or less, demonstrating that they were not meant to withstand a frontal

114. The name 'open-court' derives from the central courtyard found in such a fortress. The courtyard is always surrounded by casemate walls. The forts are almost uniformly square, with sides usually a bit over 20 meters long, and with the courtyard taking up about one-quarter of their overall area.

115. K. Hoglund, *Achaemenid Imperial Administration in Syria-Palestine and the Missions of Ezra and Nehemiah* (SBLDS, 125; Atlanta: Scholars Press, 1992), p. 203.

assault by a well-equipped army. As Hoglund points out, they do not seem to have been conceived to act as defensive islands during major military engagements, for some were positioned so as to be easily overrun by a professional army. Hoglund seems correct in his contention that the fortresses were constructed to guard roads, although his view that we may narrow the date of their construction and occupation to a few decades in the last half of the fifth century is incorrect. A comparison of his report of the dating of many of these fortresses with those given in their actual excavation reports shows that his thesis that they were constructed in a concerted effort to meet the Egyptian revolt of 465 is untenable.[116]

While we could list many other open-court fortresses either constructed or in use in Palestine during the Persian period, I will only reiterate here Hoglund's argument that the fortresses were situated to protect the roads in Palestine, as a comparison of the road system with the fortresses listed by Hoglund shows that many of them sat at crucial intersections.[117] Yet

116. It is useful in this regard to compare Hoglund's report of the dating of some of these fortresses with those given in their actual excavation reports. Cf. esp. his accounts of the dating of the following fortresses (*Achaemenid Imperial Administration*, pp. 170-201) with those given by their excavators: Tell es-Sa'idiyeh (J.B. Pritchard, *Tell es-Sa'idiyeh: Excavations on the Tell, 1964-1966* [University Museum Monographs, 60; Philadelphia: The University Museum, University of Pennsylvania, 1985], pp. 66-68), Tel Sera' (E.D. Oren, 'Sera', Tel', in *NEAEHL*, IV, pp. 1329-55 [1334]), Tell el-Hesi (W.J. Bennett and J.A. Blakely, *Tell el-Hesi: The Persian Period (Stratum V)* [ASORER; Winona Lake, IN: Eisenbrauns, 1989], p. 344), Khirbet Abu et-Twain (A. Mazar, 'Iron Age Fortresses in the Judean Hills', *PEQ* 114 [1982], pp. 87-109 [104-105]), Deir Baghl (Kochavi, *Judaea*, p. 41), and Khirbet el-Qatt, Khirbet Kabar and Khirbet ez-Zawiyye, which even by Hoglund's own admission cannot be dated more precisely than *some time* in the Persian period.

117. For information on the road system in Persian period Palestine, see D.A. Dorsey, *The Roads and Highways of Ancient Israel* (Baltimore: The Johns Hopkins University Press, 1991); and D.F. Graf, 'The Persian Royal Road System in Syria-Palestine', *Trans* 6 (1993), pp. 149-68. To list just a few examples, note the positioning of the following open-court fortresses on important roads or at the intersections of important highways: Megiddo (R.S. Lamon and G.M. Shipton, *Megiddo I: Seasons of 1925-1934, Strata I-V* [UCOIP, 42; Chicago: University of Chicago Press, 1939], p. 88), Hazor (Y. Yadin *et al.*, *Hazor I: An Account of the First Season of Excavations, 1955* [Jerusalem: Magnes Press, 1958], pp. 45-63), Khirbet el-Qatt, Beth Zur (O.R. Sellers, 'Echoes of the 1931 Campaign', in P. Lapp [ed.], *The 1957 Excavation at Beth-Zur* [AASOR, 38; Cambridge, MA: ASOR, 1968], pp. 1-3 [1]), Tell Jemmeh (L.A. Sinclair, *An Archaeological Study of Gibeah (Tell el-Ful)* [AASOR, 34; New Haven: ASOR, 1960], p. 42 n. 34), and Tell el-Hesi.

the fortresses may have provided more than simply protection. South-east of Jemmeh stood two fortresses on the Spice Road that made its way from Arabia to Gaza on the coast.[118] These may not only have acted to guard the trade that moved along this economically vital route, but also have acted as ration stops, perhaps for troops in the area, caravanners or both. The fortification tablets from Persepolis make it clear that as travelers or work groups moved from place to place, they could, if authorized by the government, draw upon the rations at various stops along the way (*PF* 1285-1579). The rations were small enough that it appears that the supply stations were only a day apart.[119] The same infrastructure is assumed by the letter Arsames, the satrap of Egypt, sent with one of his officials traveling from Babylonia to Egypt (*TAD* A6.9). It is addressed to the various *pqydn*, 'officers', on the official's route, and asks them to *hbw* [*lh p*]*tp mn byt' zyly zy bmdyntkm*, 'give [to him (the official) a ra]tion from my estate that is in your provinces'. The term *ptp*, 'ration', is also found in Aramaic summaries on the fortification tablets, where it can mean both daily rations given to workers (*PF* 855, 857, 858) or rations given to travelers (*PF* 1587, 2059).

So the fortresses along the Spice Road and elsewhere may have performed this function, as well. Another stop on the Spice Road may have been Tell el-Far'ah, from where we have a record of a number of poorly preserved ostraca. What can be read on them, however, is reminiscent of Arad Aramaic ostracon number five,[120] that begins *hb lpd' l*, 'Give to Pedael', signaling a disbursement of goods either to military or civilian personnel. At Far'ah we likely see a ration stop along the Spice Road that functioned like ration stops on roads elsewhere in Palestine and throughout the Persian empire, here enabling transportation on an important economic route. The fortresses eased the way for military and administrative personnel as well as merchants. The troops that manned them, moreover, were not under the control of the local authorities, but that of the king. The roads and their fortresses existed to break down borders, and would have facilitated the flow of all sorts of foreign commerce and

118. R. Cohen, 'Solomon's Negev Defense Line Contained Three Fewer Fortresses', *BARev* 12.4 (1986), pp. 40-45.

119. R.T. Hallock, *Persepolis Fortification Tablets* (UCOIP, 92; Chicago: University of Chicago Press, 1969), pp. 40-45.

120. Naveh, 'Published and Unpublished Aramaic Ostraca', pp. 116-17. Examples include *hb lqwsdkr*, 'Give to Qosdakar', *hb ldlwy*, 'Give to Dalluy' and so on. The names listed here are Edomite, Hebrew and possibly Persian.

people through Yehud and Palestine. The evidence of foreign trade in Yehud noted above, then, is hardly surprising, since a number of these fortresses, such as the ones at Beth Zur and Khirbet et-Twain, clearly fall within the borders of Yehud. Where we have Persian military organization we have foreigners, at the very least the Persian leaders of the degels, but more likely a far more widespread phenomenon as the Jericho ostracon suggests. And if the records from Elephantine are any guide, we should expect quite a variety of foreigners in the units that manned these garrisons.

c. *Persian Fiscal Administration*

Much of our information regarding the Persian fiscal administration depends not only on the information from Palestine but also on the more extensive records left to us from parts of the empire other than Across-the-River.[121] Records from Southern Palestine show goods distributed to military functionaries and others, much as at Tell el-Far'ah and Arad, suggesting similar collection and disbursement centers administered by the Persian government. An ostracon from Beersheba beginning *hb byt ḥpr*, 'Give to the house of *ḥpr*',[122] again shows that disbursements were given out as well as taken in. But the majority of texts from Arad, Beersheba and

121. In documents from Elephantine we know of a central storehouse for goods in kind and for silver, collected as taxes and paid out to civil servants. There may have been one or more than one such institution in each given community; at any rate, at Elephantine we have record of *bgnz' gwy'*, 'the internal treasury', to which goods were brought and paid out to military personnel (*TAD* C3.19), *ywdn' zy mlk'*, 'the storehouse of the king' (P. Grelot, *Documents araméens d'Egypte* [Literature anciennes du Proche-Orient, 5; Paris: Cerf, 1972], p. 402 reads this as *gwrn' zy mlk'*, 'the granary of the king') within the confines of the temple of YHW (A4.5), and *'wṣr' zy mlk'*, 'the treasury of the king' (B3.4). From documents recording tariffs exacted from maritime commerce in Egypt we know of tax, both in silver and in kind, deposited in *byt mlk'*, 'the storehouse of the king' (C3.7). A number of Babylonian texts mention a *nakandu šarri*, 'royal storehouse, treasury', under the control of Manushtanu, the king's nephew, while other texts from the archive mention the *bīt šarri*, 'house of the king', as the recipient of *ilku* tax paid on bow fiefs. The *bīt kari* contained rent due on royal dates and the 'king's share', while elsewhere in Babylonia we find mention of the *kaṣir*, 'treasury', supervised by the Persian Bagasaru, called the *rab kaṣir*, 'chief of the treasury' and *ganzabara*, 'treasurer' (C. Tuplin, 'The Administration of the Achaemenid Empire', in Ian Carradice [ed.], *Coinage and Administration in the Athenian and Persian Empires* [BAR International Series, 343; Oxford: BAR, 1987], pp. 109-66 [129]).

122. Naveh, 'The Aramaic Ostraca from Tel Beer-Sheba', no. 50.1 (p. 192).

Southern Palestine appear to be receipts for taxes paid in kind. The prototypical text of those in question is this Aramaic one from Southern Palestine: *b10 lkslw šnt 2 hn'l lqws br ḥwry 'škr plpws lyd 'bd'sy mšḥ s3*, 'On the tenth of Kislev, year 2, Alqos son Huri brought in the tribute of Philip to the hand of Abdisi. Oil: 3 seah'.[123] We should note that the Aramaic term *'škr*, 'tribute', is found frequently on ritual objects from Persepolis given as tribute.[124] The formula of delivery inscribed on these objects, *lyd PN gnzbr'*, 'to the hand of PN the treasurer', indicates to which fiscal administrator these objects were given as tribute. The *lyd PN* formula is also found in texts from Palestine that fall nicely into the same context: the delivery of tribute to a central storehouse.[125] Some of the texts state clearly that this is a delivery to a storehouse (*msknt'*) and name the official to whom it was delivered; others are much shorter and so less specific,[126] making it uncertain whether they document a reception of tax in kind or a disbursement of goods.

What we find in Palestine in no way differs from evidence encountered elsewhere in the empire. Taxes in kind are collected from the population for the use of the central government. Xenophon claimed that maintenance of the garrisons in a given area was supplied by local officials (*Oec*. 4.6), and Herodotus, in his list of satrapies and their annual tribute, noted that 140 talents of Cilicia's tax remained in the satrapy to maintain the cavalry stationed there (3.90), and that 120,000 units of grain were paid by Egypt as part of its yearly tax for the upkeep of Persian troops stationed in Memphis (3.91). The documents from Persepolis are mainly concerned

123. Eph'al and Naveh, *Aramaic Ostraca*, no. 98 (p. 52).

124. Raymond Brown, who first published these inscriptions, interpreted the term as a reference to haoma, the ritual drink of the Persians (*Aramaic Ritual Texts from Persepolis* [UCOIP, 91; Chicago: University of Chicago Press, 1970], pp. 53-55), but the term is clearly cognate with Hebrew, *'eškar*, 'tribute', and neo-Assyrian *iškaru*, 'tax'. See also its occurrence in the *Targum Sheni* of Est. 1.3.

125. So, e.g., *b5 lsywn šnt 7 hyty n'wm mn rmt' 'l yd 'gr' lm*[*skn*]*t' ḥs 16*, 'On the fifth of Sivan, year 7, Naum brought from Ramta to the hand of Agra, to the storehouse; wheat: 16 seah' (Eph'al and Naveh, *Aramaic Ostraca*, no. 90 [p. 49]); *b11 l'b šnt 7 'lqws lbny qwṣy lyd ḥz'l mn zpt' ḥ s 10 lmsknt' ḥ s 20*, 'On the eleventh of Ab, year 7, Alqos to the sons of Qosy, to the hand of Hazael, from the loan; wheat: 10 seah. To the storehouse; wheat: 20 seah' (no. 92 [p. 50]); etc. More frequently, however, we simply find the formula *lPN*.

126. As only one example among many, *ḥlpt lb'l 'yd qmḥ s 2 b 9 l'b šnt 14*, 'Halipat to Baalid; flour: 2 seah, on the ninth of Ab, year 14' (Lemaire, *Nouvelles inscriptions*, no. 98 [p. 21]).

with disbursements paid from the public coffers as rations to people employed by the state, but they also refer to animals received as tax (*PF* 267-273) and silver received as tax (*PT* 85). The Palestinian tax receipts mention many products accepted by the storehouses: wheat, flour, barley, oil, wine, olives, and, in one case, even silver instead of wine.[127] It appears that the tax we see represented in the receipts from Palestine is simply the government's share of what was produced in the area, in the same way that the tariffs exacted from the ships in Persian period Egypt represented a percentage of their cargo.[128] Other epigraphical finds from the region may also record taxes received in the Persian period, although in many cases this is simply a guess as to the function of particular ostraca.[129] James Christoph has concluded that the Yehud stamps were impressed upon jars that were originally used for trade purposes, believing that if they had been used for the collection of in-kind taxes they would have had a larger distribution. What he discovered, however, was a close connection between the sites he designates as 'forts' and the Yehud seals, suggesting that they were in fact used for the collection of in-kind taxes for Persian fortresses in and around the province.[130]

127. The latter text is Eph'al and Naveh, *Aramaic Ostraca*, no. 16 (p. 25): *b28 lkslw yhb ḥlpt lyhw'nh dmy ḥmr' m 8*, 'On the twenty-eighth of Kislev, Halfat gave to Yehoanah the value of the wine, 8 maah'.

128. For these records of the shipping tax in Egypt see *TAD* C3.7. The ostracon from the port city of Eilat mentioned earlier that contained the Aramaic *qrplgs*, apparently a loanword from the Greek *karpologos*, 'collector of taxes in kind', also points in this direction (Glueck, 'Ostraca from Elath', pp. 7-9).

129. An ostracon from Ashdod (written either in Aramaic or the language of Ashdod) contains the cryptic message *krm zbdyh pg*, 'the vineyard of Zebediah; half (a jar)' (J. Naveh, 'An Aramaic Ostracon from Ashdod', *Atiqot* [Eng] 9–10 [1970], pp. 200-201) a message that may be a receipt or simply a description of the contents of a jar. It is at least possible that this fifth-century ostracon is in some way related to a number of fourth-century ostraca found at Tell Jemmeh (about 50 kilometers to the south-east) that mention *ḥmr krm zby(dy)*, 'the wine of the vineyard of Zebedi' (Naveh, 'Aramaic Ostraca and Jar Inscriptions', p. 50). Notably, one of them adds the reception formula *qdm PN*, 'before PN', present also on the ritual objects at Persepolis delivered as tribute. The formula, which appears with the more common *lyd PN* or *'l yd PN*, may be added to some texts in order to indicate an official who acted as a witness to the transaction (see *PR* 5 and 18 as representative examples). A broken fragment of an Aramaic ostracon from Kadesh Barnea with the writing *'škr ṭb*, 'the tribute of *tb* [ ]' or 'good tribute' (R. Cohen, 'Kadesh-Barnea: The Israelite Fortress', in *NEAEHL*, III, pp. 843-47 [847]) is almost certainly part of a receipt for a tax payment.

130. Cited in Carter, *The Emergence of Yehud*, pp. 282-83. See especially the map

These taxes in kind would have been used to pay and supply the local garrisons—a soldier at Elephantine wrote of 'the ration that will be given to me from the storehouse of the king' (*TAD* B3.13)—and it seems that work groups obligated in some way to perform services for the government were also so reimbursed. This is most clearly demonstrated in the texts from Persepolis that are largely concerned with the payment of rations to civilian work groups of all sorts of professions.[131] Traces of a similar system may be gleaned from the Murashu texts.[132] It is only common sense to believe that the province of Yehud also contained local garrisons in the countryside and urban centers to protect the empire's interests, and that they benefited from the same taxation system we have witnessed elsewhere in Palestine and throughout the Persian-controlled areas. The groups of **pᵉlākîm* mentioned in Nehemiah 3 as contributing to the construction of Jerusalem's walls are probably an example of this. Aaron Demsky has helpfully linked the Hebrew term *pelek* to Akkadian *pilku*, 'work tax' or 'tax in the form of conscripted labor'.[133] In neo-Assyrian texts the *pilku* operate as work battalions for royal projects, especially walls and buildings, and so it appears that in this narrative of the reconstruction of Jerusalem's walls, writes Demsky, various groups were conscripted to fulfill tax obligations.[134] It is likely that these groups, while on *pilku* duty, were supported by rations from the royal storehouses, especially as Nehemiah writes that the Persian government supplied the wood that was used for the rebuilding of Jerusalem's walls (Neh. 2.8).

The biblical narrative also mentions three particular Persian period taxes by name: the series of *mndh blw whlk*, listed three times in the Aramaic portion of Ezra (4.13, 20; 7.24), the first of which is paralleled by the

on p. 284 that clearly show that the majority of the find sites were fortresses, and n. 70.

131. The treasury and fortification tablets refer to groups of many different sizes, and amounts owed to individuals of various ranks, with payment to them varying accordingly. *PF* 881, e.g., concerns payment to a group of 259 workers 'subsisting on rations', while *PF* 959–62 refer to payments to a group of 702 workers. In *PT* 9, payment is authorized for 'stoneworkers, (who) from Egypt came to Parsa', and *PT* 18 lists the differing sizes of payments granted to different workers, apparently of differing rank.

132. Stolper, *Entrepreneurs and Empire*, p. 143.

133. Scholars in the past often believed that the mention of the *pelek* and a concomitant official (such as *śr ḥṣy plk yrwšlm* 3.9, 12 or *śr plk byt hkrm* 3.14) from areas around Yehud referred to sub-districts within the bounds of the province. (So, e.g., Stern, *Material Culture*, p. 239.)

134. A. Demsky, '*Pelekh* in Nehemiah 3', *IEJ* 33 (1983), pp. 242-44.

Hebrew *mdt hmlk* in Neh. 5.4.[135] Each of these has a cognate in contemporary texts from Nippur in Babylonia, and the *hlk* and *mndh* are found also among the Aramaic texts from Egypt.[136] Our best epigraphical information from Palestine concerns taxes in kind, much of which likely remained in the province to subsidize local administrative expenses such as garrisons and work groups. We know from Herodotus that each satrapy was obligated to pay an annual sum of tribute in silver, but it is impossible to say just what effect that might have had on the province of Yehud.

We can imagine that the ubiquitous tax system of Persia was hardly beloved throughout the empire. As a drain on the populace and, in some places, a symbol of a hated regime, it should come as no surprise that when Egypt revolted in 465 the rebels, before any other act, 'cast out the Persians levying tribute from Egypt' (Diodorus 11.71.3). This is indicative of the power, both social and economic, that the Persian fiscal administration wielded. Because it was omnipresent, it paid no respect to borders. People were forced to respect its authority, and would have been well aware of its presence whenever they paid it or whenever they saw the military and *pilku* forces that benefited from it. The ubiquitous tax system would have contributed to the anxiety of the Jerusalem temple community for, as Neh. 9.36-37 interpreted it, it was part of God's punishment for the community's past and present sins. It was understood by the community as a visible sign of God's anger for the failure to observe social morality, an expression of the power of the Persians to destroy the community should

135. Note that Ezra 4.20 has *middâ* rather than *mindâ*.

136. The *hlk* known from Egypt is, as I mentioned earlier, the kind of tax one pays on semi-feudal holdings that are alienable subject to the command of the Persian authority. The term is cognate with Akkadian *ilku*, as is evident from neo-Babylonian texts where an Aramaic summary is given of the Akkadian contents. (E.g. one Akkadian text [BE 10.78] begins *10 šiqlu kaspu ni-din-*tu_4 *ar-ki-*tu_4 *il-ki gamrūtu ša šatti 3* KAM^{LU}*da-ri-ia-muš šarri*, '10 shekels of silver, the latter gift, the complete tax of the year 3 of Darius the king', and in its Aramaic summary [*šṭr bnḥ zy ksp ḥlk' zy pry' zy šnt 3 dryhwš*, 'the record of the gift of silver, the tax that was paid of the year 3 of Darius'] *bnh* seems to parallel Akkadian *nidintu arkitu* and *hlk* to parallel *ilki gamrūtu*). Only rarely in Babylonia do we find this tax levied on non-feudal holdings or paid in a commodity other than silver (Tuplin, 'The Administration of the Achaemenid Empire', p. 154). The *mndt* also appears in a text from Egypt in an order from Arsames that commands that the *mndt* be sent from his lands to him (*TAD* A6.13). The Akkadian *mandattu* appears in Murashu texts dealing with husbandry, where it appears to stipulate an annual surcharge paid over and above the rent paid for a particular piece of land (Stolper, *Entrepreneurs and Empire*, p. 140).

God desire it, and so an incentive to induce members to strengthen social integration.

d. *Persia and Foreign Religious Institutions*

Persian religious tolerance is widely touted by scholars, the paradigm example usually advanced being the Cyrus Cylinder discovered in Babylon, on which Cyrus proclaims his loyalty to Marduk and his care of the sanctuaries of Babylonia neglected by Nabonidus. There is actually nothing on the cylinder itself that addresses any general policy of a return of exiles or support of any sanctuary outside of Babylonia. The cities named in the cylinder were in fact those located in politically sensitive areas, and Cyrus hoped to win the good will of the populace by restoring the status quo ante there.[137] In general, political amelioration appears to govern the attitude of the Persian leadership to foreign religious institutions. It would permit and even promote the flourishing of local cults if this provided them with political capital. But gods and their temples were often dangerous institutions, centers of nationalism and revolt and, more benignly, economic drain, and the Persian kings did not hesitate to check any danger such cults posed to their empire. As the Nabonidus Chronicle makes clear, Nabonidus had taken up residence in Teima, meaning that it was impossible to conduct the Akitu festival in Babylon in his absence.[138] There was political sense in Cyrus's courtship of the good feelings of the powerful priests of Esagila, the temple of Marduk, for he, a foreigner, proved a more pious king than Nabonidus who neglected the Marduk cult. Udjahorresnet, an officer of the Egyptian navy who defected to Cambyses during the Persian invasion of Egypt in 525, wrote in 518 that Cambyses actively supported the cult of the goddess Neith at Sais, worshipping before the goddess and restoring her cult and working to eliminate ritual impurities.[139] It is possible that Cambyses also participated in the worship of Marduk at Esagil, although the chronicle is broken at this point.[140] Seals and reliefs of Cambyses from Egypt show him in local rather than Elamite dress, kneeling before the local gods and proclaiming himself as their

137. A. Kuhrt, 'The Cyrus Cylinder and Achaemenid Imperial Policy', *JSOT* 25 (1983), pp. 83-97.

138. Text in Grayson, *Assyrian and Babylonian Chronicles*, no. 7.2.5-24 (pp. 124-27).

139. Translation of text in M. Lichtheim, *Ancient Egyptian Literature*, III (Berkeley: University of California Press, 1980), pp. 36-41.

140. Grayson, *Assyrian and Babylonian Chronicles*, no. 7.3.24-28 (p. 127).

favorite,[141] even as Cyrus so proclaimed himself in relation to Marduk.[142]

On the other hand, Cambyses did not always enact policies in favor of the temples, if doing so was deleterious to his empire. The Demotic Chronicle records Cambyses's order to end government subsidies to all the temples of Egypt with three exceptions, and even these temples' income is sharply curtailed.[143] The letter of the Jewish community in Elephantine to the governors of Yehud and Samaria at the end of the fifth century boasts that the temple of YHW stood before the coming of Cambyses, by whom *'gwry 'lhy mṣryn kl mgrw*, 'all the temples of the gods of Egypt were overthrown' (*TAD* A4.7), implying that their temple was favored by the Persian kings. That all the Egyptian temples were destroyed is obviously hyperbole, but one understands thereby that Cambyses's reputation cannot be judged solely on the basis of Udjahorresnet's inscription, and that Herodotus's account of Cambyses's impious actions in Egypt may not be wrong on all accounts. The Persians would destroy temples that were involved in nationalistic rebellions against the empire (Herodotus 6.18-20; Strabo, *Geog.* 16.1.5; Arrian, *Anab.* 3.16.4). The Persian administration also regulated the income of the temples in Babylonia, which were absorbed into the Persian taxation network.[144] Fiscal and political concerns would seem to dominate the monarchy's approach to foreign religious institutions.

141. M.A. Dandamaev, *A Political History of the Achaemenid Empire* (trans. W.J. Vogelsang; Leiden: E.J. Brill, 1989), pp. 76-77.

142. All of this suggests, then, that the portrait that Herodotus paints of Cambyses's violently eccentric sojourn in Egypt (3.27-38) and that is followed by other classical sources may not be wholly accurate. His concluding statements regarding the king's actions there—'In every way it therefore seems to me that Cambyses was quite mad, for he would not have otherwise attempted to deride religion and custom' (3.38)—may in part be the result of anti-Persian sentiment that circulated in Egypt after Cambyses's death.

143. Text and translation in W. Spiegelberg (ed.), *Die sogenannte demotische Chronik: Des Pap. 215 der Bibliotheque Nationale zu Paris* (Leipzig: J.C. Hinrichs, 1914), pp. 32-33.

144. Texts from Ur refer to land as simultaneously belonging to Sin and as bow land, while other Ur texts refer to taxes on temple lands as *baru*, a kind of tax that was a subdivision of the *ilku* tax charged on feudal holdings. It appears, in short, that the crown treated some Babylonian temples as administrative estates, placing them within government regulated land tenure (M. Stolper, 'Mesopotamia, 482–330 B.C.', in D.M. Lewis *et al.* [eds.], *The Cambridge Ancient History*, VI [Cambridge: Cambridge University Press, 2nd edn, 1994], pp. 234-60 [250]).

Temple construction was also monitored and approved by the central government. One of the best examples of this comes from the city of Xanthos in Lycia, where a fourth-century trilingual inscription was discovered.[145] The Aramaic, Greek and Lycian texts are roughly similar. They tell of the intention of the citizens of Xanthos and the neighboring towns to establish a temple and cult for Basileus Kaunioi and Arkesimai, including the appointment of a hereditary priesthood, the gift of land from the city to the cult, and an annual donation from city and citizens to the cult. The Greek and Lycian texts record the town's appeal to establish the cult, and the Aramaic text records the government's approval, repeating to a great extent the original request in its own text. Notably, the Greek text ends with the plea *Pixōtaros de kurios estō*, 'may Pixodoros establish it as lawful', while the corresponding line in the Aramaic text is *dth dk ktb zy mh<ḥ>sn*, 'he (Pixodoros) wrote this law that he is enforcing'.[146] (The end of the Lycian text contains hapaxes of unknown meaning.) As the official order approving the request, the Aramaic text publicly established it as law, naming all the stipulations outlined therein as *dth* or *data*, 'law' (a loanword from Old Persian), and prefacing the request with the authoritative *pgswd*[*r*]... *ḥštrpn'*... *'* [*mr*], 'Pixodoros the satrap says...'

This literary style of a Persian official issuing an order and including verbatim an earlier correspondence in the order occurs a number of times in the Arsames correspondence from Egypt.[147] The same style is employed in Ezra 6.1-12 which records correspondence between Darius and Tattenai, the governor of Across-the-River. In his letter, Darius quotes an original decree from Cyrus that authorized the construction of the temple in Jerusalem, specifying its dimensions and ordering that the vessels plundered by Nebuchadnezzar be restored (6.3-5). J. Briend has suggested that this decree itself was actually the verbatim repetition of a request of the Aaronid priests to Cyrus at the end of the exile,[148] much in the same

145. H. Metzger, 'La stèle trilingue récemment découverte au Létoon de Xanthos: Le texte grec', *CRAIBL* (1974), pp. 82-93; E. Laroche, 'La stèle trilingue récemment découverte au Létoon de Xanthos: Le texte lycien', *CRAIBL* (1974), pp. 115-25; A. Dupont-Sommer, 'La stèle trilingue récemment découverte au Létoon de Xanthos: Le texte araméen', *CRAIBL* (1974), pp. 132-49.

146. This follows Dupont-Sommer's emendation of the text, which is the only way I can make sense of it.

147. See, e.g., *TAD* A6.3, 6.8.

148. J. Briend, 'L'édit de Cyrus et sa valeur historique', *Trans* 11 (1996), pp. 33-44 [44].

way that the Aramaic text at Xanthos that authorizes the institution of the cult there quotes the request first issued to the government in Greek.[149] This also makes it clear, as does the correspondence of Ezra 4–6, that the temple in Jerusalem was reconstructed only with the authorization of the Persian government.

We also have evidence that the Persian administration insisted on having a voice in the appointment of important temple officials. On 21 April 492, Pherendates, the satrap of Egypt, writes to the *wab*-priests of Khnum, the chief deity of Syene, stating that he will appoint the *lesonis*, an important temple administrator in charge of deliveries to the temple and burnt offerings for Khnum, and that Darius had already set the requirements an individual must meet in order to become *lesonis*.[150] At Xanthos, too, it seems that the person who would act as high priest for Basileus Kaunioi and Ankesimai had to be approved by the satrap. A letter from a Hananiah to the Jewish community in Elephantine in 419 (*TAD* A4.1) concerning the details of how Passover was to be celebrated states that even these cultic stipulations were approved by the crown and satrap. Hananiah writes that the order *mn mlk' šlyḥ 'l 'rš*[*m*], 'has been sent from the king to Arsa[mes]'.

We have no reason to doubt that the Persian administration kept as close a watch on the cultic affairs in Jerusalem as they did in other parts of the empire. The story of Ezra 5.3–6.15, in which Tattenai, the governor of Across-the-River, asks that the official archives in Babylon be searched for authorization regarding the reconstruction of the Jerusalem temple, is as good an example of this proposition as any. It is at least possible that Jerusalem's priests were exempt from taxes (certainly the Artaxerxes letter of Ezra 7.12-26 insists that they were), and that the government authorized the transfer of the sacred vessels to the temple that Nebuchadnezzar had robbed, and it is at least within the realm of possibility that the Persians

149. Perhaps the edict of Ezra 1.2-4 is also a royal restatement of a request for repatriation and restoration of the temple on the part of the Israelite exiles, although, as Briend has noted, its language suspiciously suits the theological agenda of the redactor of Ezra 1–6 ('L'édit de Cyrus', p. 43). More likely it is a freer rendition into Hebrew of an original ordinance issued in Aramaic (perhaps Ezra 6.3-5).

150. Translation in B. Porten, *The Elephantine Papyri in English* (DMOA, 22; Leiden: E.J. Brill, 1996), no. C1 (p. 290). The *wab*-priests actually reject Pherendates's authority, for they appoint one Eskhnumpemet as *lesonis* on or before 7 May 492, but do not inform the satrap of this decision until 25 December. See Porten, *The Elephantine Papyri*, nos. C2, C3 (pp. 290-91) and p. 289.

demanded a say in the appointment of the chief priest, or approved certain ritual practices, as was the case elsewhere in the empire. And since at least one of the Jerusalem priests minted his own coins in the second half of the fourth century,[151] we should not be surprised if the Persians monitored both the economy and the leadership of the temple. While the Persian central authority allowed religious freedom where it made political and economic sense, it otherwise kept a close watch on temple priesthoods and finances. The Persians' ability to interfere in temple affairs made it clear to the temple assembly that another destruction and exile could occur at the whim of the monarch. Nothing, not even God's house, was exempt from the transgressive power of Persia. And like the unavoidable presence of the Persian military and taxation system, Persian oversight of the temple would only have increased the anxiety of a community worried that foreign influences were destroying it. The presence of the Persians was one influence of which the assembly could never rid itself, and it was an influence that penetrated to the center of the community's holiness. It was also taken as a sign, as the anxiety expressed in Ezra–Nehemiah makes clear, that foreign control was God's punishment for the society's lax internal integration.

4. *Conclusion: Foreign Influences in Yehud and the Witch-craze Anxiety*

We have seen a picture in this work of a temple assembly with a strong desire to separate from its neighbors. Through its theology and its use of genealogies and even, to some extent, the placement of its settlements, we find a community adamant that its members not associate with the people around it. Even by the time of Nehemiah, a century after the return from exile, the community understands itself as the exiles, the captives from the captivity. It is the remnant, and no one but these people who have formed their identity through the rhetoric of divine punishment, who are considered Yehudim or members of the *qāhāl*.

151. A coin inscribed *yḥn*[*n*] *hkhn*, 'Yohanan the priest', belongs to the fourth-century Philisto-Arabian group of coins, and closely resembles the *yhd* coins with the inscription *yḥzqyh hpḥh*, 'Hezekiah the governor', that date to the mid-fourth century. See D. Barag, 'Some Notes on a Silver Coin of Johanan the High Priest', *BA* 48 (1985), pp. 166-68; and *idem*, 'A Silver Coin of Yohanan the High Priest and the Coinage of Judea in the Fourth Century B.C.', *Israel Numismatic Journal* 9 (1986/1987), pp. 4-21.

This separation, and all the theological ideas and experiences that undergirded it, was an ideal, but it was hardly one to which the community could seriously live up. Yehud, like the rest of Palestine, was pervaded by foreigners and their goods, by Persian soldiers and administrators, and by all the cultural products, material and otherwise, that accompanied such a flow of foreigners. How could the community remain separate when merchants, with the apparent protection and support of the Persian administration, wandered through the province and into Jerusalem? How could it remain pure when some of its members lived in foreign areas, or when Persian garrisons were stationed throughout the country?

The assembly's attempt to create absolutely strong external boundaries remained in the realm of fantasy. It is not so difficult to explain the anxiety that we see in the Persian period texts regarding the neglect of the temple cult and social collapse. The fact of the matter is that the temple assembly was a competitive community. It had to compete for the loyalty of its members who had plenty of exposure to foreign worldview and sources of power. The situation of Persian period Palestine was such that one did not have far to go to encounter foreigners and their religions and ideas and cultures. The marketplace of one's hometown, even if it was Jerusalem, would likely suffice. And so we find a society that again and again expresses the fear that its members do not pay enough attention to the temple cult—an issue of no little importance since, as we know, it is participation in its rites and contribution to its needs that signals an acceptance of social morality and obeisance to the social order. When a society's law is thought to come from God, and many within that society abandon the worship of God, the threat this poses to social integration is not difficult to interpret.

Social anxiety would hardly have been lessened by Persian oversight of the assembly and its cult. What Cyrus has given Artaxerxes may take away; in a society founded upon an exile interpreted as God's punishment every manifestation of Persian power seems just another indication of the ease with which the destruction of the society could be effected. Ezra–Nehemiah does not paint the Persian monarchy the way Daniel portrays Anitochus as the enemy of God—indeed, the picture in Ezra–Nehemiah is quite the opposite, as Japhet has shown.[152] So the assembly consists of 'slaves', graciously granted a probationary period by God in which it may either atone for the sins of Israel or face utter destruction at the hands of

152. Japhet, 'Sheshbazzar and Zerubbabel', p. 73.

the Persians, the instrument of divine wrath. The very present arms of the Persian administration were adopted as evidence for this point of view: one slip-up, one egregious flaunting of God's law, and into captivity it goes, this time forever. This is precisely the point of Ezra 9 and Nehemiah 9. And since the community interpreted foreign control as a sign of God's displeasure, the prevalence of the Persian administration would have been seen as a further sign of Israel's sin and its need to curb it—or, as an anthropologist would put it, its need to increase social integration.

Faced with this collapse of social morality—what the community called a failure to follow God's law—and sure that divine punishment was to follow—for that was how the community interpreted the Persian presence—the temple assembly took precisely the action we would expect a community with its particular social boundaries and concomitant worldview to take: it engaged in a ritualized act of purification, and this is recorded in Ezra 9–10. In such an action the community works together and its members implicitly recommit themselves to the social order and thus shore up the weakening internal integration. So many were the sources of foreign influence responsible for this anxiety, though, that the community could not find an obvious group of dissidents to blame. Its anxiety led to a witch-hunt for precisely that reason. The community turned its focus to the foreign women because it had nowhere obvious to turn. The issue was resolved only when the community purified itself of these contaminants, forcing a modicum of public expressions of allegiance to the social order.

BIBLIOGRAPHY

Ackroyd, P.R., *I and II Chronicles, Ezra, Nehemiah* (TBC; London: SCM Press, 1973).

Alt, A., 'Die Rolle Samarias bei der Entstehung des Judentums', in *idem*, *Kleine Schriften zur Geschichte des Volkes Israel*, II (Munich: C.H. Beck, 1953), pp. 316-37.

Ariel, D.T., 'Coins from Excavations at Tel Nahariya, 1982', *Atiqot* (Eng) 22 (1993), pp. 125-32.

Avigad, N., *Bullae and Seals from a Post-Exilic Judean Archive* (Qedem Reports, 4; Jerusalem: Hebrew University, 1976).

Avner, R., and E. Eshel, 'A Juglet with a Phoenician Inscription from a Recent Excavation in Jaffa, Israel', *Trans* 12 (1996), pp. 59-63.

Balensi, J. *et al.*, 'Le niveau perse à Tell Abu Hawam, résultats récents et signification dans le contexte regional cotier', *Trans* 2 (1990), pp. 125-36.

Barag, D., 'A Silver Coin of Yohanan the High Priest and the Coinage of Judea in the Fourth Century B.C.', *Israel Numismatic Journal* 9 (1986/1987), pp. 4-21.

—'Some Notes on a Silver Coin of Johanan the High Priest', *BA* 48 (1985), pp. 166-68.

Batten, L.W., *The Books of Ezra and Nehemiah* (ICC; New York: Charles Scribner's Sons, 1913).

Bell, C., *Ritual Theory, Ritual Practice* (Oxford: Oxford University Press, 1992).

Bennett, W.J., and J.A. Blakely, *Tell el-Hesi: The Persian Period (Stratum V)* (ASORER; Winona Lake, IN: Eisenbrauns, 1989).

Berger, P., *The Sacred Canopy: Elements of a Sociological Theory of Religion* (New York: Anchor, 1969).

Berquist, J.L., *Judaism in Persia's Shadow: A Social and Historical Approach* (Minneapolis: Fortress Press, 1995).

Bikai, P.M., 'Observations on Archaeological Evidence for the Trade between Israel and Tyre', *BASOR* 258 (1985), pp. 71-72.

Blakely, J.A., and F.L. Horton, Jr, 'South Palestinian Bes Vessels of the Persian Period', *Levant* 18 (1986), pp. 111-19.

Blenkinsopp, J., *Ezra–Nehemiah: A Commentary* (OTL; Philadelphia: Westminster Press, 1988).

—'The Social Context of the "Outsider Woman" in Proverbs 1–9', *Bib* 72 (1991), pp. 457-73.

—'Temple and Society in Achaemenid Judah', in P.R. Davies (ed.), *Second Temple Studies: 1. Persian Period* (JSOTSup, 117; Sheffield: JSOT Press, 1991), pp. 22-53.

Bloch, M., 'Death, Women and Power', in M. Bloch and J. Parry (eds.), *Death and the Regeneration of Life* (Cambridge: Cambridge University Press, 1982), pp. 211-30.

—*Ritual, History and Power: Selected Papers in Anthropology* (London School of Economics Monographs on Social Anthropology, 58; London: Athlone Press, 1989).

Bongenaar, A.C.V.M., *The Neo-Babylonian Ebabbar Temple at Sippar: Its Administration and its Prosopography* (Uitgaven van het Nederlands Historisch-Archaeologisch Instituut te

Instanbul, 80; Leiden: Nederlands Historisch-Archaeologisch Instituut te Instsanbul, 1997).

Bonnet, C., 'Antipatros l'Ascalonite dévoré par un lion: Commentaire de *CIS* I, 115', *Sem* 38 (1990), pp. 39-47.

Borger, R., *Die Inschriften Asarhaddons Konigs von Assyrien* (*AfO*, 9; Osnabruck: Biblio, 1967).

Bourdieu, P., *Outline of a Theory of Practice* (trans. Richard Nice; Cambridge Studies in Social Anthropology, 16; Cambridge: Cambridge University Press, 1977).

Briend, J., 'L'édit de Cyrus et sa valeur historique', *Trans* 11 (1996), pp. 33-44.

—'L'occupation de la Galilee occidentale à l'époque perse', *Trans* 2 (1990), pp. 109-23.

Broshi, M., 'Megadim, Tel', in *NEAEHL*, III, pp. 1001-1003.

Brown, R., *Aramaic Ritual Texts from Persepolis* (UCOIP, 91; Chicago: University of Chicago Press, 1970).

Cameron, G., *Persepolis Treasury Tablets* (UCOIP, 65; Chicago: University of Chicago Press, 1948).

Carter, C.E., *The Emergence of Yehud in the Persian Period: A Social and Demographic Study* (JSOTSup, 294; Sheffield: Sheffield Academic Press, 1999).

Clines, D.J.A., *Ezra, Nehemiah, Esther* (NCBC, 15; Grand Rapids: Eerdmans, 1984).

—'The Nehemiah Memoir: The Perils of Autobiography', in *idem*, *What Does Eve Do to Help? And Other Readerly Questions to the Old Testament* (JSOTSup, 94; Sheffield: JSOT Press, 1990), pp. 124-64.

Cohen, R., 'Kadesh-Barnea: The Israelite Fortress', in *NEAEHL*, III, pp. 843-47.

—'Solomon's Negev Defense Line Contained Three Fewer Fortresses', *BARev* 12.4 (1986), pp. 40-45.

Conder, C.R., 'The Prayer of Ben Abdas on the Dedication of the Temple of Joppa', *PEQ* (1892), pp. 170-74.

Cross, F.M., 'A New Aramaic Stele from Tayma', *CBQ* 48 (1986), pp. 387-94.

—'The Papyri and their Historical Implications', in P.W. Lapp and N.L. Lapp (eds.), *Discoveries in the Wadi ed-Daliyeh* (AASOR, 41; Cambridge: ASOR, 1974), pp. 17-29.

—'A Reconstruction of the Judean Restoration', *JBL* 94 (1975), pp. 4-18.

—'Samaria Papyrus 1: An Aramaic Slave Conveyance of 335 B.C.E. Found in the Wadi ed-Daliyeh', *EI* 18 (1985), pp. 7*-17*.

Dandamaev, M.A., *A Political History of the Achaemenid Empire* (trans. W.J. Vogelsang; Leiden: E.J. Brill, 1989).

Dar, S., *Landscape and Pattern: An Archaeological Survey of Samaria 800 BCE-636 CE* (BAR International Series, 308; Oxford: BAR, 1986).

Demsky, A., '*Pelekh* in Nehemiah 3', *IEJ* 33 (1983), pp. 242-44.

Deutsch, R., and M. Heltzer, *Forty New Ancient West Semitic Inscriptions* (Tel Aviv: Archaeological Center, 1994).

—'Numismatic Evidence from the Persian Period from the Sharon Plain', *Trans* 13 (1996), pp. 17-20.

Dorsey, D.A., *The Roads and Highways of Ancient Israel* (Baltimore: The Johns Hopkins University Press, 1991).

Dothan, M., 'Akko: Interim Excavation Report First Season, 1973/4', *BASOR* 224 (1976), pp. 1-48.

—'An Attic Red-Figured Bell-Krater from Tel 'Akko', *IEJ* 29 (1979), pp. 148-51.

—'A Phoenician Inscripton from 'Akko', *IEJ* 35 (1985), pp. 81-94.

Douglas, M., *Natural Symbols: Explorations in Cosmology* (New York: Vintage Books, 1973).

—*Purity and Danger: An Analysis of the Concepts of Pollution and Taboo* (London: Routledge & Kegan Paul, 1966).

Dumbrell, W.J., 'The Tell el-Maskhouta Bowls and the "Kingdom" of Qedar in the Persian Period', *BASOR* 203 (1973), pp. 33-44.

Dupont-Sommer, A., 'La stèle trilingue récemment découverte au Létoon de Xanthos: le texte araméen', *CRAIBL* (1974), pp. 132-49.

Durkheim, E., *The Elementary Forms of the Religious Life* (trans. J.W. Swain; New York: George Allen & Unwin, 1915).

Dyck, J.E., *The Theocratic Ideology of the Chronicler* (BIS, 33; Leiden: E.J. Brill, 1998).

Elayi, J., 'La diffusion des monnaies phéniciennes en Palestine', in E.-M. Laperrousaz and A. Lemaire (eds.), *La Palestine a l'époque perse* (Paris: Cerf, 1994), pp. 289-315.

—'Le phénomène monétaire dans les cites phéniciennes à l'époque perse', in T. Hackens and G. Mouchante (eds.), *Numismatique et histoire économique phéniciennes et puniques* (Studia Phoenicia, 9; Louvain-la-Neuve: Université Catholique de Louvain, 1992), pp. 21-31.

—'Presence grecque sur la côte palestinienne', in E.-M. Laperrousaz and A. Lemaire (eds.), *La Palestine à l'époque perse* (Paris: Cerf, 1994), pp. 245-60.

Elayi, J., and A.G. Elayi, *Treśors de monnaies phéniciennes et circulation monétaire (V^{e}-IVe siècles avant J.-C.)* (TransSup, 1; Paris: J. Gabalda, 1993).

Elgavish, J., 'Shiqmona', in *NEAEHL*, IV, pp. 1373-78.

Eph'al, I., *The Ancient Arabs: Nomads on the Borders of the Fertile Crescent 9th–5th Centuries B.C.* (Leiden: E.J. Brill, 1982).

Eph'al, I., and J. Naveh, *Aramaic Ostraca of the Fourth Century B.C. from Idumaea* (Jerusalem: Magnes Press, 1996).

Erikson, K., *Wayward Puritans: A Study in the Sociology of Deviance* (New York: John Wiley & Sons, 1966).

Eskenazi, T., *In an Age of Prose: A Literary Approach to Ezra–Nehemiah* (SBLMS, 36; Atlanta: Scholars Press, 1988).

—'Out from the Shadows: Biblical Women in the Post-Exilic Era', *JSOT* 54 (1992), pp. 25-43.

Eskenazi, T., and E.P. Judd, 'Marriage to a Stranger in Ezra 9–10', in T.C. Eskenazi and K.H. Richards (eds.), *Second Temple Studies: 2. Temple and Community in the Persian Period* (JSOTSup, 175; Sheffield: JSOT Press, 1994), pp. 266-85.

Fenn, R., *The End of Time: Religion, Ritual, and the Forging of the Soul* (Cleveland: Pilgrim, 1997).

Finkelstein, I., 'The Land of Ephraim Survey 1980–1987: Preliminary Report', *TA* 15–16 (1988/1989), pp. 117-83.

Finkelstein, I., and Y. Magen, *Archaeological Survey of the Hill Country of Benjamin* (Jerusalem: Israel Antiquities Authority, 1993).

Foley, R., *Humans before Humanity: An Evolutionary Perspective* (Oxford: Basil Blackwell, 1995).

Gal, Z., 'Galilee: Chalcolithic to Persian Periods', in *NEAEHL*, II, pp. 448-51.

Geertz, C., *The Interpretation of Cultures: Selected Essays* (New York: HarperCollins, 1973).

Geva, S., 'Archaeological Evidence for the Trade between Israel and Tyre?', *BASOR* 248 (1982), pp. 69-72.

Gibson, J.C.L., *Textbook of Syrian Semitic Inscriptions.* II. *Aramaic Inscriptions* (Oxford: Clarendon Press, 1975).

Glueck, N., 'Ostraca from Elath', *BASOR* 80 (1940), pp. 3-10.

Gophna, R., and M. Kochavi, 'An Archaeological Survey of the Plain of Sharon', *IEJ* 16 (1966), pp. 143-44.

Grabbe, L.L., *Ezra–Nehemiah* (London: Routledge, 1998).

—*Judaism from Cyrus to Hadrian* (2 vols.; Minneapolis: Fortress Press, 1992).

—'What was Ezra's Mission?', in T.C. Eskenazi and K.H. Richards (eds.), *Second Temple Studies: 2. Temple and Community in the Persian Period* (JSOTSup, 175; Sheffield: JSOT Press, 1994), pp. 286-99.

Graf, D.F., 'The Persian Royal Road System in Syria-Palestine', *Trans* 6 (1993), pp. 149-68.

Grayson, A.K., *Assyrian and Babylonian Chronicles* (Texts from Cuneiform Sources, 5; Locust Valley, NY: J.J. Augustin, 1975).

Greenfield, J.C., 'A Group of Phoenician City Seals', *IEJ* 35 (1985), pp. 129-34.

Grelot, P., *Documents araméens d'Egypte* (Literature anciennes du Proche-Orient, 5; Paris: Cerf, 1972).

Hallock, R.T., *Persepolis Fortification Tablets* (UCOIP, 92; Chicago: University of Chicago Press, 1969).

Hanson, P., *The Dawn of Apocalyptic* (Philadelphia: Fortress Press, 1975).

Heltzer, M., 'A Recently Published Babylonian Tablet and the Province of Judah after 516 B.C.E.', *Trans* 5 (1992), pp. 57-61.

Herzog, Z., 'Michmal, Tel', *NEAEHL*, III, pp. 1036-41.

Hill, A., 'Dating the Book of Malachi: A Linguistic Reexamination', in C.L. Meyers and M. O'Connor (eds.), *The Word of the Lord Shall Go Forth* (Festschrift D.N. Freedman; Winona Lake, IN: Eisenbrauns, 1983), pp. 77-89.

Hoglund, K., 'The Achaemenid Context', in P.R. Davies (ed.), *Second Temple Studies*: 1. *The Persian Period* (JSOTSup, 117; Sheffield: JSOT Press, 1991), pp. 54-72.

—*Achaemenid Imperial Administration in Syria-Palestine and the Missions of Ezra and Nehemiah* (SBLDS, 125; Atlanta: Scholars Press, 1992).

—'The Chronicler as a Historian: A Comparativist Perspective', in M.P. Graham, K.G. Hoglund and S.L. MacKenzie (eds.), *The Chronicler as Historian* (JSOTSup, 238; Sheffield: Sheffield Academic Press, 1997), pp. 19-29.

Janzen, D., 'The Meaning of *porneia* in Matthew 5.32 and 19.9: An Approach from the Study of Ancient Near Eastern Culture', *JSNT* 80 (2000), pp. 69-83.

—'The "Mission" of Ezra and the Persian Period Temple Community', *JBL* 119 (2000), pp. 619-43.

Japhet, S., *I and II Chronicles* (OTL; Louisville, KY: Westminster/John Knox Press, 1993).

—'Sheshbazzar and Zerubbabel: Against the Background of the Historical and Religious Tendencies of Ezra–Nehemiah', *ZAW* 94 (1982), pp. 66-98; 95 (1983), pp. 218-29.

—'Supposed Common Authorship of Chronicles and Ezra–Nehemiah Investigated Anew', *VT* 18 (1968), pp. 330-71.

Jaussen, A., and R. Savignac, *Missions archéologique en Arabie II* (Paris: Paul Geuthner, 1914).

Jay, N., *Throughout your Generations Forever: Sacrifice, Religion, and Paternity* (Chicago: University of Chicago Press, 1992).

Kaplan, J., 'The Archaeology and History of Tel Aviv-Jaffa', *BA* 35 (1972), pp. 66-95.

Katzenstein, H.J., 'Gaza in the Persian Period', *Trans* 1 (1989), pp. 67-86.

Keil, C.F., and F. Delitzsch, *The Books of Ezra, Nehemiah, and Esther* (trans. Sophia Taylor; Edinburgh: T. & T. Clark, 1888).

Kellermann, U., *Nehemia: Quellen, Uberlieferung und Geschichte* (Berlin: Alfred Töpelmann, 1967).

Kelly, T., 'Herodotus and the Chronology of the Kings of Sidon', *BASOR* 268 (1987), pp. 39-56.

Kent, R.G., *Old Persian: Grammar, Texts, Lexicon* (AOS, 33; New Haven: American Oriental Society, 1953).

Kippenberg, H.G., *Religion und Klassenbildung im antiken Judaea* (Göttingen: Vandenhoeck & Ruprecht, 1978).

Klingbeil, G.A., 'The Aramaic Ostraca from Lachish: A New Reading and Interpretation', *AUSS* 33 (1995), pp. 77-84.

Knauf, E.A., 'The Persian Administration in Arabia', *Trans* 2 (1990), pp. 201-17.

Kochavi, M. (ed.), *Judaea, Samaria and the Golan: Archaeological Survey 1967–1968* (Publications of the Archaeological Survey of Israel, 1; Jerusalem: Carta, 1972).

Kuhrt, A., 'The Cyrus Cylinder and Achaemenid Imperial Policy', *JSOT* 25 (1983), pp. 83-97.

Lamon, R.S., and G.M. Shipton, *Megiddo I: Seasons of 1925–1934, Strata I–V* (UCOIP, 42; Chicago: University of Chicago Press, 1939).

Laroche, E., 'La stèle trilingue récemment découverte au Létoon de Xanthos: Le texte lycien', *CRAIBL* (1974), pp. 115-25.

Leach, E., *Culture and Communication: The Logic by which Symbols are Connected* (Cambridge: Cambridge University Press, 1976).

Lemaire, A., 'Histoire et administration de la Palestine à l'époque perse', in E.-M. Laperrousaz and A. Lemaire (eds.), *La Palestine à l'époque perse* (Paris: Cerf, 1994), pp. 11-53.

—'Les Minéens et la Transeuphratène à l'époque perse: Une première approche', *Trans* 13 (1997), pp. 123-39.

—'Un nouveau roi arabe en Qedar dans l'inscription de l'autel à encens de Lachish', *RB* 81 (1974), pp. 63-72.

—'Un nouvel ostracon araméen du Ve siècle av. J.-C.', *Sem* 25 (1978), pp. 87-96.

—*Nouvelles inscriptions araméenes d'Idumée au Musée d'Israel* (TransSup, 3; Paris: J. Gabalda, 1996).

—'L'ostracon "Ramat-Negeb" et la topographie historique du Negeb', *Sem* 23 (1973), pp. 11-26.

—'Populations et territoires de la Palestine', in E.-M. Laperrousaz and A. Lemaire (eds.), *La Palestine à l'époque perse* (Paris: Cerf, 1994), pp. 31-74.

—'Populations et territoires de la Palestine à l'époque perse', *Trans* 3 (1990), pp. 31-74.

—'Les transformations politiques et culturelles de la Transjordanie au VIe siecle av. J.-C.', *Trans* 8 (1994), pp. 9-27.

—'Le trésor d'Abu Shusheh et le monnyage d'Ashdod avant Alexandre', *Revue Numismatique* (6th series) 32 (1990), pp. 257-63.

Lemaire, A., and H. Lozachmeur, 'La Cilicie à l'époque perse, recherches sur les pouvoirs locaux et l'organisation du territoire', *Trans* 3 (1990), pp. 143-55.

Lichtheim, M., *Ancient Egyptian Literature*, III (Berkeley: University of California Press, 1980).

Lund, J., 'The Northern Coastline of Syria in the Persian Period: A Survey of the Archaeological Evidence', *Trans* 2 (1990), pp. 13-36.

Macalister, R.A.S., *The Excavation of Gezer*, II (London: Palestine Exploration Fund, 1912).

Magen, I., 'Gerizim, Mount', in *NEAEHL*, II, pp. 484-92.

Malbran-Labat, F., *La version akkadienne de l'inscription trilingue de Darius à Behistun* (Documenta Asiana, 1; Rome: Gruppo editoriale internazionale, 1994).

Marchese, R., 'Athenian Imports in the Persian Period', in E. Stern (ed.), *Excavations at Dor, Final Report*. IB. *Areas A and C: The Finds* (Qedem Reports, 2; Jerusalem: Hebrew University, 1995), pp. 127-33.

Mazar, A., 'Iron Age Fortresses in the Judean Hills', *PEQ* 114 (1982), pp. 87-109.

—'Qasile, Tel', in *NEAEHL*, IV, pp. 1204-12.

McEwan, G.J.P., *Priest and Temple in Hellenistic Babylonia* (Freiburger Altorientalische Studien, 4; Wiesbaden: Franz Steiner, 1981).

Merquior, J.B., *The Veil and the Mask: Essays on Culture and Ideology* (London: Routledge & Kegan Paul, 1979).

Meshorer, Y., 'The Mints of Ashdod and Ashkelon during the Late Persian Period', *EI* 20 (1989), pp. 287-91, 205*.

Meshorer, Y., and S. Qedar, *The Coinage of Samaria in the Fourth Century B.C.E.* (Jerusalem: Numismatic Fine Arts, 1991).

Metzger, H., 'La stèle trilingue récemment découverte au Létoon de Xanthos: Le texte grec', *CRAIBL* (1974), pp. 82-93.

Meyer, E., *Die Entstehung des Judenthums* (Halle: Max Niemeyer, 1896).

Michaeli, F., *Les livres des Chroniques, d'Esdras et de Nehemie* (CAT, 16; Neuchâtel: Delachaux & Niestlé, 1967).

Mildenberg, L., 'Gaza Mint Authorities in Persian Time: Preliminary Studies of the Local Coinage in the 5th Persian Satrapy. Part 4', *Trans* 2 (1990), pp. 137-46.

—'Notes on the Coin Issues of Mazday', *Israel Numismatic Journal* 11 (1990/1991), pp. 9-17.

—'Petra on the Frankincense Road?', *Trans* 10 (1995), pp. 69-72.

—'The Philisto-Arabian Coins—A Preview: Preliminary Studies of Local Coinage in the 5th Persian Satrapy. Part 3', in T. Hackens and G. Mouchante (eds.), *Numismatique et histoire economique phénicienne et puniques* (Studia Phoenicia, 9; Louvain-la-Neuve: Université Catholique de Louvain, 1992), pp. 33-40.

Milgrom, J., *Leviticus 1–16* (AB, 3; New York: Doubleday, 1991).

Milik, J.T., 'Textes hebreux et araméenes', in P. Benoit *et al.* (eds.), *Les grottes de Murabba'at* (DJD, 2; Oxford: Clarendon Press, 1961), pp. 67-205.

Millard, A., 'Note on Two Seals Impressions on Pottery', *Levant* 21 (1989), pp. 60-61.

Mullen, E.T., 'A New Royal Sidonian Inscription', *BASOR* 216 (1974), pp. 25-30.

Myers, J.M., *Ezra–Nehemiah* (AB, 14; Garden City, NY: Doubleday, 1965).

Naveh, J., 'The Aramaic Ostraca', in Yohanan Aharoni (ed.), *Beer-Sheba I: Excavations at Tel Beer-Sheba (1969-1971 Seasons)* (Tel Aviv: Tel Aviv University, 1973), pp. 79-82.

—'Aramaic Ostraca and Jar Inscriptions from Tell Jemmeh', *Atiqot* (Eng) 21 (1992), pp. 49-53.

—'The Aramaic Ostraca from Tel Arad', in Yohanan Aharoni (ed.), *Arad Inscriptions* (Judean Desert Studies; trans. Judith Ben-Or; Jerusalem: Israel Exploration Society, 1981), pp. 153-76.

—'The Aramaic Ostraca from Tel Beer-Sheba (Seasons 1971–1976)', *TA* 6 (1979), pp. 182-98.

—'An Aramaic Ostracon from Ashdod', *Atiqot* (Eng) 9–10 (1970), pp. 200-201.

—*The Development of the Aramaic Script* (Proceedings of the Israel Academy of Sciences and Humanities, 5.1; Jerusalem: Israel Academy of Sciences, 1970).

—'Gleanings of Some Pottery Inscriptions', *IEJ* 46 (1996), pp. 44-51.

—'A Phoenician Inscription from Area C', in E. Stern (ed.), *Excavations at Dor, Final Report*, IB (Qedem Reports, 2; Jerusalem: Hebrew University, 1995), p. 489.

—'Published and Unpublished Aramaic Ostraca', *Atiqot* (Eng) 17 (1985), pp. 114-21.

—'The Scripts of Two Ostraca from Elath', *BASOR* 183 (1966), pp. 27-30.
North, R., 'Civil Authority in Ezra', in *Studi in onore di Edoardo Volterra*, VI (Milan: A. Giuffre, 1971), pp. 377-404.
Noth, M., *The Chronicler's History* (JSOTSup, 50; trans. H.G.M. Williamson; Sheffield: JSOT Press, 1987).
Oeming, M., *Das wahre Israel: Die 'genealogische Vorhalle' 1 Chronik 1–9* (BWANT; Stuttgart: W. Kohlhammer, 1990).
Ofer, A., 'Judean Hills Survey', in *NEAEHL*, III, pp. 815-16.
Oren, E.D., 'Sera', Tel', in *NEAEHL*, IV, pp. 1329-35.
Ortner, S.B., *Making Gender: The Politics and Erotics of Culture* (Boston: Beacon Press, 1996).
—'Theory in Anthropology since the Sixties', *Comparative Studies in Society and History* 26 (1984), pp. 126-65.
Peckham, J.B., *The Development of the Late Phoenician Scripts* (HSS, 20; Cambridge, MA: Harvard University Press, 1968).
Petersen, D., *Zechariah 9–14 and Malachi: A Commentary* (OTL; Louisville, KY: Westminster/John Knox Press, 1995).
Porath, Y. *et al.*, 'Mikhmoret, Tel', in *NEAEHL*, III, pp. 1043-46.
Porten, B., *Archives from Elephantine: The Life of an Ancient Jewish Military Colony* (Berkeley: University of California Press, 1968).
—*The Elephantine Papyri in English* (DMOA, 22; Leiden: E.J. Brill, 1996).
Pritchard, J.B., *Tell es-Sa'idiyeh: Excavations on the Tell, 1964–1966* (University Museum Monographs, 60; Philadelphia: The University Museum, University of Pennsylvania, 1985).
Purvis, J.D., *The Samaritan Pentateuch and the Origin of the Samaritan Sect* (Cambridge, MA: Harvard University Press, 1968).
Raban, A., 'A Group of Imported "East Greek" Pottery from Locus 46 at Area F on Tel Akko', in M. Heltzer *et al.* (eds.), *Studies in the Archaeology and History of Ancient Israel* (Festschrift Moshe Dothan; Haifa: Haifa University, 1993), pp. 73-98.
Raban, A., and E. Linder, ''Atlit: Maritime 'Atlit', in *NEAEHL*, I, pp. 117-20.
Rappaport, R.A., *Ritual and Religion in the Making of Humanity* (Cambridge Studies in Social and Cultural Anthropology, 110; Cambridge: Cambridge University Press, 1999).
Rappaport, U., 'Gaza and Ascalon in the Persian and Hellenistic Periods in Relation to their Coins', *IEJ* 20 (1970), pp. 75-80.
Rolli, I., and E. Ayalon, 'Appolonia-Arsuf', in *NEAEHL*, I, pp. 72-75.
Roth, M.T., *Babylonian Marriage Agreements 7th–3rd Centuries B.C.* (AOAT, 222; Neukirchen–Vluyn: Neukirchener Verlag, 1989).
Rowe, A., *A Catalogue of Egyptian Scarabs* (Jerusalem: Palestine Archaeological Museum, 1936).
Rudolph, W., *Esra und Nehemia* (HAT, 20; Tübingen: J.C.B. Mohr, 1949).
Schultz, F.W., *The Book of Ezra* (J.P. Lange Commentaries, 7; trans. C.A. Briggs; New York: Scribner, Armstrong and Co., 1877).
Seitz, C., 'On the Question of Divisions Internal to the Book of Isaiah', in E.H. Lovering, Jr (ed.), *Society of Biblical Literature 1993 Seminar Papers* (Atlanta: Scholars Press, 1993), pp. 260-66.
Sellers, O.R., 'Echoes of the 1931 Campaign', in P. Lapp (ed.), *The 1957 Excavation at Beth-Zur* (AASOR, 38; Cambridge, MA: ASOR, 1968), pp. 1-3.

Sinclair, L.A., *An Archaeological Study of Gibeah (Tell el-Ful)* (AASOR, 34; New Haven: ASOR, 1960).

Smith-Christopher, D.L., 'The Mixed Marriage Crisis in Ezra 9–10 and Nehemiah 13: A Study of the Sociology of the Post-Exilic Judaean Community', in T.C. Eskenazi and K.H. Richards (eds.), *Second Temple Studies: 2. Temple and Community in the Persian Period* (JSOTSup, 175; Sheffield: JSOT Press, 1994), pp. 243-65.

Spiegelberg, W. (ed.), *Die sogenannte demotische Chronik: Des Pap. 215 der Bibliotheque Nationale zu Paris* (Leipzig: J.C. Hinrichs, 1914).

Stager, L., 'Ashkelon', in *NEAEHL*, I, pp. 103-12.

Stern, E., 'The Beginning of the Greek Settlement in Palestine in Light of the Excavations of Tel Dor', in S. Gitin and W.G. Dever (eds.), *Recent Excavations in Israel: Studies in Iron Age Archaeology* (AASOR, 49; Winona Lake, IN: Eisenbrauns, 1989), pp. 107-24.

—'Dor', in *NEAEHL*, I, pp. 357-68.

—*Excavations at Dor, Final Report*. IA. *Areas A and C* (Qedem Reports, 1; Jerusalem: Hebrew University, 1995).

—*Excavations at Tel Mevorakh (1973–1976): Part One* (Qedem Reports, 9; Jerusalem: Hebrew University, 1978).

—*Material Culture of the Land of the Bible in the Persian Period 538–332 B.C.* (Jerusalem: Israel Exploration Society, 1982).

—'A Phoenician Art Centre in Post-Exilic Samaria', in Piero Bartolini *et al.* (eds.), *Atti del I Congresso Internazionale di Studi Fenici e Punici*, I (Collezione di Studi Fenici, 16; Rome: Consiglio Nazionale delle Richerche, 1983), pp. 211-12.

—'Two *Favissae* from Tel Dor', in C. Bonnett *et al.* (eds.), *Religio Phoenicia* (Studia Phoenicia, 4; Namur: Societe des études classiques, 1986), pp. 277-87.

Stern, M., *Greek and Latin Authors on Jews and Judaism*, III (Jerusalem: Israel Academy of Sciences and Humanities, 1984).

Stolper, M.W., 'Belšunu the Satrap', in F. Rochberg-Halton (ed.), *Language, Literature, and History* (Festschrift Erica Reiner; New Haven: American Oriental Society, 1987), pp. 389-402.

—*Entrepreneurs and Empire: The Murašu Archive, the Murašu Firm, and Persian Rule in Babylonia* (Nederlands Historisch-Archaeologisch Instituut te Instanbul, 54; Leiden: Uitgaven van Het, 1985).

—'The Governor of Babylonia and Across-the-River in 486 B.C.', *JNES* 48 (1989), pp. 283-305.

—'Mesopotamia, 482–330 B.C.', in D.M. Lewis *et al.* (eds.), *The Cambridge Ancient History*, VI (Cambridge: Cambridge University Press, 2nd edn, 1994), pp. 234-60.

Strathern, A., *One Father, One Blood: Descent and Group Structure among the Melpa People* (London: Tavistock, 1972).

—'Witchcraft, Greed, Cannibalism and Death: Some Related Themes from the New Guinea Highlands', in M. Bloch and J. Parry (eds.), *Death and the Regeneration of Life* (Cambridge: Cambridge University Press, 1982), pp. 111-33.

Thompson, J.B., *Studies in the Theory of Ideology* (Berkeley: University of California Press, 1984).

Tillich, P., *The Dynamics of Faith* (New York: Harper & Row, 1957).

Throntveit, M.A., *Ezra–Nehemiah* (Interpretation; Louisville, KY: Westminster/John Knox Press, 1992).

—'Linguistic Analysis and the Question of Authorship in Chronicles, Ezra and Nehemiah', *VT* 32 (1982), pp. 201-16.

Torrey, C.C., *Ezra Studies* (New York: Ktav, 1970).

Trevor-Roper, H., 'The European Witch-Craze of the Sixteenth and Seventeenth Centuries', in *idem*, *The European Witch-Craze of the Sixteenth and Seventeenth Centuries and Other Essays* (New York: Harper & Row, 1967), pp. 90-192.

Tuplin, C., 'The Administration of the Achaemenid Empire', in Ian Carradice (ed.), *Coinage and Administration in the Athenian and Persian Empires* (BAR International Series, 343; Oxford: BAR, 1987), pp. 109-66.

Turner, V., *Dramas, Fields, and Metaphors: Symbolic Action in Human Society* (Symbol, Myth, and Ritual Series; Ithaca, NY: Cornell University Press, 1974).

Valeri, V., *Kingship and Sacrifice: Ritual and Society in Ancient Hawaii* (trans. Paula Wissing; Chicago: University of Chicago Press, 1985).

Washington, H., 'The Strange Woman of Proverbs 1–9 and Post-Exilic Judean Society', in T.C. Eskenazi and K.H. Richards (eds.), *Second Temple Studies: 2. Temple and Community in the Persian Period* (JSOTSup, 175; Sheffield: JSOT Press, 1994), pp. 217-42.

Watts, J.D.W., *Isaiah 34–66* (WBC, 25; Waco, TX: Word Books, 1987).

Weinberg, J., 'Das Wesen und funktionelle Bestimmung der Listen in I Chr 1–9', *ZAW* 93 (1981), pp. 91-114.

Welten, P., *Geschichte und Geschichtsdarstellung in der Chronikbüchern* (WMANT, 42; Neukirchen–Vluyn: Neukirchener Verlag, 1973).

Wenning, R., 'Attische Keramik in Palastina: Ein Zwischenbericht', *Trans* 2 (1990), pp. 157-67.

Westbrook, R., *Old Babylonian Marriage Law* (*AfO* Beiheft, 23; Horn: Ferdinand Berger & Sohne, 1988).

Westermann, C., *Isaiah 40–66* (OTL; Philadelphia: Westminster Press, 1969).

Whybray, R.N., *Isaiah 40–66* (NCBC, 23.2; Grand Rapids: Eerdmans, 1975).

Williamson, H.G.M., 'The Composition of Ezra i–vi', *JTS* NS 34 (1983), pp. 1-30.

—*Ezra, Nehemiah* (WBC, 16; Waco, TX: Word Books, 1985).

—'The Governors of Judah under the Persians', *TynBul* 39 (1988), pp. 59-82.

—*Israel in the Book of Chronicles* (Cambridge: Cambridge University Press, 1977).

Wuthnow, R., *Meaning and Moral Order: Explorations in Cultural Analysis* (Berkeley: University of California Press, 1987).

Yadin, Y. *et al.*, *Hazor I: An Account of the First Season of Excavations, 1955* (Jerusalem: Magnes Press, 1958).

Yassine, K. and J. Texidor, 'Ammonite and Aramaic Inscriptions from Tell el-Mazar in Jordan', *BASOR* 264 (1986), pp. 45-50.

Yogev, O., 'Tel Nahariya', *ESI* 2 (1983), pp. 75-76.

Zemer, A., *Storage Jars in Ancient Israel* (Haifa: National Maritime Museum Foundation, 1977).

Zertal, A., 'The Pahwah of Samaria (Northern Israel) during the Persian Period: Types of Settlement, Economy, History and New Discoveries', *Trans* 3 (1990), pp. 9-30.

INDEXES

INDEX OF REFERENCES

OLD TESTAMENT

OTHER ANCIENT REFERENCES

Index of Authors

JOURNAL FOR THE STUDY OF THE OLD TESTAMENT
SUPPLEMENT SERIES

268 Linda S. Schearing and Steven L. McKenzie (eds.), *Those Elusive Deuteronomists: 'Pandeuteronomism' and Scholarship in the Nineties*
269 David J.A. Clines and Stephen D. Moore (eds.), *Auguries: The Jubilee Volume of the Sheffield Department of Biblical Studies*
270 John Day (ed.), *King and Messiah in Israel and the Ancient Near East: Proceedings of the Oxford Old Testament Seminar*
271 Wonsuk Ma, *Until the Spirit Comes: The Spirit of God in the Book of Isaiah*
272 James Richard Linville, *Israel in the Book of Kings: The Past as a Project of Social Identity*
273 Meir Lubetski, Claire Gottlieb and Sharon Keller (eds.), *Boundaries of the Ancient Near Eastern World: A Tribute to Cyrus H. Gordon*
274 Martin J. Buss, *Biblical Form Criticism in its Context*
275 William Johnstone, *Chronicles and Exodus: An Analogy and its Application*
276 Raz Kletter, *Economic Keystones: The Weight System of the Kingdom of Judah*
277 Augustine Pagolu, *The Religion of the Patriarchs*
278 Lester L. Grabbe (ed.), *Leading Captivity Captive: 'The Exile' as History and Ideology*
279 Kari Latvus, *God, Anger and Ideology: The Anger of God in Joshua and Judges in Relation to Deuteronomy and the Priestly Writings*
280 Eric S. Christianson, *A Time to Tell: Narrative Strategies in Ecclesiastes*
281 Peter D. Miscall, *Isaiah 34–35: A Nightmare/A Dream*
282 Joan E. Cook, *Hannah's Desire, God's Design: Early Interpretations in the Story of Hannah*
283 Kelvin Friebel, *Jeremiah's and Ezekiel's Sign-Acts: Rhetorical Nonverbal Communication*
284 M. Patrick Graham, Rick R. Marrs and Steven L. McKenzie (eds.), *Worship and the Hebrew Bible: Essays in Honor of John T. Willis*
285 Paolo Sacchi, *History of the Second Temple*
286 Wesley J. Bergen, *Elisha and the End of Prophetism*
287 Anne Fitzpatrick-McKinley, *The Transformation of Torah from Scribal Advice to Law*
288 Diana Lipton, *Revisions of the Night: Politics and Promises in the Patriarchal Dreams of Genesis*
289 Jože Krašovec (ed.), *The Interpretation of the Bible: The International Symposium in Slovenia*
290 Frederick H. Cryer and Thomas L. Thompson (eds.), *Qumran between the Old and New Testaments*
291 Christine Schams, *Jewish Scribes in the Second-Temple Period*
292 David J.A. Clines, *On the Way to the Postmodern: Old Testament Essays, 1967–1998 Volume 1*

293 David J.A. Clines, *On the Way to the Postmodern: Old Testament Essays, 1967–1998 Volume 2*
294 Charles E. Carter, *The Emergence of Yehud in the Persian Period: A Social and Demographic Study*
295 Jean-Marc Heimerdinger, *Topic, Focus and Foreground in Ancient Hebrew Narratives*
296 Mark Cameron Love, *The Evasive Text: Zechariah 1–8 and the Frustrated Reader*
297 Paul S. Ash, *David, Solomon and Egypt: A Reassessment*
298 John D. Baildam, *Paradisal Love: Johann Gottfried Herder and the Song of Songs*
299 M. Daniel Carroll R., *Rethinking Contexts, Rereading Texts: Contributions from the Social Sciences to Biblical Interpretation*
300 Edward Ball (ed.), *In Search of True Wisdom: Essays in Old Testament Interpretation in Honour of Ronald E. Clements*
301 Carolyn S. Leeb, *Away from the Father's House: The Social Location of na'ar and na'arah in Ancient Israel*
302 Xuan Huong Thi Pham, *Mourning in the Ancient Near East and the Hebrew Bible*
303 Ingrid Hjelm, *The Samaritans and Early Judaism: A Literary Analysis*
304 Wolter H. Rose, *Zemah and Zerubabbel: Messianic Expectations in the Early Postexilic Period*
305 Jo Bailey Wells, *God's Holy People: A Theme in Biblical Theology*
306 Albert de Pury, Thomas Römer and Jean-Daniel Macchi (eds.), *Israel Constructs its History: Deuteronomistic Historiography in Recent Research*
307 Robert L. Cole, *The Shape and Message of Book III (Psalms 73–89)*
308 Yiu-Wing Fung, *Victim and Victimizer: Joseph's Interpretation of his Destiny*
309 George Aichele (ed.), *Culture, Entertainment and the Bible*
310 Esther Fuchs, *Sexual Politics in the Biblical Narrative: Reading the Hebrew Bible as a Woman*
311 Gregory Glazov, *The Bridling of the Tongue and the Opening of the Mouth in Biblical Prophecy*
312 Francis Landy, *Beauty and the Enigma: And Other Essays on the Hebrew Bible*
313 Martin O'Kane (ed.), *Borders, Boundaries and the Bible*
314 Bernard S. Jackson, *Studies in the Semiotics of Biblical Law*
315 Paul R. Williamson, *Abraham, Israel and the Nations: The Patriarchal Promise and its Covenantal Development in Genesis*
316 Dominic Rudman, *Determinism in the Book of Ecclesiastes*
317 Lester L. Grabbe (ed.), *Did Moses Speak Attic? Jewish Historiography and Scripture in the Hellenistic Period*
318 David A. Baer, *When We All Go Home: Translation and Theology in* LXX *56–66*
319 Henning Graf Reventlow and Yair Hoffman (eds.), *Creation in Jewish and Christian Tradition*
320 Claudia V. Camp, *Wise, Strange and Holy: The Strange Woman and the Making of the Bible*

321 Varese Layzer, *Signs of Weakness: Juxtaposing Irish Tales and the Bible*
322 Mignon R. Jacobs, *The Conceptual Coherence of the Book of Micah*
323 Martin Ravndal Hauge, *The Descent from the Mountain: Narrative Patterns in Exodus 19–40*
324 P.M. Michèle Daviau, John W. Wevers and Michael Weigl (eds.), *The World of the Aramaeans: Studies in Honour of Paul-Eugène Dion*, Volume 1
325 P.M. Michèle Daviau, John W. Wevers and Michael Weigl (eds.), *The World of the Aramaeans: Studies in Honour of Paul-Eugène Dion*, Volume 2
326 P.M. Michèle Daviau, John W. Wevers and Michael Weigl (eds.), *The World of the Aramaeans: Studies in Honour of Paul-Eugène Dion*, Volume 3
327 Gary D. Salyer, *Vain Rhetoric: Private Insight and Public Debate in Ecclesiastes*
328 James M. Trotter, *Reading Hosea in Achaemenid Yehud*
329 Wolfgang Bluedorn, *Yahweh Verus Baalism: A Theological Reading of the Gideon-Abimelech Narrative*
330 Lester L. Grabbe and Robert D. Haak (eds.), *'Every City shall be Forsaken': Urbanism and Prophecy in Ancient Israel and the Near East*
331 Amihai Mazar (ed.), with the assistance of Ginny Mathias, *Studies in the Archaeology of the Iron Age in Israel and Jordan*
332 Robert J.V. Hiebert, Claude E. Cox and Peter J. Gentry (eds.), *The Old Greek Psalter: Studies in Honour of Albert Pietersma*
333 Ada Rapoport-Albert and Gillian Greenberg (eds.), *Biblical Hebrew, Biblical Texts: Essays in Memory of Michael P. Weitzman*
334 Ken Stone (ed.), *Queer Commentary and the Hebrew Bible*
335 James K. Bruckner, *Implied Law in the Abrahamic Narrative: A Literary and Theological Analysis*
336 Stephen L. Cook, Corrine L. Patton and James W. Watts (eds.), *The Whirlwind: Essays on Job, Hermeneutics and Theology in Memory of Jane Morse*
337 Joyce Rilett Wood, *Amos in Song and Book Culture*
338 Alice A. Keefe, *Woman's Body and the Social Body in Hosea 1–2*
339 Sarah Nicholson, *Three Faces of Saul: An Intertextual Approach to Biblical Tragedy*
341 Mark W. Chavalas and K. Lawson Younger Jr (eds.), *Mesopotamia and the Bible*
343 J. Andrew Dearman and M. Patrick Graham (eds.), *The Land that I Will Show You: Essays on the History and Archaeology of the Ancient Near East in Honor of J. Maxwell Miller*
345 Jan-Wim Wesselius, *The Origin of the History of Israel: Herodotus' Histories as Blueprint for the First Books of the Bible*
346 Johanna Stiebert, *The Construction of Shame in the Hebrew Bible: The Prophetic Contribution*
347 Andrew G. Shead, *The Open Book and the Sealed Book: Jeremiah 32 in its Hebrew and Greek Recensions*
350 David Janzen, *Witch-hunts, Purity and Social Boundaries: The Expulsion of the Foreign Women in Ezra 9–10*
352 William John Lyons, *Canon and Exegesis: Canonical Praxis and the Sodom Narrative*